Post-Truth, Philosophy and Law

In the wake of Brexit and Trump, the debate surrounding post-truth fills the newspapers and is at the centre of the public debate. Democratic institutions and the rule of law have always been constructed and legitimized by discourses of truth. And so the issue of "post-truth" or "fake truth" can be regarded as a contemporary degeneration of that legitimacy. But what, precisely, is post-truth from a theoretical point of view? Can it actually change perceptions of law, of institutions and political power? And can it affect our understanding of society and social relations? What are its ideological premises? What are the technical conditions that foster it? And most importantly, does it have anything to teach lovers of the truth? Pursuing an interdisciplinary perspective, this book gathers both well-known and newer scholars from a range of subject areas, to engage in a philosophical interrogation of the relationship between truth and law.

Angela Condello is Adjunct Professor at the Department of Philosophy of the University of Turin, Italy.

Tiziana Andina is Associate Professor of Philosophy at the University of Turin, Italy.

Law And Politics: Continental Perspectives

Series editors:

Mariano Croce, Sapienza University of Rome, Italy
Marco Goldoni, University of Glasgow, UK

for information about the series and details of previous and forthcoming titles, see https://www.routledge.com/law/series/LPCP

Post-Truth, Philosophy and Law

Edited by
Angela Condello and Tiziana Andina

Routledge
Taylor & Francis Group
a GlassHouse book

First published 2019
by Routledge
2 Park Square, Milton Park, Abingdon, Oxon OX14 4RN

and by Routledge
605 Third Avenue, New York, NY 10017

First issued in paperback 2020

A GlassHouse book

Routledge is an imprint of the Taylor & Francis Group, an informa business

British Library Cataloguing in Publication Data
A catalogue record for this book is available from the British Library

Library of Congress Cataloging-in-Publication Data
Names: Condello, Angela, 1984- editor. | Andina, Tiziana, editor.
Title: Post-truth, philosophy and law / edited by Angela
Condello and Tiziana Andina.
Description: Abingdon, Oxon ; New York, NY : Routledge, 2019. |
Series: Law and politics: continental perspectives |
Includes bibliographical refreences and index.
Identifiers: LCCN 2019002256 (print) | LCCN 2019006617 (ebook) |
ISBN 9780429450778 (ebk) | ISBN 9781138324664 (hbk)
Subjects: LCSH: Law--Political aspects. | Truth--Political aspects. |
Political science--Philosophy.
Classification: LCC JA75 (ebook) | LCC JA75 .P67 2019 (print) |
DDC 323.44/501--dc23
LC record available at https://lccn.loc.gov/2019002256

ISBN 13: 978-0-367-72902-8 (pbk)
ISBN 13: 978-1-138-32466-4 (hbk)

Typeset in Galliard
by Taylor & Francis Books

Contents

Illustrations

Figure

Table

Contributors

Tiziana Andina is Associate Professor of Philosophy at the University of Turin (Italy). Since 2018 she is the director of the research center, LabOnt – Center for Ontology at the University of Turin (www.labont.it). She has been a fellow of Columbia University (2008–2009) and Käte Hamburger Kolleg, University of Bonn (2015) as well as Visiting Professor at ITMO University, Russia (2014). She has published many articles on philosophy and the philosophy of art in several internationals journals. Her recent work concerns the definition of art and social ontology. Her publications include: *Il volto Americano di Nietzsche*, La Città del Sole, 1999; *Il problema della percezione nella filosofia di Nietzsche*, Albo Versorio, 2005; *Arthur Danto: Philosopher of Pop*, Cambridge Scholars Publishing, 2011; *The Philosophy of Art: The Question of Definition. From Hegel to Post-Dantian Theories*, Bloomsbury Academy, 2013; *An Ontology for Social Reality*, Palgrave-Macmillan, 2016; *What is Art? The Question of Definition Reloaded*, Brill, 2017; and (ed. by) *Bridging the Analytical Continental Divide. A Companion to Contemporary Western Philosophy*, Brill, 2014. She is co-editor of the international series *Brill Research Perspectives in Art and Law* and of the international series *Analytic Aesthetics and Contemporary Art* (Bloomsbury Academic).

Sanja Bojanić is a researcher immersed in philosophy of culture and queer studies, with an overarching commitment to comprehend contemporary forms of gender, racial and class practices, which underpin social and affective inequalities specifically increased in the current political contexts. She studied philosophy and expanded and tailored her interests as a graduate student at the University of Paris 8, where she obtained an M.A. in Hypermedia Studies at the Department of Science and Technology of Information, and an M.A. and Ph. D. at Centre d'Etudes féminines et d'etude de genre, a process that ultimately led to interdisciplinary research based on experimental artistic practices, queer studies and particularities of Affect Theory. She has served as the Information Engineer at the Institut National d'Histoire de l'Art (Louvre, Paris), Nouvel Observateur (Paris), and Laboratory for Evaluation and Development of Digital Editing, Maison des Sciences de l'Homme (Paris Nord, St. Denis). She is the Executive Director of the Center for Advanced Studies Southeast Europe (CAS

SEE) and the vice-dean for international cooperation of the Academy of Applied Art at the University of Rijeka.

Angela Condello, Ph.D. (1984), is a legal philosopher. She is an Adjunct Professor at the University of Torino and University of Roma Tre. She is a Jean Monnet Module Holder (www.cultureofnormativity.unito.it/) at the University of Torino, Department of Philosophy. She has been teaching law and humanities and legal philosophy since 2013. Her work covers critical approaches to classical legal theoretical themes, and in particular metaphor and analogy. She has published widely on exemplarity, casuistry in law, law and literature, law and humanities. She was awarded fellowships among which the "Law as Culture" Fellowship (Bonn), Fernand Braudel (EHESS), "Jean Monnet Project" and "Jean Monnet Module", and others to teach and work at University of California at Berkeley, Max Planck Institute for International and Public Law (Heidelberg), Australian University at Canberrra, Cardozo Law School (New York), and McGill Law School. Her monograph, *Analogica. Il doppio legame tra diritto e analogia*, was published by Giappichelli in 2018 and her other monograph, *Between Ordinary and Extraordinary. The Normativity of the Singular Case in Art and Law*, was published by Brill in 2018. Email: angela.condello@unito.it

Jacopo Domenicucci, *normalien* (Ecole normale supérieure, Paris) and *professeur agrégé de philosophie*, has studied trust since 2014 and digital trust since 2015. On trust, he published *Trust As a Two-Place Relation*, co-authored with Richard Holton, Oxford University Press, 2017; and *Trust, Agency and Discrimination*, Rivista di Estetica, 2017; and edited *Trusting Institutions*, Rosenberg&Sellier, 2018. On digital trust, he published *Trust, Extended Memories and Social Media*, Palgrave Macmillan, 2018; and edited *La confiance à l'ère numérique*, Berger-Levrault and Rue d'Ulm, 2018, with Milad Doueihi. His research was presented at the University Paris I Panthéon-Sorbonne, University of Cambridge, University of Manchester, University of Minho, University of Turin, Ecole des Hautes Etudes en Sciences Sociales (EHESS), FMSH, and CEM (Paris). At the Leverhulme Centre for the Future of Intelligence (Cambridge), he has run with Rune Nyrup the "Trust and AI Seminar". He is a member of the Cambridge Trust & Technology SRI.

Maurizio Ferraris is full Professor of Philosophy at the University of Turin since 1999 and Deputy Rector for Humanities Research. He is President of LabOnt – Center for Ontology, Directeur de recherche at the Collège d'études mondiales (Paris) and advisory member of the Center for Advanced Studies of South East Europe (Rijeka) and of the Internationales Zentrum Für Philosophie NRW. He is doctor honoris causa in Humanities at the University of Flores (Buenos Aires) and at the University of Pécs from 2017. He has been Fellow of Käte-Hamburger Kolleg "Recht als Kultur" (Bonn) and Fellow of the Italian Academy for Advanced Studies in America (Columbia University, New York) and of the Alexander von Humboldt Stiftung. He has also been

Directeur d'études of the Collège International de Philosophie and Visiting Professor at the École des Hautes Études en Sciences Sociales (Paris) as well as other European and American universities. He is columnist for *La Repubblica*, Director of *Rivista di Estetica, Critique, Círculo Hermenéutico editorial* and of the *Revue francophone d'esthétique*. He wrote more than 50 books that have been translated into several languages. He has worked in the field of Aesthetics, Hermeneutics, and Social Ontology, with a focus on the theory of Documentality and contemporary New Realism.

Anna Elisabetta Galeotti is Full Professor of Political Philosophy in the Department of Humanities at the University of Eastern Piedmont, Vercelli. Her research interests range from toleration, multiculturalism, equal respect, to deception and self-deception in politics. Among her English publications: *Toleration as Recognition*, Cambridge University Press, 2002; "Autonomy and Cultural Practices: The Risk of Double Standards" *European Journal of Political Theory*, 2015; "The Range of Toleration" *Philosophy and Social Criticism*, 2015; "Cultural Conflicts: A Deflationary Approach" *Critical Review of International Social and Political Philosophy*, 2017; *Political Self-Deception*, Cambridge University Press, 2018.

Sara Guindani earned a Ph.D. in Philosophy and has an expertise in aesthetics. She has devised and is currently leading the *Politics of Images* programme at FMSH in Paris. Her research relates to arts, philosophy and psychoanalysis, and notably on the relationship between image and writing in the rememoration process. She has applied this area of expertise to the works of Marcel Proust and its influence on French contemporary philosophy (Merleau-Ponty, Deleuze, Barthes). She has translated several philosophy and art theory essays from French into Italian by such authors as André Chastel, Louis Marin and Georges Didi-Huberman. She is also a psychoanalyst and a co-therapist in analytical psychodrama. Her publications include: *Lo stereoscopio di Proust. Pittura, fotografia e fantasmagoria nella* Recherche, Mimesis, 2005; *Effetti di verità: documenti e immagini tra storia e finzione*, ed. with M. Piazza, Roma TrE-Press, 2016; *Jacques Derrida: la dissémination à l'oeuvre*, ed. with Alexis Nuselovici, Paris, Editions de la MSH, forthcoming in spring 2019.

Diego Marconi, Ph.D. (Pittsburgh 1980), was a professor of Philosophy of Language in the University of Torino until 2017; he had taught Logic, Philosophy of Science and Philosophy of Language at other universities, both in Italy and in other European countries. His main work is on Wittgenstein's philosophy, Hegel's dialectic, paraconsistent logic, and several topics in the philosophy of language, particularly lexical meaning (*Lexical Competence*, MIT Press, 1997). He is a member of the Accademia delle Scienze of Torino and the Academia Europaea. Prof. Diego Marconi, Center for Logic, Language and Cognition, University of Torino, Italy. Email: diego.marconi@unito.it

Luke Mason is Associate Professor at Birmingham City University. Luke is a lawyer and philosopher whose work spans a range of intersecting areas. He has published widely in the fields of labour law, social policy, the nature of legal knowledge, and the law's connection with the arts, humanities, philosophy and science. A thread which unites his research is the nature of legal reasoning and its relationship with law's social function. He has held permanent and visiting positions in various universities across Europe.

Davide Pala is a Ph.D. Student and Teaching Assistant at the Department of Politics of the University of Manchester. He works within the Manchester Center for Political Theory (MANCEPT) in the field of normative political theory applied to international and transnational questions. He is currently developing a neo-republican approach to human rights. Previously, he was a Ph.D. Student at the Department of Political Studies of the University of Turin. His research focussed on global justice, world poverty and socio-economic inequalities. His publications include articles on institutional cosmopolitanism, capability approach and liberal nationalism.

Tracy B. Strong is Professor of Political Theory and Philosophy at the University of Southampton (UK) and University of California, San Diego, Distinguished Professor emeritus. He is the author of books or essays on topics in political theory as well as monographs on Nietzsche, Rousseau, Hobbes, Carl Schmitt and others. He is also the editor of seven books. His *Politics Without Vision: 'Thinking without a Banister' in the Twentieth Century* won the American Political Science Association David Easton prize in 2012. His *Learning Our Native Tongue: Citizenship, Contestation and Conflict in America* is presently in press at the University of Chicago. From 1990 until 2000 he was editor of *Political Theory. An International Journal in Political Philosophy.*

Enrico Terrone is Juan de la Cierva Postdoctoral Fellow at the LOGOS Research Group, Universitat de Barcelona. He works on philosophical issues concerning aesthetics, ontology and technology. His main area of research is philosophy of film. He has published papers on international journals such as *British Journal of Aesthetics, Erkenntnis, The Monist, Philosophy of the Social Sciences.*

Post-truth: what is it about? Introduction

Tiziana Andina and Angela Condello

I.1 Fake images, fake narratives, fake facts (by A. Condello)[1]

With the present book, we aim to discuss the relationship between law, socio-political relations and institutions, and truth. In particular, we will focus on the consequences produced by various phenomena of truth-deformation and on their impact on the political equilibrium and on democracy. The topic, indeed, requires a timely theoretical analysis: legal and political legitimation are quite evidently going through a crisis.

Starting from some concrete cases, the present introduction aims at drawing a general framework for the theoretical cornerstones underlying the relationship between law, post-truth and democracy. In particular, the concrete cases show the impact of post-truth on the political and legal legitimation of authority and power in contemporary societies.

Before proceeding, one clarification needs to be made. Throughout the chapters collected here, authors often use the expression "fake news" in order to refer to the most recurrent phenomenon associated to the more general linguistic and epistemic practice known as "post-truth". This practice consists of many different actions: for instance, commenting on an image, reporting concrete facts and data, or analyzing phenomena through a distorted perspective in order to evidentiate some aspects and neglect others.

For instance, let us take the Italian public discourse on migration evidently, if a whole category of subjects is depicted as being dangerous, sick, untrustworthy and scary, the political agenda and the legal policies proposed and carried out will reflect the type of consensus produced by the mainstream public opinion about these subjects. Here we will consider in particular one fake image, two fake narratives and some fake data.

1 I wish to thank Valentina Calderone (Director of *A Buon Diritto* Onlus) and Valentina Brinis (UNHCR Italy) for their advice on the information discussed in this paragraph and (more importantly) for their work to make migration policies more humane and just.

I.1.2 Fake image

Who is Josefa? Her full name is Josephine and she comes from Cameroon. The image of her rescue in the Mediterranean in summer 2018 went immediately viral on the web for two reasons: (i) she was the only one to survive the shipwreck of a boat coming from Libya, a tragedy whose victims included a mother and her little boy; (ii) Josefa, before the rescue, spent two days floating in the sea, holding on to a piece of wood until the volunteers of the Spanish NgO *Open Arms* recovered her in the waters off the cost of Libya.

Josefa's eyes and tears then appeared all over the world. A detail was noticed: there was another picture of Josefa circulating on the web, showing her after the rescue, and at a closer look one could notice that she was wearing nail polish. This picture also went viral, and a comment started turning Josefa's tragic story into a mystery. A woman commented on her Twitter page that the story of Josefa's rescue might have been a fake: how could Josefa's hands look so clean after two days in the sea? How could she be wearing red nail polish? *Something was wrong, something had to be false.*

Annalisa Camilli, journalist at *Internazionale*, immediately replied to the comment (she was on the boat with the *Open Arms* volunteers and had witnessed the rescue): the picture circulating on the web, where Josefa wears nail polish, was not taken right after the rescue, but four days later. The boat, after the rescue, navigated to Spain, where some female volunteers helped Josefa recover, and thought nail polish could help her feel a little better. She wore no nail polish whatsoever when she was rescued.

I.1.3 Fake narratives

There are various narratives concerning migrants that, today, are quite popular in Italy and Europe: some concern health, others public safety. It seems to be a widespread (false) belief that migrants bring dangerous diseases: for instance, malaria and tuberculosis. They allegedly come from Africa with their diseases and spread them in healthy Europe. This is false, and a clear product of what a report of the Council of Europe defined "information disorder".[2] As for malaria, the National Institute for Health reports that the cases of malaria diseases in Italy were not caused by infected migrants, but very likely by an insect that travelled with European tourists and that was brought back through their luggage.

The false narrative concerning public safety, instead, is that migrants tend to be criminals. Actually, this has become an equation often taken for granted in public discourse. Data confirm the opposite: in relation to the percentage on the Italian population, the number of migrants (which is an imprecise category, because not all of them are refugees, nor are all of them illegal migrants) shows that they do

2 Information disorder: towards an interdisciplinary framework for research and policy making: https://rm.coe.int/information-disorder-toward-an-interdisciplinary-framework-for-researc/168076277c.

not *tend* to commit crimes. More likely, whenever a migrant commits a crime, *that individual event* is immediately reported and goes viral more quickly.

I.1.4 Fake facts

In a video uploaded on her Facebook page, the leader of the right-wing party "Fratelli d'Italia", Giorgia Meloni, re-published a fake news piece that had been circulating for months on right-wing webpages. The piece of news reports that philanthropist millionaire George Soros (disliked by Trump and by right-wing European leaders), in collaboration with MasterCard, would have distributed a certain number of credit cards to migrants in order to help them flee from their home countries and reach Europe. These credit cards allegedly bear the logo of UNHCR, the UN agency working for refugee policies. How did the fake fact emerge? It seems that the xenophobic Slovenian website Nova24, which had spread other conspiracy theories and false facts, was the first to publish the news. According to *The New York Times*, this website is controlled by other media companies financed by politicians close to Viktor Orbán, the extreme right-wing Hungarian leader. In October 2018, this website reported a Croatian policeman's declaration that many of "these migrants" entering the European border were well dressed (as if it that was a crime, and as if one could not flee from war or famine with a decent shirt), but most importantly they had MasterCard credit cards. A policeman's personal opinion thus became a (post-)true fact, which was naively reported by a political leader in Italy. Without checking the source.

In short, what matters is the *function* performed by images, narratives, or facts.

I.2 Is post-truth only fake or is it something more? (by T. Andina)

The notion of "post-truth" seems to share some of the meanings that identify the concept of "fake". However, two points must be underlined: as emerges from the examples we have just discussed, some fakes, for various reasons, take on a more structured form than others; this form coincides with what we call "post-truth". The second point we must try to keep in mind is that this transition from truth to post-truth seems to be subject to two conditions: first of all the idea that truth is often placed, or perhaps hidden, in inaccessible or hardly accessible places. This idea then generates a fundamental distrust, accompanied by the feeling that the truth is often intermingled with deceit and that there is no way to separate the two areas: truth and lies tend to overlap and it is seemingly impossible, from an epistemological point of view, to keep them separate.

This intuition has sceptical roots and was mainly introduced in philosophy by Friedrich Nietzsche: to speak of truth and falsehood as two sides of the same coin means to argue that there is no way to draw a line between truth and lies because we do not have the epistemological tools to do so. This epistemological concern created the conditions for the development of post-truth. In this sense, post-truth is what emerges after we have discovered that the epistemological horizon of truth must be replaced because, somewhat paradoxically, it is not true, or because it cannot be understood using the classical notions of truth and falsehood. In this sense – this is the idea – the truth should be replaced with post-truth: that is, with something that we know to be fluid, constructed and subject-dependent.

If Nietzsche laid down the premises for this sort of epistemological turn, postmodern philosophy has completed and defined the horizon of post-truth, paving the way for this conception of "fluid truth" to be applied outside the perimeter of philosophy. To clarify this idea I think it is useful to take an example: namely the narratives surrounding the issue of climate change. This is a typical case in which the radical weakening of truth has allowed for the implementation of a precise strategy, which has clear objectives in terms of economic repercussions. But let's take a step back and see how we've come to this situation.

I.2.1 On certainty: from fake news to post-truth

In principle, certainty would seem like a good guideline to follow; the problem, however, lies in the idea of "absolute certainty". What does it mean to have absolute certainty when considering, for example, scientific problems? Absolute certainty does not exist in science – which rather relies on a verifiable and shareable method. In essence, science proceeds by trial and error, in order to get closer and closer to a good degree of certainty. In other words, science has developed a method that provides for the possibility of error and its correction: it therefore provides for a margin of uncertainty without this jeopardizing the possibility of producing objective knowledge.

However, it is precisely this margin of uncertainty that has given rise to the radical and quite imaginative theses used by the many negationists of climate change. In particular, their criticism is focused on two issues: firstly, on the unreliability of scientific studies that deal with climate change; secondly, on the idea that taking this uncertainty into account means accepting that any other hypothesis has the same degree of legitimacy as those studies and, therefore, can be supported as a plausible and founded alternative.

In reality, all evidence shows that this is not the case. Climate science has been telling us for years now that climate change is taking place and that its origin is anthropogenic. From the scientific point of view the trustworthiness of these theses is very high. About 97% of the scientific production on these issues converges to support three theses: (1) there is no doubt that the phenomenon of climate change is underway, (2) that it is anthropogenic, namely that a substantial part of it can be traced back to human choice, and, finally, (3) that it is extremely dangerous. On the basis of such a broad convergence of scientific literature, it is more than founded to believe that scientific knowledge offers reasonably certain conclusions in this regard. Yet the 3% of discordant scientific opinions has been sufficient to produce a negationist rhetoric, aimed at precise economic and development strategies.

Climate negationism began to take on an organized form in 1998, the year of formation of the Intergovernmental Panel on Climate Change (IPCC). The panel was made up of hundreds of scientists from around the world who had been assigned the goal of studying climate change by providing empirical data. In all its reports, the IPCC has always been consistent in supporting the anthropogenic origin and the danger of climate change. The United States was the one to strongly oppose the IPCC's conclusions. In 1989 the Global Climate Coalition was created, encompassing five oil companies as well as the Chamber of Commerce and the national association of US manufacturing industries. Beginning in 1995, when the second IPCC report was released, the association systematically attacked the work of the panel undermining the credibility of the scientists who were part of it. The communication strategy that they decided to adopt was extremely simple and effective: the idea was to show that if there was no complete consensus among scientists it was not possible to consider the results of those studies completely certain. And since such total consensus was not present, it was necessary to conclude that those researches had no sufficient scientific validity.

Now, as we have already pointed out, any researcher knows well that that kind of consensus – that is, a consensus based on absolute certainty – is neither possible nor necessary to produce certain knowledge. Nonetheless, the arguments of the negationists have found significant consensus in the public opinion and this consensus has been easily transformed into political action, that is, into social and political pressure. Following this, the political decisions of the US government have marked the choices that have affected and are still affecting climate change at the global level, in decisive and fundamentally negative ways.

This story has all the ingredients for the transition from truth to post-truth: a well-founded and reasonably certain scientific research is discredited using arguments that have no meaning in the scientific community, but are rhetorically effective and convincing for the general public; an economic and political objective (producing wealth through a certain economic model) is lucidly pursued by some economic-social actors; finally, extremely powerful and effective mass communication tools are used to create broad consensus. So, the strategy put in place for the formation of the post-true narrative about climate change (as in the case of narratives about migrants in Europe) was roughly the following: scientific knowledge (or, in the case of migrants, social-historical knowledge) has been strategically weakened in the pursuit of a precise goal. On this basis, a certain narrative was constructed and communicated, one that was functional to the purpose and to the formation of social consensus. Finally, once the social context had been adequately prepared, political action has been able to follow through – being able to count on a wide consensus consolidated by continuous artificial "constructions" of the truth (and falsehood).

1 Truth, lies, and post-truth

Tiziana Andina

1.1 Post-truth

Post-truth is a mysterious object that has become part of our epistemologies for some years now. As often happens, the term was coined to solve a problem, namely the fact that the distinction between truth and lies, in some contexts and situations, seems to have become particularly fluid and subtle, up to vanishing altogether occasionally. True and false would be a whole in which everything is confused together, depending on the perspective we adopt. Of course, no one argues that lies should be preferred to the truth, but the concept of truth is undoubtedly not doing too well given that it was thought useful to add to the traditional pair of truth and lies a third concept, that of post-truth, which somewhat plays with the idea that there is "something" beyond the truth.

As is known, the function of theories in philosophy is to elaborate hypotheses to offer arguments in support of an explanation. Now, the fact that theories have been conceived that, in some way, refer to the concept of post-truth means two things: first, that the concept of truth, in itself, has seemed to some insufficient to explain the type of relationship that exists between human beings and the world. Second, that the traditional concept of truth, which – to be clear – certifies the correspondence between the human representations of reality and reality itself, has seemed too rigid, too anthropocentric, to actually account for the complexity of the real. Therefore – at least ever since Immanuel Kant – philosophers have begun to formulate the hypothesis that there is something else, something that is placed beyond what the truth is able to capture.

Is there something beyond the truth? And if so, what is it exactly? It does not seem easy to answer this question, but the concept of post-truth appears to result from a certain dissatisfaction about the definitions of truth and lies: a dissatisfaction similar to that which must have driven Kant to introduce the concept of noumenon next to that of reality. At the other end of the reality of phenomena, Kant placed something that goes beyond them, pointing at perfection: beyond the imperfect and partially unknown world in which we find ourselves, beyond what we construct and organize in that world, there we find the noumenon which is perfect and complete and which perhaps we will never see or know. Yet, somehow, we know that it exists and that it has (at least) those characteristics. I think Kant introduced the noumenon into his theory because of his idea of perfection of being: in some way, the world had to be better than we know it to be. The hypothesis of the existence of a noumenal reality expresses this conviction.

The idea of post-truth, at least in its first approximation, on the one hand seems to react to the Kantian conviction about the perfection of being, on the other hand seems to radicalize Kant's skepticism about the possibility of developing true judgments about the knowledge of the external world, or relative to the knowledge of phenomenal reality. The general thesis is rather simple: since we have reason to doubt that it is accessible or even that it serves something, we consider the truth a bad *telos*, something to which it is not necessary to aspire. Instead, post-truth seems to be, on the one hand, a more modest and much more realistic objective, on the other hand, a more useful perspective to organize the sense of reality. In short, if truth is a high and unrealistic concept, that of post-truth seems to be a more circumscribed, consoling domain, because it is more accessible and, in some way, ecumenical.

Post-truth is thus a type of truth that is for everyone, because – as we know all too well – the truth understood in the traditional sense of the adaptation of the proposition to the thing can be very hard both to achieve and to support. So, a version of it at everyone's reach, also suitable for the weaker, less radical, spirits, can perhaps make us happier, make us feel less inadequate and – most importantly – open up a world characterized by a plurality of ideas and points of view. Most of the latter, in the view of post-truth supporters, can aspire to a legitimacy that is proportional to the rhetorical and polemical vehemence with which they are expressed. In other words, the more one supports a post-true thesis, the more one will be able to claim it should be considered true.

That is to say: if we admit that the truth as such does not exist, we must replace it with individual versions of post-truth. In other words, post-truth becomes the measure of the fact that in our particular perspective we have placed a meaning in relation to our life; a meaning that is true for us and only for us or, at most, for those with whom we share the same perspective. In some ways, the commitment to claim post-truth is stronger than that to support the truth which, in fact, in many circumstances speaks for itself. The point, as I will try to show, is this: the post-true perspective has the objective of debilitating or, if you will, weakening the truth, replacing it in the name of tolerance, democracy, and respect. Now, these are all very shareable values, when applied to the practical sphere of human life, but perhaps are less appropriate in relation to truth. Yet, we often tend to confuse the epistemological and ethical levels.

Finally, according to some hermeneutical philosophies, that of post-truth seems to be the only domain in which we ought to be interested, because it is a non-ideological domain, which consciously rejects the rigor and harshness of any judgment that claims to be true and therefore definitive and certain.[1] The underlying intuition is that humans should abandon the search for truth as a practice capable of giving them an identity, simply because each individual corresponds to a particular identity, style, and character; while, conversely, the truth seems unique, something that must be achieved and shared and that, sometimes, was even imposed by force.

1 Richard Rorty, *Philosophy and the Mirror of Nature* (Princeton, Princeton University Press.

1.2 Definition and genealogy

To approach the notion of post-truth and to capture the constellation of meanings to which it refers, let's examine the definition of the concept and then go backwards, reconstructing the genealogy of the term through the history of ideas.

"**Post-truth**. Argumentation characterized by a strong appeal to emotionality, based on widespread beliefs and not on verified facts, which tends to be accepted as truthful, influencing public opinion". This is the definition of post-truth that we find on the Treccani encyclopedia. The Oxford dictionary describes the concept in much the same way: "Relating to or denoting circumstances in which objective facts are less influential in shaping public opinion than appeals to emotion and personal belief".

The two definitions share more than one element, but mainly the idea that post-truth involves a strong emotional reaction in relation to what the post-true judgment is about. In other words, post-truth, more than truth, is emotionally connoted: emotions help post-truth come into being; we could say that they favor it. As is known, traditionally, a strong emotional connotation is considered an element of disturbance to the formulation of true judgments, since emotion is able to alter the objectivity of the formulation of the judgment. In the case of post-truth, on the contrary, the emotional connotation would be the most useful element to convince people to support post-true opinions.

The second assumption shared by both definitions regards the idea that, in the domain of post-truth, objective facts have very little weight and, in any case, much less importance than what we attribute to unfounded opinions. In other words, the facts that we consider objective as verified are irrelevant. A third assumption concerns the sphere of influence of post-true judgments and opinions. In fact, the latter seems to be a very wide sphere indeed. The formulation of post-true judgments, in general, does not concern experts in a certain domain; it rather concerns non-experts, that is, practically all of us, formulating judgments whose objects are not things we can claim to be competent in.

To summarize: the formulation of post-true judgments generally depends on people who are not competent in the area in which they formulate judgments – which means that, concretely, we are all exposed to the possibility of formulating post-true judgments. Furthermore, the exposure to post-truth grows along with the degree of emotionality that characterizes the issues we are dealing with. To be clear, the more we are dealing with things that concern and involve us, but in which we are not competent, the higher the risk of formulating post-true observations or opinions. In essence, therefore, nobody seems to be effectively protected from the risk of formulating post-true opinions and judgments and, therefore, from contributing to muddying the waters of truth.

The last element that needs to be emphasized is the necessary link between truth and post-truth. In both definitions it is possible to speak of post-truth because, in the final analysis, we are still speaking of truth, or rather because the concept of truth continues to offer the background of reference. There is a post-true domain because there is a true domain – at least according to the definitions we have seen earlier. So, it seems to be indispensable to clarify what is meant by truth in order to foster a better understanding of the concept of post-truth.

Truth is one of those concepts that has always run through the history of philosophy. Plato, in the *Cratylus*, specified that "that speech which says things as they are is true"[2], while Aristotle, in *Metaphysics*, put forward the very famous definition by which: "To say that what is is not, or that what is not is, is false; but to say that what is is, and what is not is not, is true."[3] The Aristotelian definition would later be the reference of Thomas Aquinas who, as we know, articulated the theory of truth as *adaequatio rei et intellectus*, formulated for the first time by the philosopher Isaac Ben Israeli.[4] Post-true judgments are independent of the will to describe things as they are; the goal of those who formulate them is instead that of constructing a narrative that presents them to us as we wish, imagine, hope, or fear them to be.

As for the authors of post-true judgments, we must consider at least three cases. The first is that in which the authors of post-true judgments believe that the formulation of their judgments corresponds to the truth. So, in essence, they end up mistaking post-truth (opinion, Plato would say) for the truth. Ultimately, they do not question the truth, nor do they doubt that the truth exists: they simply confuse what is true with what, at most, is only verisimilar. A second case is given by those who formulate post-true judgments while being aware that they are post-true judgments and using them as such. In essence, they lie knowing they are lying and do so for a purpose. A third case, the most complex and philosophically interesting, is that of those who believe that there is only post-truth, while truth is a kind of false myth that philosophy should deconstruct and investigate genealogically. In this case, post-truth completely replaces truth. Let's consider the issue in more detail.

1.3 Truth pushed to the edge

One of the tasks traditionally assumed by philosophy is to subject everything to critical scrutiny, even things that come with reasonable certainty. One of the most striking examples of this deconstruction is René Descartes' famous suspicion towards the existence of the external world, which he developed with increasing radicality, up to contemplating hypotheses that a person of common sense would not even dream of formulating. Let us say, Descartes suggests, that what we call reality is, in fact, a dream.[5] After all, we could very well fail to notice the difference

2 Plato, *Cratylus* in *Plato in Twelve Volumes*, Vol. 12 translated by Harold N. Fowler (Cambridge, MA, Harvard University Press; London, William Heinemann Ltd. 1921), 385b.

3 Aristotle, *Metaphysics* in *Aristotle in 23 Volumes*, Vols.17, 18, translated by Hugh Tredennick (Cambridge, MA, Harvard University Press; London, William Heinemann Ltd. 1933, 1989), IV,7 1011b.

4 Thomas Aquinas, *Quaestiones Disputatae De Veritate*, q. 1. a. 1.

5 René Descartes, *Meditations on First Philosophy*, in *The Philosophical Works of Descartes* (Cambridge University Press, 1911). Friedrich Nietzsche's insight is brilliant in this respect: "*Misconception of Dreams.*—In the dream, mankind, in epochs of crude primitive civilization, thought they were introduced to a second, substantial world: here we have the source of all metaphysic. Without the dream, men would never have been

between reality and dream, since it sometimes happens that our dreams have elements of reality: it does happen that while we dream we mistake the dream for reality. How can we rule out that this is not always the case and, indeed, that there is no mysterious entity, perhaps evil, that deceives us systematically, causing us to confuse dream and wakefulness? If this is the case – and no one, according to the skeptical argument, can really exclude that it is – then it will be necessary to formulate a theoretical and heuristic hypothesis that addresses the matter. This is one of Descartes' fundamental arguments in his *Meditations*.

It is not easy to deconstruct the skeptical argument because it asserts a possibility that, as such, cannot be excluded. If we accept, from an epistemological point of view, the possibility of this paradox, it is not easy to get out of it, or rather it is not easy to demonstrate that in reality this possibility is only possible (or even impossible). Common sense has been widely used as a foothold to combat skepticism which, however, cannot be silenced altogether. What common sense can easily achieve is to show that it is not worthwhile to follow the skeptical path, since it adds nothing to what we know with some degree of reasonable certainty. On the other hand, the risks we run if we try to solve the skeptical doubts and take them seriously are very high: in fact, to do so we should question the minimal core of knowledge that allows us to dwell in the world and make value judgments.

George Edward Moore was of the idea that through common sense we know certain things about the world with reasonable certainty, which philosophical analysis could never find in a better and more convincing way. In essence, there is no way that philosophy could bring our fundamental knowledge to a higher degree of certainty. Epistemologists will not be satisfied – as is inevitable – but ordinary people have no need to justify their knowledge of, say, the existence of material objects in ways other than those they already know and practice. On the basis of these intuitions, Moore committed to show the high degree of uncertainty and implausibility implicit in skeptical arguments, compared to the certainty that instead accompanies some statements of ordinary language.[6] If Tom wants to show Dick that there are three printing errors on page 11 in his book, what he should do is go to page 11 and show him the errors, indicating them. In this way, Dick would see the errors and easily convince himself that there are indeed three printing errors in that book, on page 11. Moore believes that we must behave in the same way with regard to the skeptical arguments about the existence of the external world. Suppose we have to prove the existence of things in the world. It is enough to show the existence of something in the world – it would not be necessary to do anything else.

incited to an analysis of the world. Even the distinction between soul and body is wholly due to the primitive conception of the dream, as also the hypothesis of the embodied soul, whence the development of all superstition, and also, probably, the belief in god." F. Nietzsche, *Human, All Too Human* (Chicago, Charles H. Kerr & Company 1908), § 5.

6 G. E. Moore, *Philosophical Papers*, Muirhead Library of Philosophy (London, New York, Allen and Unwin; Macmillan, 1959), 32–59.

Some have noted[7] that Moore's argument would leave the skeptic unsatisfied, since it says nothing about the existence of external objects, but at most argues for the existence of a certain external object – the book containing the errors on page 11. However, Moore's purpose is clearly not to follow the skeptic into the folds of his doubt, but to offer reasons not to get lost in it in the first place, i.e. to escape that sterile deconstructive path. To put the question differently: is it really convenient, in terms of economy of thought, to accept the skeptical doubt? In other words: given that the goal is knowledge rather than deconstruction, what advantage would skepticism bring? I think this is a legitimate question, whose answer is the only bulwark we can oppose to the skeptic's deconstructive drive. There has been a time in the history of philosophy in which not only the reality of the outside world was questioned, but the truth itself began to be viewed with suspicion and distrust. It has been doubted whether people can access it, partially or completely, or, more radically, whether it even exists. In other words, some have questioned whether the world in which we live is the true world, or whether it is only the product of appearance or deception. Moreover, and more radically, it has been asked if it made sense to speak of truth. The first question (about the real world), actually seems paradoxical, at least from the point of view of common sense. The second, on the very possibility of formulating true judgments, seems radically absurd since the truth is intrinsic to our way of knowing the world.

Let's start with the first one. One of the reasons that has led philosophers to systematically ask the question of truth and to often put it in terms of the relationship between reality and appearance, translating it into the relationship between truth and deception, is the suspicion about the limits and fallibility of sensible knowledge. If we accept the fact that sensitive knowledge is somewhat problematic and accidental – namely that it can be subject to deception due to perceptual dysfunctionalities or cognitive errors in the brain's processing of information – then it seems necessary to find some grounds for knowledge that are safe from the fallibility of the senses.

The senses, moreover, depend largely on one's species: at a macro level the information produced by perception is shared, but at a closer look human beings perceive the world differently from (say) bats, cats, or fish. So, Kant investigated the modalities of sensible and intellectual knowledge, relativizing them to the human being. However, after circumscribing the perimeter of human knowledge, bringing it back to its conditions of possibility, Kant also asserted that what there is does not coincide with what humans can know. In other words, he hypothesized that there are limits to what we can know and that what lies beyond these limits – and of which we only have some negative intuition – is somehow more real, more true, and more consistent than the reality to which we confer meaning through reason and the senses.

In short, part of Kantian metaphysics is the idea that there is, or may be, a reality that is more true than the phenomenal reality that we also call true. Now, it is

7 P. A. Schilpp, *The Philosophy of G. E. Moore* (Open Court Publishing Company, 1999), 397–417.

evident that this intuition does not make sense if transposed in the terms of ordinary language, since for the common person it makes no sense to maintain that there is a reality more real than that in which we live, or to make this reality a transcendent reality separated from the human one. From the perspective of common sense, we can hypothesize that there are things that escape our senses because they are too big or too small or too complex, but in some sense, what is there is all there is, and it is true.

Kant cautiously circumscribes the domain of what we can know, and limits it to what can be encountered through our senses and explored through our intellect. On the other hand, he is also certain that outside of this perimeter there is something more, which, however, we are destined to know only as a negative limit. We know that there is something, but we do not know what it is, so we must consider that limit as a regulatory principle. Kant thus overthrows the traditional framework long upheld by philosophy, where the *episteme* prevailed on the *doxa*, so that the former was seen as the only area in which it actually makes sense to speak of knowledge. Rather, Kant circumscribes the scope of possibility to metaphysics, somehow undermining the ultimate value of knowledge and keeping space for the truth, while denying that it is a space that human knowledge can access. Essentially, he introduces the idea of a truth circumscribed to the sense domain constructed by human beings – therefore, in the final analysis, a truth true to them, but not absolutely true.

This idea is clearly guided by a principle of prudence, which involves certain consequences, some desired by Kant himself – above all, the limitation of the scope of investigation of metaphysics – others, in some way, unforeseen, such as those produced by the introduction of a concept of truth that declares itself limited to a specific domain, that of human life. What is true is true, but it is true for us who know things through senses and categories that work in our typical and standardized ways. Humans know the world precisely within this domain which they themselves create in the exact moment they organize it. Prudence, however, concealed certain dangers that emerged promptly when the Kantian theory was taken further.

This particular side of Kantianism was drawn on and developed by Friedrich Nietzsche, who radicalized the subject taking it to extremes and trying to base it on two distinct levels: physiology and the critique of culture. Once clarified that only humans care about the truth, since only humans use languages and only humans exist in the world reflecting on the meaning of their relationship with it, we can deduce that the truth only exists for humans and relatively to their relationship with the world. Furthermore, we cannot exclude that, having a meaning only for us, the truth is relative to our needs, or even depends on those needs. Therefore, Nietzsche suggests that the truth is nothing other than the outcome of a strategy aimed at survival. Let me quote here a somewhat long but particularly meaningful passage, taken from *Human, All Too Human*:

> *Metaphysical World.*—It is true, there may be a metaphysical world; the absolute possibility of it can scarcely be disputed. We see all things through the

> medium of the human head and we cannot well cut off this head: although there remains the question what part of the world would be left after it had been cut off. But that is a purely abstract scientific problem and one not much calculated to give men uneasiness: yet everything that has heretofore made metaphysical assumptions valuable, fearful or delightful to men, all that gave rise to them is passion, error and self deception: the worst systems of knowledge, not the best, pin their tenets of belief thereto. When such methods are once brought to view as the basis of all existing religions and metaphysics, they are already discredited. There always remains, however, the possibility already conceded: but nothing at all can be made out of that, to say not a word about letting happiness, salvation and life hang upon the threads spun from such a possibility. Accordingly, nothing could be predicated of the metaphysical world beyond the fact that it is an elsewhere, another sphere, inaccessible and incomprehensible to us: it would become a thing of negative properties. Even were the existence of such a world absolutely established, it would nevertheless remain incontrovertible that of all kinds of knowledge, knowledge of such a world would be of least consequence—of even less consequence than knowledge of the chemical analysis of water would be to a storm tossed mariner.[8]

So, Nietzsche accepts the Kantian hypothesis: that is, he accepts the idea that there could be a metaphysical world to which we usually associate a metaphysical truth, which we know we cannot access. What we call truth is the fruit of the perspective from which we formulate it, and more precisely, it is the fruit of the structure of that perspective and of the idea of utility that it expresses. Hence a minimal and prudent truth which – and this is the point – is the "owl" of post-truth.

1.4 Game over for the truth

Thus, Nietzsche pushes the truth from the edge of metaphysics, where it had already been relegated by Kant's decentralization, even further to outside the realm of philosophy. The way he does so is rather simple. While granting the possibility of the existence of being in itself, he decisively distances himself from metaphysics on some specific questions concerning, roughly, the limits and characteristics of human knowledge, the irrelevance of the metaphysical question for common sense and, finally, for life. In other words, he does not simply claim that it is true that being is when it is, but goes so far as to affirm that we call true that which is useful – for us, that is. The revolution initiated by Kant thus becomes Copernican with Nietzsche. Let's see the fundamental questions around which it revolves.

The relativity of perspective. Nietzsche believes that human beings, the only creatures for which the word "truth" has any meaning, consider the world and the truth from their own point of view. They can know their point of view and the

8 Nietzsche, *Human, All Too Human*, § 9.

ways in which it is determined, as well as the conditions that determine it, but they cannot in any way come out of it, nor can they transcend it. This situation is immutable: it cannot be changed or corrected. So, we have no way of knowing what we would know if we were in different conditions. This situation – which is a fact – makes the metaphysical question about the thing in itself irresolvable: it is virtually possible that our knowledge is marked by imperfection, typicality, and incompleteness and we may never notice. This is evidently the skeptical hypothesis, transposed to the question of truth.

The limits of perspective. The knowledge that we usually produce when seeking the truth is affected by the imperfect components of our humanity: typically, passions and emotions. All this exposes us to error. We are interested in metaphysics precisely because of our passion for building worlds: we are passionate about this, so we create imaginative and false explanations, i.e. fantastic worlds. It should be noted that, rather curiously, Nietzsche continues to use the distinction between truth / error / lie in this context, even after having completely dismissed the truth. He dismisses it by rejecting the hypothesis that it is possible to reach the truth with the hypothesis that truth is a theoretical construct subordinated to utility.

We do not and cannot know what is absolutely true, but generally each of us knows what is useful for them, which may or may not be in agreement with the utility of the species. So, in the name of survival, reason tricked us into treating utility as if it were the truth. Therefore, it passed off a circumscribed benefit as absolute truth. In this context, the task of philosophy consists precisely in describing this shift in all its significance, so as to take any residual grounds away from metaphysics. The truth is no longer even a regulative principle: it has turned into a lie which must be believed so as not to deprive human beings of their purpose. In the long run, however, this "truth" will inevitably come out and reveal itself as a lie.

The limits of the metaphysical question. For Nietzsche, the question of truth and the real world, as it is posed by metaphysics, is only relevant to philosophy, whereas for common sense these are largely secondary questions. The reason for this lies in utility: the question about the conditions of possibility or knowledge of the thing in itself does not affect daily life. It could affect the moral sphere, but as Nietzsche shows, the latter is a typically man-made construct which, significantly, derives from what humans consider useful for life.

The truth is now completely pushed aside: not only is it a secondary concept, but it is also false,[9] because it is the outcome of manipulation driven by bad conscience, which transforms utility into reality. This manipulation has disruptive effects, because the faith in the truth – as Nietzsche says – has given rise to the most powerful energies. What happens is that we, human animals, only care about things in their relationship with the human sphere, especially with regard to their ability to bring pleasure or pain. If we ourselves are the criterion of truth, while

9 Friedrich Nietzsche, *On Truth and Lying in An Extramoral Sense* (Oxford, Oxford University Press, 1989).

the yardstick of judgment is given by utility, it follows that what our species perceives as useful is seen as true. If anyone ever revealed the truth to us, not only would we not know what to do with it, but we would be deeply disappointed:

> Whoever should disclose to us the essence of the world would be undeceiving us most cruelly. Not the world as thing-in-itself but the world as idea (as error) is rich in portent, deep, wonderful, carrying happiness and unhappiness in its womb. This result leads to a philosophy of world negation: which, at any rate, can be as well combined with a practical world affirmation as with its opposite.[10]

As you can see, Nietzsche is deeply interested in the needs of the human being, and therefore focuses on the question of happiness, creating an ambivalent tension: if someone revealed to us the essence of the world, if such a thing exists, it would make us unhappy. Only the lie – which is also infinite freedom, because it coincides with absolute creativity – gives us a colorful, interpretable world, with which we can play and create endlessly. This childish creativity towards the truth also seems to be the only guarantee of happiness. After all, this is the meaning of the famous aphorism 125 of *The Gay Science*: "the madman."[11] In Nietzsche's view, the madman is such precisely because he has unmasked the most gigantic deception of metaphysics, namely the existence of God and, as a result of this unmasking, he tries to tell the world about this fact. The metaphysical world, of which God's existence would be a guarantee, provides shelter to human beings, giving them some form of serenity. However, this comes at a dear price, a price that we have all paid: human beings are content to live within protective lies, and the madman pays with madness for his search for the truth.

However, even though Nietzsche dismisses the truth, calling it artisticity and deception if not even a useless frill, the truth remains there: it is told by the madman who strives to make it known to all. The madman knows that whoever hears his story is destined to unhappiness; therefore, he also knows that, to defend themselves from the truth of his story, his listeners will call him insane. This tension constitutes the backbone of the whole Nietzschean theory: on the one hand there is the idea that the real world is a metaphysical construction that has been developed by humans to defend themselves from the instability of a reality that they fear and cannot control, and the idea that breaking free from that construction would allow those who have a strong enough spirit to live in a state of fuller happiness because they would be more exposed to life, which is all there is.

On the other hand, there is a constant reference to the truth, because saying that reality is neither captured nor described by the categories of true and false means to argue against the theoreticians of truth with a specific truth – Nietzsche's own truth. There is no way out here, and Nietzsche knew this: any description of being, however weakened or provisional, refers to a structure, albeit that of a

10 Nietzsche, *Human, All Too Human*, § 29.
11 Friedrich Nietzsche, *The Gay Science* (Cambridge, CUP, 2001), § 125.

world without structure. Moreover, Nietzsche himself could only draw his conclusions by taking the skeptical doubt seriously, in other words, by postulating that reality may be radically different from how we experience it, because there may be living beings who experience it and construct it in ways that are totally different from ours. This could be the case, of course, but there is no evidence that it is so.

1.5 The effects of the Nietzschean dynamite: the downfall of truth and the rise of post-truth

"I am no man, I am dynamite". In fact, the question of truth as Nietzsche inherits it from Kant and then develops it in his own way is explosive to say the least in terms of its consequences. Let's try to recap the theoretical cores of the Nietzschean discourse:

1 The push of metaphysics to truth has no reason to exist for two reasons: first, because even if it existed, the truth expressed in absolute terms would be a negative concept: something about which, in the final analysis, we cannot state anything. Second, because the only truth about which we can affirm something is a truth circumscribed to the domain of the human being, the only creature for which it makes sense to speak of truth and falsehood.
2 This type of investigation, so dear to philosophers, is absolutely indifferent to common people, for whom the only perspective that counts is that of utility, and secondly that of happiness. Therefore, it would be appropriate for philosophers, too, to learn to deal with common sense rather than metaphysics.
3 Since truth in the absolute sense does not exist, it is entirely legitimate for human beings to take care of their happiness by pursuing their own utility. As for what kind of utility can convey happiness or at least serenity, Nietzsche explains it extensively through his genealogical reflections aimed at discussing the cornerstones of traditional metaphysics: the substantial subject, substance, and God. Given this gigantic deconstruction of the foundations of reality and the consequent reworking of the main concepts that make up traditional ontologies, it is obvious, from the Nietzschean point of view, that happiness should go through unhappiness – that which derives from the loss of any object endowed with a comforting function. In these terms, the happiness that Nietzsche has in mind is something that is only possible for the chosen spirits – a happiness for the few.

These are the fundamental elements of Nietzsche's theory. What is most interesting with regard to the discourse about post-truth are the consequences of his idea of the truth. First of all, it is important to note one point: although Nietzsche undertakes to deconstruct the idea of truth understood in the traditional sense and to limit its scope to a very circumscribed area – the human one – the truth remains in the background as the horizon that makes the Nietzschean reasoning possible. Nietzsche cannot eliminate the truth: he can weaken it, marginalize it, he can talk about its twilight, but he cannot overshadow its light completely. While dismissing the truth, he tells us that utility and happiness (in the particular sense that Nietzsche ascribes to the term) are more important than a truth whose power has been tremendously reduced. If the truth is pushed to the edge of the scene, what we should focus on is happiness.

Happiness is the core of the concept of post-truth as we understand it today. Given that truth is not possible, since it may not be possible in absolute terms, post-truth is there to make us, or allow us to be, happy, though not in Nietzsche's terms.[12] Nietzsche's conception of happiness was extremely burdensome: he dismissed the truth, but he made happiness something extremely demanding – practically elitist. His model of happiness required commitment to shape one's character, to control one's instincts, to forge one's will: a work that has an ascetic aspect and that has a certain idea of human perfection as its natural *telos.* The idea that it is legitimate to replace truth with utility and happiness is inherently problematic and full of implications, but Nietzsche somehow limited the consequences of it – at least those implied by his theory – by proposing an ethics of self-improvement that preserves the ideal of the human being, although it too is full of consequences (many of which are questionable).

If, however, we redefine happiness in less demanding terms than those that Nietzsche had in mind and bring it down to common sense – the same common sense that is generally the focus of politics when it comes to creating consensus – then the formulation of post-true judgments implies the adoption of absolutely individualistic criteria that are tailored to the happiness of those who formulate the post-true judgment. The domain of post-truth is not aimed at the truth: it is content with a modest utility which, moreover, is functional to the achievement of an equally modest happiness. Its core is equality – any judgment has equal legitimacy as long as it is useful to those who formulate it. Still Nietzsche, somewhat paradoxically, captures well the mediocre nature of this typicalization:

> Now, the great majority of mankind endure life without any great protest, and believe, to this extent, in the value of existence, but that is because each individual decides and determines alone, and never comes out of his own personality like these exceptions: everything outside of the personal has no existence for them or at the utmost is observed as but a faint shadow. Consequently the value of life for the generality of mankind consists simply in the fact that the individual attaches more importance to himself than he does to the world.[13]

12 Here's an example: "What I wish for those men who are of any concern to me at all is that they experience suffering, desolation, sickness, ill-treatment and indignities—that profound self-contempt, the torment of self-distrust and the misery of the vanquished not remain unknown to them: I have no pity for them because I wish them the only thing which can prove today whether one has any value or not—that he stands firm." Nietzsche, *The Will to Power* (London, Penguin, 2017), § 910.

13 Nietzsche, *Human, All Too Human*, § 33.

In this further stretch of his theory, Nietzsche recalls a doctor prescribing a cure while knowing very well what side effects it will present.

In post-truth, any judgment should be heard and legitimized simply because it has been formulated. Therefore, the best-formulated post-true judgments are those that are rhetorically more effective and arouse emotions capable of making them incisive. There are two objections, in my opinion decisive, to the two versions of the post-truth theory, namely the Nietzschean, broader variant and today's one, which is a less refined and less noble subspecies of the former. The first is a sort of diffused mist that permeates a universe in which everything has the same legitimacy. In the mist, the coordinates are lost and we lose direction even more than in the dark. The second is that the post-true world will not produce a better humanity: on the contrary it will produce a second-rate humanity, one for which nothing matters except one's own happiness. Nietzsche had a vague suspicion, a presentiment, that this could happen: in a world where everything has the same value – the value that each of us give it – we need Baron Münchhausen's initiative not to sink in the swamp.

Bibliography

Aquinas, Thomas. *Quaestiones Disputatae De Veritate.* Mariette, 1949.

———. *The Summa Theologiæ of St. Thomas Aquinas*, Second and Revised Edition, Literally translated by Fathers of the English Dominican Province, 1920 (newadvent.org).

Aristotle. *Metaphysics*, in Aristotle in 23 Volumes, Vols.17, 18, translated by Hugh Tredennick. Cambridge, MA, Harvard University Press; London, William Heinemann Ltd.1933, 1989.

Descartes, René. Meditations on First Philosophy, in *The Philosophical Works of Descartes.* Cambridge, Cambridge University Press, 1911.

Moore, G. E. *Philosophical Papers.* Muirhead Library of Philosophy. London, New York, Allen and Unwin; Macmillan, 1959.

Nietzsche, Friedrich. *Human, All Too Human.* Chicago, Charles H. Kerr & Company, 1908.

———. *The Will to Power.* London, Penguin, 2017.

———. *The Gay Science.* Cambridge, CUP, 2001.

———. *On Truth and Lying in An Extramoral Sense.* Oxford, Oxford University Press, 1989.

Plato. *Cratylus*, in Plato in Twelve Volumes, Vol. 12 translated by Harold N. Fowler. Cambridge, MA, Harvard University Press; London, William Heinemann Ltd. 1921.

Rorty, Richard. *Philosophy and the Mirror of Nature.* Princeton: Princeton University Press, 1979.

Schilpp, P. A. *The Philosophy of G. E. Moore.* Open Court Publishing Company, 1999.

Vattimo, Gianni. *Addio Alla Verità.* Melusine. Roma: Meltemi, 2009.

2 Certain trouble

Mockumentaries and truth

Sanja Bojanić

2.1 Certain trouble: mockumentaries and truth

We are so eager for "truth". But neither in life, nor theory, nor arts or politics is truth given, and figuring out what appears to be true and what appears to be false requires approaches that demand time and persuasive skills; not only rational and argumentative proficiencies, but also artistic ones, which deal with a series of elements of aesthetic nature, and above all, of affective and emotional accuracy. Indeed, producing or evidencing any material, information or fact, even artistic fact, is somewhere in the midst of a framework that deals with both truth and accuracy but also persuasiveness and acceptance.

Still, the truth and the accuracy I am dealing with in this chapter is not scientific nor is it philosophical. The protocols of truth and accuracy don't only imply particular argumentative correctness and exactness but also a certain structure of affective acceptability built through a specific framework of timing and conditioning of the truth/falsehood relationship. By demonstrating functionality of a particular genre of cinema and its relation to truth, outlined throughout the twentieth century, my intention is to highlight difficulties of unmet affective accuracies that sometimes documentaries and specifically mock-documentaries, channel while creating what has been seen, heard and experienced as true. More precisely, and for the purpose of this chapter, the question is under which conditions we are revealing the truth and what are the conditions under which the truth has been accepted, on one hand in documentary, and on the other, in mockumentary. Finally, my main objective remains to question the persuasiveness and affective expressiveness of the message they deliver. Why does this message need to be true and what are the consequences if it doesn't meet spectators' expectations?

But firstly, as the accuracy of what truth is should not be ambiguous, it is impossible to say that something could be "more true"; even though it is possible to say that it could be more accurate. It is well known in philosophy, and specifically in the theory of "truthmaking" (see Beebee and Dodd, 2005) at the intersection between ontology, metaphysics and semantics, that scholars deal with acceptance and rejection of arguments about truth-makers' maximalism where every truth has a truth-maker. Generally, truth is made true in relation to a fact. But this making or producing of the structure of facts becomes more complex when dealing with the representation of facts that have certain accuracy and still a problematic relationship with truth. Nevertheless, the goal here is not to go into a long-standing and internal debate on truth and the accuracy of philosophers but to point out the affective and emotional complexity of representing and accepting truth in a particular genre of cinema (documentary and mockumentary).

In his 1995 book on some of television's most controversial ways of addressing the viewer as citizen and consumer, John Corner asked vital questions about the nature of what appears on the screen and how it varyingly engages, informs and entertains viewers. By retracing ways of reproducing informative facts, he pointed out that:

> the core mode of documentation from the 1930's through to today is the employment of the *recorded images and sounds of actuality* to provide the viewer with a distinctive kind of 'seeing' and 'hearing' experience, a distinctive means of knowledge.
>
> (Corner, 1995: 78, author's italics)

The particularity of such knowledge is thus produced through "a distinctive kind of 'seeing' and 'hearing' experience" supported by "recorded images" and screened evidences. Processes of supporting facts using the camera thus enable a long list of specific cinematic "truth-makers" which differentiates at least two major categories: what is seen and screened is evidential (i.e. real) and what is constructed and screened is fictional (not-real or fake).

To illustrate this practice of "recorded images and sounds of actuality" belonging to these cinematic "truth-makers", I introduce a few remarks on one of the pillars of the documentary in the history of cinema, Dziga Vertov and his *Kino-Pravda* (1922–25) comparing it in a further step to one recent mockumentary (or fake documentary) by Ziga Virc, entitled *Houston, We Have a Problem!* (2016, 98'). The aim of their brief presentations and comparison is to stress how affective and emotional accuracy (which both examples remarkably carry each in their own particular manner) influences "truth-making" and blurs the distinction between factual and fictional in documentaries. Furthermore, it also introduces a certain ineffectiveness of argumentative and factual persuasiveness when it comes to recorded and screened footages and their overwhelmingly affective expressiveness. If in the first case of Vertov our affective reactions meet the expectations of spontaneity of life, sophisticated and technically successful mockumentary leaves us emotionally unsatiated.

Kino-Pravda/Kino Istina (literally translated, "film-truth") is the translation for "cinema *verité*", "direct cinema" and a synthagm describing a subject moving through the world with a camera. Dziga and Ziga, likewise Vertov and Virc may sound alike but these authors are on the opposite sides of a similar genre.

It was in 1922 that in the Soviet Union, Dziga Vertov started the *Kino-Pravda* series. The series of 23 newsreels-documentaries took its title from the official government newspaper *Pravda* and expressed Vertov's agitprop preoccupations serving the communist idea. On the one hand the *Kino-Pravda* was linked to the old newsreel, but on the other, it was a contemporary mouthpiece of the cinematic eye of the author who in a period of several years left an incredibly rich heritage for the history of the world cinema. His experimental silent documentary *The Man with the Movie Camera* (1929) shoot with the same zeal as *Kino-Pravda* is famous for the range of cinematic techniques it invented. Vertov's well-known resistance to the Capitalist film industry in the early years of cinema opened a clear path to depicting life as such with statements such as: "The body of cinema is numbed by the terrible poison of habit. We demand an opportunity to experiment with this dying organism, to find an antidote" (Barnouw, 1993: 54). His antidote was "reality". Together with his younger brother Mikhail Kaufman and his wife Yelizaveta Svilova (who actually covered the opening of Auschwitz by the Red Army in January 1945), they were to shoot what seemed important and to catch life "unaware". *Kino-Pravda* needed the camera eye, a kind of a truth-maker considered as a miraculous tool and a "machine for seeing" which could help the human eye perceive things it could not otherwise see. Vertov's specific vision was to capture "film truth" – i.e. fragments of actuality which, when organized together, have an accuracy that cannot be seen with the naked eye. In his book published in 1936, he affirmed "showing the truth is far from easy," even though "the truth itself is simple."

> Our eyes see very poorly and very little – and so men conceived of the microscope in order to see invisible phenomena; and they discovered the telescope in order to see and explore distant, unknown worlds. The movie camera was invented in order to penetrate deeper into the visible world, to explore and record visual phenomena, so that we do not forget what happens and what the future must take into account.
>
> (Vertov, 1984: 67)

With its dynamic, swift camera movements, double exposures, jump cuts, self-reflexive visuals and rapid close-ups, *Kino-Pravda* was considered livelier than most newsreels. Focusing on everyday experiences and shunning bourgeois concerns, Vertov filmed marketplaces, bars and schools instead, sometimes with a hidden camera, without asking permission first. The episodes of *Kino-Pravda* usually did not include reenactments or any staging (with a few exceptions: the people reading the journals in the trolley and the scenes of the selling of the newspapers on the streets). The cinematography was simple, functional, unelaborate, an obvious result of Vertov's disinterest in both "beauty" and the "grandeur of fiction." It dealt with "the prose of life" (Vertov, 1984: 67–69) but processed with certain elements that would convey symbolic values. So in issue No. 24 (1925), on the first anniversary of the death of Lenin, we see people streaming past the dead leader in his coffin. Meanwhile the living Lenin appears by superimposure in the corner of the screen as though still speaking to them. Here the "simplicity" of truth has been covered by sophisticated and tricky double exposure, presence of the absent with intentions of symbolically comforting mourning masses. The *Kino-Pravda* series considerably influenced the development of the documentary as a genre and likely contributed to *Time*'s decision to create *The March of Time*. The inspiration to the *cinema vérité* movement of the 1960s was not evident solely by its name but in the aspiration of capturing life "on the run". Content of life has been satiated by details and affective spontaneity. The stories were typically descriptive, not narrative, and included vignettes and exposés, showing for instance the renovation of a trolley system, the organization of farmers into communes and the trial of Social Revolutionaries; one story even shows starvation in the nascent Communist state.

This was to be a cinema of the seen, recorded and screened fact, of life unscripted, and the cinematographer rejected any attempt to introduce fictional or narrative elements as rearguard. For Vertov, cinema rose to its full potential as a medium only when it "was built on the organization of documentary footage recorded by the camera" (Vertov, 1984: 103). Affective and emotional persuasiveness of the screened material fulfilled all expectations and the film was shown with extreme directness and candor. On the contrary to his understanding of capturing these life instances, the narrative cinema was "a phenomenon of a secondary, theatrical nature" as it was "founded upon the organization of acted footage recorded by the camera" (*ibid.*). This incredible energy and speed invested in the creation of the cultural policies of the Soviet government actually followed the interest in film expressed by Vladimir Ilyich Lenin, resulting in subsidizing film production and creating state film schools to train personnel for the new industry. It was known that Lenin preferred the educational content found in newsreels and documentaries, and argued for the establishment of a "fixed ratio between entertainment pictures and scientific [documentary] ones" (Vertov, 1984: 88). This protocol identified as a "Leninist ratio" followed the idea according to which if you have good newsreels and serious educational films, then "it doesn't matter if some useless film is shown to attract an audience" (Vertov, 1984: 113).

Clearly, Vertov's ideological faith didn't only respect technological progress but also certain pre-formalist elements which treated the cinematic eye as "the possibility of making the invisible visible, the unclear clear, the hidden manifest, the disguised overt, the acted non-acted" (Vertov, 1984: 82), finally constructing reality from sometimes falsely spontaneous situations and directing raw screened material into truth. *Kino-Eye* was to show truth on the screen and this truth was given as the *Kino-Pravda* (film-truth). Avoiding any form of prearranged narrative, emotional and affective persuasiveness make their way to the spectators in a purely formalist, technological and repetitive manner. Obviously, these proceedings matched Victor Shklovsky's (1923) words from his manifesto: "Now (in 1923) words are dead, and language is like a graveyard, but an image was once alive in the newly-born word". A few lines later we read, "every word is basically — a trope" and "we live as if coated with rubber." The only imperative should be to recover the world. The author continues:

> The purpose of the image is to call an object by a new name. To do this, to make the object, an artistic fact must be abstracted from among the facts of life. We must first of all 'shake up' things... We must rip things from their

> ordinary sequence of associations. Things must be turned over like logs in a fire.
>
> (Shklovsky, 1923: 24–26)

Vertov's words from *A Report to the Cine-Eyes* (Kahana, 2016: 171–173) are less metaphoric even though they grasp the same radical necessity of epistemic change and call for certainty that he finds in technology: "The technical quality, the social and historical value of the material and, subsequently, the quality of the whole thing depend on how and when we submit life to the lens and how we reinforce the trace that it leaves" (Vertov, 1984: 113).

"Shaking up things" and quite intriguingly "submitting life to the lens", face the same goal of materially reinforcing the traces of life that subsequently didn't work later in the Stalinist and Zhdanov era of social realism. Truth then ceased to be a product of hard work and investigation, and contrary to Vertov's first intentions, it only remained a highly constructed ideology packed into the hermetic narrative. His position of cinematographer who produced and made naked truth contrasted the opposing tendencies of substituting the cinematic eye with a well-developed story. In the rest of the twentieth century the new documentary age prevailed with various subgenres combining exactly the same tropes Shklovsky fustigated as a waste of time and creative energy.

Documentary story-telling gradually contaminated screening of what has been seen, heard and experienced as evident and true. In fact, it culminated in different docufiction forms and the development of the mockumentary which eventually found its ways as a genre combining facts and fiction, i.e. fiction and facts in a form of chiasm. Comparing it to previously exposed Vertov's intentions, new documentaries started lacking the whole "reality" or "evidential" part of the construction. This is the nuance between the construction of the truth effects and the accuracy to the facts. Smoothly composed narration thus feeds the spectator's need for affective satiety. It urges the spectator's satisfaction but doesn't meet his/her need for truth nor for the reality. Unlike most docufictions which are by definition considered and treated as documented story-telling, the trouble with mockumentary starts when it appropriates much more closely the look and feel of a basic form of documentary. Mockumentary uses all documentary devices such as voiceover narrations, on-camera interviews and reenactments in order to provide appearance of documentary authenticity to events that are actually staged and scripted (see Lipkin, Paget, and Roscoe, 2006: 11–27). It pretends going through the research and investigation by citing the sources and providing disclaimers. Tricky enough, it remains reality based and eventually, what it should mark it out from the "hoax" or "fakeness" is the unwritten contract set up between producer and audience (see Schantz, 2018). Still, this lookalike attitude distances it from a position of the truth-maker and obstructs its intentions. Consequently, even though mockumentary's basic incentives are to deconstruct, criticize and mock certain reality, its relation to truth becomes distorted.

But, let us first check what *Houston, We Have a Problem!* is about. The whole film is extremely well packed and staged. All we read in its spoiler, we could watch on screen. The story starts with:

> the discovery of the newly declassified information proving that in the 1960s the United States government paid $ 2.5 billion to buy the Yugoslav space program, under the mistaken impression that it was far in advance of where it was.

The plot is furthermore developed by introducing historical figures of John F. Kennedy, Lyndon B. Johnson and even Richard Nixon, threatening president of then Yugoslavia, Tito, "trying to get the tech to work or to get the money back." Along the way, Ziga Virc intercuts the story as being told by supposed historian Roger McMillan, providing piles of "evidences" and archive footage. It chooses a main character, a smart and obscure engineer "Ivan Pavic" who has been supposedly smuggled to the United States. More or less, the narrative is based on the main character's testimony during the visit to his abandoned birthplace in Yugoslavia and his first encounter with a daughter he never met. Americans patiently kept the engineer alive, as he was supposedly helping them to crack the moon-race code during the Cold War. By the end of the film, Slavoj Zizek (involved in the process of production and certainly because of the notoriety mentioned as one of the main protagonists), while commenting what has been screened proclaims: "Even if it didn't happen, it's true."

This ambiguously strange formula comes to an end and confirms the parody of the whole script. Its ill tuned satirical tones leave most of the audience unfulfilled at spending some time witnessing a film that mocked up, not only the conspiracy theories and roles that certain figures had in a recent history of the Balkans region, but also collective beliefs. The seemingly Lacanian statement with McLuhan's nuances not only pretends to propose a better understanding of the Real (as unattainable) but puts truth on the opposite side of the Vertov's "simplicity" and the understanding that "showing truth is not easy" even though "truth is simple." Regretfully, nowadays the post-truth ambiance encourages biases, which appear as truth. It allows situations that pretend to be true and represent truth and results in the parodying of truth to the point of inventing it. Distortion of truth and its highly constructed narratives reminds us of Shklovsky's words: "we live as if coated with rubber."

References

Barnouw, Erik, 1993, *Documentary: A History of the Non-fiction Film*, Oxford: Oxford University Press.

Beebee, Helen and Dodd, Julian (eds.), 2005, *Truthmakers: The Contemporary Debate*, Oxford: Clarendon Press.

Corner, John, 1995, *Television Form and Public Address*, London: Edward Arnold.

Kahana, Jonathan ed., 2016, *The Documentary Film Reader: History, Theory, Criticism*, Oxford and New York: Oxford University Press.

Lipkin, Steven, Paget, Dereck, and Roscoe, Jane, 2006, "Docudrama and Mock-Documentary: Defining Terms, Proposing Canons" in *Docufictions: Essays on the Intersection of Documentary and Fictional Filmmaking*, Rhodes, Gary D., Springer, John Parris (eds.), Jefferson, North Carolina and London: McFarland & Company, Inc., Publishers.

Schantz, Miriam von, 2018, *The Doc, the Mock, and the What? Events of Realing, Mockumentalities and the Becoming-Political of the Viewing Subject*, "Örebro Studies in Media and Communication 23", Örebro University.

Shklovsky, Viktor, 1923, "Form and Material in Art" in Blake, Patricia and Hayward, Max 1975 (eds.), *Dissonant Voices in Soviet Literature*, Westport, Conn.: Greenwood Press.

Vertov, Dziga, 1984, "Kino-Eye" in *Kino-Eye: The Writings of Dziga Vertov*, ed. and intro. Michelson, Annette, Berkeley, Los Angeles and London: University of California Press.

3 After the ordeal

Law and the age of post-truth

Angela Condello

> *a* uniformly valid and binding
> designation is invented for things,
> and this legislation of language likewise
> establishes the first laws of truth
> [Nietzsche 1873]

3.1 Preliminary remarks

Few things are probably more risky for a jurist than theorizing on the nature of truth, (plus) starting from remarks on *language*; and, if it was not sufficient, within a book composed by a relevant number of philosophical contributions. Yet, it is precisely from language that I intend to begin and, in addition to this, it is with some remarks on language that I shall conclude. In this book, we are called to discuss the functions and values of post-truth today, and to question its meaning from different disciplinary perspectives; the composed term 'post-truth' has been used very frequently in the last couple of years, and it keeps being used quite frequently nowadays. Why did this word emerge? What makes the use of the expression "post-truth" relevant?

Emergence. New words emerge when new concepts or objects need to be defined; when our vocabulary, in other words, is not enough. The emergence of the expression "post-truth", which in English is used as an attribute (like in the phrase "post-truth politics") while in Italian (and in French and in other romance languages) is used as a noun, expresses the need to name a new form of knowledge, of truth production, and of circulation of information–especially in the public realm; more precisely, and more often, especially on the web. The Oxford English Dictionary has decreed that "post-truth" was the word of the year for 2016 – the year of Brexit and of Trump's elections. The word indicates a circumstance in which objective facts and the correspondence between reality and what is said about reality is less influential in the shaping of public opinion than emotions or personal beliefs.

Generally, the main remark made about post-truth is that such a linguistic-rhetorical practice has a specific purpose, today: it is aimed, supposedly, at constructing a new reality out of whole cloth. A new reality in which data are (or might be) wrong, and yet are manipulated in order to reach specific goals (mainly, and mostly, to achieve consensus for political purposes). In other terms, currently post-truth is an *instrument*: it is no coincidence that in recent works about post-truth (Ferraris 2017), philosophers have focused on the processes through which truth is made, produced, created.

Post-truth requires a certain discipline and willingness to tell many lies that add up to one bigger, and more inclusive, lie. This is why we do not speak about *one* or *two* specific sentences which do not correspond to the truth and that are aimed at achieving a precise political goal, but we refer instead to a broader and more inclusive *system* of propositions that do not correspond to reality or that are not coherent with reality. All these, together, build what has been defined as "post-truth" politics.[1] If legitimation through truth, lies, faith, and similar complex structures of belief has always characterized the management of power through politics, the contemporary era is particularly interesting since new media and social networks – with the systems for filtering the news and for creating groups that resemble Leibniz's monads (speaking to themselves redundantly) – have increased together with the increase of the communicative force of communication in truth production and in political legitimation.

Connections. Post-truth is generally understood as a deviation from truth. But its basic structure and system of production are the same as for truth (Ferraris 2017). Truth is, in fact, always based on the connection between a subject and a predicate (Plato defined it with the term "*symplokè*"): truth defines the connection between these two and such a connection can be, depending on the case, more or less correspondent to reality. The reason why I introduce the function of connection in language is that such specific connection and correspondence explain the emergence, today, of post-truth – since new media (in general) and the web (in particular) multiply the number of possible connections between subjects and predicates. Thus, judgments proliferate, together with the system of voices and sources contributing to truth-making.

3.2 After truth

Post-truth indicates what comes *after* truth: a sort of "under-truth", or minor form of truth. The procedures aimed at making or producing truth (Ferraris 2017), which are fundamental characters of the age called "post-truth", lead to the creation of un-realities that exist parallel to "real" reality, one "riddled with falsity, inconsistency, and confusion" (Fitzpatrick 2017). The majority of commentators agree on the fact that the main aim of such a "passage" – from truth to post-truth – is to confuse the perceptions of reality and to break down trust in order to achieve the dependence of individuals on the dominating powers. Fitzpatrick reads

1 As an anonymous Bush official declared in an interview to *The New York Times* in 2004 (Ron Suskind, October 14): "We're an empire now, and when we act, we create our own reality".

this transition through the Foucauldian intuition that liberal democracy would have produced the singularization of individuals (Foucault 2007: 89, 106).

Similarly, Ferraris reads this moment of change through the metaphor of the monads (Leibniz): each individual lives in a sort of "bubble" in which he or she can produce truth autonomously. This is made possible by the fact that verification processes through epistemic authorities are losing credibility. What is particularly striking in Fitzpatrick's and Ferraris' reflections on the consequences of post-truth on socio-legal studies, is that post-truth politics have an impact that goes much beyond the mere sphere of "public discourse", or of political debates. Post-truth constitutes an alternative way for depicting reality, a way that creates room for different forms of legitimation, and that thus has a relevant impact on the value attributed to the force and power of institutions. The common characteristic of post-truistic communication is that it works at a double level: on the one hand, it produces consensus and legitimizes actions, choices, and judgments based on consensus. A typical example is Trump's way of communicating via Twitter or other social networks. On the other hand, the consensus is so powerful that it de-legitimizes other forms of power, such as institutional or legal power. This allows for the creation of a different dimension in which the correspondence between language and reality is not verifiable, but is instead based on the authority and charisma of the individual that conveys the truth. This produces a clash between different forms of truth, which could be described with the categories of "truth" and "post-truth", where the main difference between the two categories lies in the source of the *connection* between language and reality. In the case of truth, there are epistemic authorities that control the process of truth production; in the case of post-truth, the validity of the connections between language and reality is only guaranteed by the rhetorical force and charismatic attitude of the individual-leader and by the consensus deriving from such force and charismatic attitude.

A recent episode will hopefully help clarify this double movement and, at the same time, will bring the former reflections more towards the specificity of law in relation to post-truth today. It is mid-August 2018 and the vessel *Diciotti*, of the Italian Coast Guard (Guardia Costiera), arrives close to the Italian coast, near Catania in Sicily. A hundred and seventy-seven people are on the vessel: almost all of them are in the conditions to be granted the humanitarian protection by international law. The *Diciotti* remains docked for one day, and then for two days, and up to more than five days. The migrants are not allowed to disembark because – this is the argument used by the Minister of the Interior, Matteo Salvini – they cannot disembark since they do not have guarantees from Brussels on their distribution in other EU countries. The Minister of the Interior wants the other European states to take responsibility for the care of the refugees and migrants on the ship. During 2018, it is the third time already that the *Diciotti* is prevented from landing migrants into an Italian port. This time, at the end of August 2018, most of the people on board the *Diciotti* in Catania are from Somalia and Eritrea. The spokesmen of various international NgOs, such as Save the Chidren and Amnesty International, denounce the episode in terms of an extremely serious violation of fundamental human rights.

Matteo Salvini, Minister of the Interior, insists on his position despite the intervention of intellectuals, politicians, civil society, activists, and NgOs. So, prosecutors start investigating on the legality of his behavior, travelling to Rome to question Salvini and some members of his staff. *The Guardian* reports (August 25, 2018) his words: "I heard prosecutors asked for my details. Here you go. I was born in Milan, March 9 1973. I'm ready and proud to be arrested because I'm fighting to defend the Italian border" – this is what Salvini wrote on Facebook as the news emerged about the investigation. In any case, after a couple days he let the refugees disembark.[2]

3.2.1 After the ordeal

That is the prelude. Then the attack against the judiciary begins. The Minister begins by writing posts on Twitter and Facebook against Luigi Patronaggio, the Prosecutor of Agrigento who started the investigation. He writes that Patronaggio had recently (actually, he writes "very recently") declared that there could be, in some specific situations, the risk of terrorism related to clandestine boats (out of control of any authority). Actually, the interview he refers to had been released almost one year before (first non-corresponding fact); and Patronaggio had been discussing, in that interview, about a completely different situation: he had not spoken about refugees fleeing the war, but about little clandestine boats carrying completely different subjects in completely different conditions and for different reasons (second non-corresponding fact). Salvini cuts parts and single propositions in Patronaggio's speeches about a different situation and context, and re-uses them in order to demonstrate the alleged lack of coherence of the Prosecutor. He uses the words that he needs to use, withdrawing titles and sentences from old newspapers and building a collage that can support his current intentions: the migrants must not disembark. His symbolic war against migration must be carried on with all means and in particular with means not based on correct data, but aimed at increasing support and unconditional consensus.

All this prelude leads at the core of an ancient contrast: that between opinion, individual will and values, on the one hand; and convention, law, procedure, on

2 In January 2019, the story continues. Catania's Court for Ministers requests authorization to proceed with the Diciotti case, for which Matteo Salvini is accused of kidnapping for refusing to allow that large number of migrants to get off the Diciotti ship. "They are trying again," League leader Salvini said in a live Facebook broadcast. "Once again I am under investigation for kidnapping people and minors, with a possible term of between three and 15 years (…) I wouldn't get that even if I were a drug dealer or a rapist. (…) Now it's up to the Senate and the Senators will have to say yes or no, free or innocent, trial or not.". He continues "But I say right away that my position is not changing one centimetre - I ask the Italian people if they think I should keep being minister, exercising rights and duties, or if should ask this court or another about immigration policy. (…) I admit it, I confess it and I stand by it - I stopped the disembarkment - And I declare myself guilty of the crimes of the coming months, because I'm not changing". [source www.ansa.it/english/news/2019/01/24/court-requests-to-proceed-with-salvini-diciotti-case_3f6dbbc8-1463-4fb6-9770-da4a6ac7c048.html].

the other hand – that between irrational choices and the rationality of procedure. It is by now well known that the "art of the lie" (post-truth politics, in other words) is built on mechanisms like "filter bubbles", which are made possible by the fact that netizens tend to form self-contained groups which circulate precise information crafted precisely for those groups. Algorithms can detect preferences and web surfing behaviors and this can keep people from finding countervailing views and opinions (and data and facts corresponding to what is real). So, for instance, during the referendum in the UK campaign, leavers mostly saw pro-Brexit news. Obviously, these algorithms and the way they are used can construct groups that "make" truth independently of any epistemic authority and procedure of verification or legitimation. The function of truth is no longer the best interest of the community, but it becomes the best interest of the individual.

I consider the conflict between Minister Salvini and Prosecutor Patronaggio a good example of different attitudes towards truth: that of law and that of politics. Social media, in fact, enable members of groups to strengthen each other's beliefs, by shutting out contradictory information: unlike legal procedures (I would say: opposite to legal procedures) post-truth politics have been made possible by a loss of trust in institutions and by a loss of grounding and legitimation of truth-making procedures and systems. This has caused an extremely serious consequence: truth has lost its *raison d'être*, which should have been the capacity of establishing connections between language and reality. The contrast between the Prosecutor and the Minister is interesting because it shows two different ways of approaching truth: a proceduralized way, and an emotional and instinctive way. Such a contrast proves that post-truth politics produce a deviation from the very nature of truth, which lies also in the validation of truth-making processes. Such a validation and control over the procedures that build the connection between language and reality got lost in post-truth politics. Perhaps, this has to do with a loss of the function of politics.

The function of law and of legal procedures, on the other hand, remains pretty clear since there is no doubt about the consequences that a decision of a judge can have on reality: law is not concerned with a final, universal truth (which, we will see also following Nietzsche, is not something that can be discovered or possessed by human beings), but with a sort of "everyday" truth. More importantly, legal truth has clear *consequences*: it is because of the consequences that it could produce that truth in law needs to be the product of clear procedures – of evidence, of proceduralized investigations, of continuous verification. The consequences and the concrete impact of truth, in law, are directly related to its proceduralization and deliberately recognized artificiality. What is different in current post-truth politics, instead, is that the procedures of truth-making and the constructed nature of truth are often concealed because otherwise post-truth politics would lose their rhetorical force. As a technique, instead, law permanently builds connections between language and reality and leads to the attribution of values to propositions and facts: the *iuris prudentia* is indeed a *technè*.

The *prudentia* of modern law is proceduralized for a reason. Such a knowledge and capacity of judgment comes after the *ordeal*, which symbolically represents irrationality. Late Medieval ordeals used in the Langobardic legal system are an interesting paradigm of a legal procedure based on completely irrational principles. The correspondence between language and reality, in Medieval ordeals, was a secondary value: what counted most was that a decision was reached – and as quickly as possible. Individuals and individual interests and values, in those ordeals, had a very active role in helping the judge to reach the truth: self-confirmation counted more than truth in itself. Before the Gregorian reformation (XI century), the official value of a trial was thought to be given by the Holy Spirit, which was supposed to be diffusely present everywhere. The validity of judicial truth-making procedures was certified by this kind of "mystical" force, invisible and yet extremely powerful, in order to reach a conclusion as soon as possible. After the Gregorian reformation, the Church established that the Holy Spirit is not present diffusely and everywhere, and this entails that it must be embodied by someone, by an authority that certifies its presence and truthfulness. Ordeals were officiated before the Gregorian reformation and were based on a probatory system entirely different from the Roman law procedure: where Roman procedural law was based upon proofs, witnesses, and documents, the late Medieval (mainly Germanic) ordeal – on the contrary – was based upon the outcome of duels, on oaths, and on random natural facts. While ancient Roman procedure was aimed at finding truth – or, better, at *making* truth – properly, that is to say according to the same series of actions, the ordeal had the following characteristics (Loschiavo, in press): (i) it was mainly oral; (ii) the activity of the parts was more relevant than the opinion and the activity of the judge; (iii) the parts would communicate directly, without much mediation of the judge; (iv) courage, faith, passions would count more than truth-making procedures. Often guilt or innocence were determined by subjecting the accused to painful or unpleasant and dangerous experiences. For instance, a very common proof consisted in asking the accused to put his hand into a cauldron with boiling water. Other times, it was the accuser being asked to put his hand into boiling water. If the hand remained uninjured, he was considered innocent; otherwise, he was considered guilty. The trial by ordeal was a judgment of God: a procedure based on the idea that God would help the innocent by performing a miracle on his behalf.

After the ordeal came modernity. With it, law was returned to rationality – which entailed procedure: a standardized way of *making truth*. From that moment on, democracy and truth-making were no longer separated and this interconnection is now showing the risks of its misinterpretation and abuse.

3.3 Making truth. The legal perspective

When speaking about the relationship between law and truth, we must preliminarily draw a distinction between the truth-value of a proposition of law, on the one hand, and the procedure through which truth is made *via* procedure by the judiciary – what has been named "judicial truth" (Viola 1995) – on the other (Patterson 1996). What does it mean to say that a proposition of law is true? Answering this question entails exploring the complex relationship between realism and truth in law, a relationship broadly explored in this book. Also, to simplify what appears to be a conundrum of diverse perspectives on the relationship between law and truth, we can recall H. L. A. Hart's claim on legal positivism, according to which truth in law is always (and must always be) a question of form and of correspondence between form and content. It is widely known, at least among legal scholars, that such a positivist and formalist perspective on law was based on the idea that legal norms are part of a system within which the primary value is *internal coherence*: that is to say, a system in which each norm is made valid (and, in this sense, also "true") by norms of a higher level. The rule of recognition is the paradigm of such a formal and systematized relationship between law and truth: Hart's rule of recognition is a kind of secondary rule which validates a legal system and which is central, foundational, and essential to every legal system. Law, from the perspective of legal positivism, is *constituted* by form (Patterson 1996, 25):

> form renders juridical relationships intelligible as such. Form is what makes something intelligible, making it what it is and distinguishing it from all other things. In other words, form makes the object or idea intelligible to a subject capable of cognition. As an object of consciousness, form must be grasped as a unity, that is, as a unity of content.

And yet, the specific nature of the interconnection between law and truth is not *only* a matter of legal positivism, nor of legal formalism. Legal procedure has much to do with the unique nature of legal truth too, as I shall argue in this paragraph.

What can we thus gain by looking at the relationship between law and truth, in the age of post-truth? I am tempted to answer: "the very nature of truth", but this might sound as an exaggeration. Without idealizing law, which is itself a system embedded with power and which of course is much more complex an object than just a general and abstract *Stufenbau* – the "law", as it is referred to in this synthetic series of remarks – I am still inclined to answer that politics and public discourse would gain something by observing how law relates to truth. The general remark is that law – both in its "static" version, the positive norm which generalizes an obligation and is valid because of norms of higher rank, and in its "dynamic" version, the judgment that connects facts and norms – is intrinsically artificial and deliberately considers truth as the product of a convention. Jurists speak, in fact, of "judicial truth" (Viola 1995). The legal process (at least ideally), as noted by many legal theorists including Luigi Ferrajoli, does not aim at persuading anyone, but at justifying the decision: judicial truth, thus, entails the artificiality of the connection between language and the world. The legal arguments are not – and must not be – valued for their persuasive force. On the contrary, they should be valued for their conformity to objective criteria and procedures, as the example of the conflict between Salvini and Patronaggio discussed earlier should prove.

The judicial decision concerns both facts and norms and thus truth-making must be deconstructed into a *quaestio facti* (factual truth) and *quaestio iuris* (legal truth). The judicial decision is indeed a very interesting example of a mixed system of truth production (Viola 1995), in which both the correspondence between language and reality and the coherence of the final judgment with the more general values and functions of the legal system (first and foremost, to guarantee justice) are relevant. From the point of view of the law, there are no true and false facts or true and false norms, but only correct judgments (or non-correct judgments). Italian legal philosopher Francesco Viola has perfectly recalled the centrality of the competent authority in making legal truth, which was discussed by Hans Kelsen. Viola writes:

> In place of the empirical verification, through which the scientist knows and constitutes the natural facts, there is the fact of the ascertainment by the judge, who is the competent authority (Kelsen, *Reine Rechtslehre* 244). A *legal fact* is not a natural fact ascertained by a judge in a legal process, but it is the *ascertainment* itself. Thus, the legal judgment has specific truth-criteria that are parallel to those of natural science, but distinct from it. The most relevant difference does not reside in particular methods, but in the normative appointment of a subject authorized to produce legal facts. Therefore, Kelsen restores total autonomy to the world of legal knowledge and of legal reality.
>
> (Viola 1995: 252)

The legal paradigm is particularly interesting, when observed today, since it breaks down the alleged division between philosophical theories of correspondence and of coherence. Within the philosophical tradition, in fact, different theories on truth have emerged and developed over time. The two main theories are known as "correspondence theory" and "coherence theory". On the one hand, the main idea of *correspondence* theory, which is then diversified into various correspondence theories (Glanzberg 2018), is that what we believe and say is either true or false if it corresponds – or not – to the way things actually are, that is to say to facts of reality. From the perspective of correspondence theory, facts are propositions that are always true, since they always have factual correspondence. On the contrary, propositions are not always true since their correspondence with facts must always be verified. It has to be noted that the correspondence theory of truth is (at its core) an ontological thesis: a belief is true if there exists an appropriate entity – a fact – to which it corresponds (Glanzberg 2018).

On the other hand, the *coherence* theory of truth implies that truth in its essential nature concerns systematic coherence. Truth, in other words, must be considered as one aspect of a larger frame. Thus, from the perspective of the coherence theory, a belief is true if and only if it is part of a coherent system of beliefs.

Law seems to stand between these two theories (Lynch 2008): both in the case of the positive, abstract legal norm, and in the case of the judicial decision, the relationship with truth is characterized by (i) the connection with reality and factuality; (ii) the coherence with a larger system of values and with the function and *raison d'être* of law more generally, i.e. guaranteeing order and peaceful coexistence. Because of the functions that it is aimed at achieving, law indicates the convergence between correspondence and coherence and thus indicates a different perspective on truth. Such connection with a task, and final objective, seems to emerge in particular in legal texts that explicitly mention *truth as a value* for future generations.

For instance, in section 26 of the Act on the German Federal Constitutional Court (*Bundesverfassungsgerichtsgesetz* – BverfGG, 1951) we read:

> *(1)* The Federal Constitutional Court shall take the evidence necessary to establish the truth. It may, outside of the oral hearing, instruct a member of the Court to do so or may request another court to do so in respect of specific facts and individuals.

Truth is, here, a value that must be protected and guaranteed and that, thus, must be based on evidence, which in turn shall be selected according to specific conventional criteria (Bellucci 2005). Around truth, in law, there is a system of protection: a labyrinth that, at each turning point, entails institutional responsibility towards a community. Especially after the historical experience of totalitarian regimes, truth is considered a fundamental apparatus of the rule of law: contemporary constitutions often mention truth as a sort of precious value that must be preserved against the risk of tyranny.

Correspondence. Law rejects the existence of an absolute truth and builds ways of dealing with what has been defined "pretention of truth" (Tuzet 2013). The verification of such pretention is based on narratives (by the parts, by witnesses, by the judge): this is due to the very structure of juridical norms, which are composed – like every conditional proposition – by a protasis and by an apodosis (*if X, then P*). Legal procedure aims at verifying the factual conditions and at connecting them to the normative consequences.

Facts, in legal procedure, are necessarily reconstructed – this explains the "ordinary" artificiality of judicial truth. Reconstruction is possible thanks to narratives which come from different sources. These sources, in turn, are selected: thus, also the source of the narratives on which the correspondence between language and reality is evaluated is conventional and established a priori. Mainly, four types of subjects participate in the reconstruction of legal truth (Taruffo 2009; Pastore 1996): the parts (especially attorneys); witnesses; experts and consultants; judges.

Coherence. As far as the relationship with coherence is concerned, law relates to truth in a way which is entirely different from, for instance, history or literature (Viola and Zaccaria 1999). Unlike history or literature, which are also based on narratives and on various sources, law performs a specific task and thus it shows the need to be anchored to solid systems of value and to precise tasks. It is mainly for this reason that judicial narratives, by all participants in the trial, are tied by the need to reach a coherent conclusion which balances the interests of the parts – which is, in other words, just. In order for this correspondence and coherence to be assured, there is no transcendental value or institution involved in the procedure: it is sufficient that some basic conditions are respected – more specifically, that narratives come from qualified subjects (i) and that they have an authoritative force once the decision is "constructed" (ii). The concrete and practical nature of their consequences is, in other words, what makes them unique.

Truth is thus relevant for law, and for procedure in particular, because what counts is not to reach whatever decision or truth. What counts is to reach a *just* decision and a *just* truth, that is to say a very specific and qualified type of truth: this is possible if correspondence to facts and reality and coherence with a more structured system of values converge.

3.4 A "movable host of metaphors"

Often, post-truth has been associated with postmodernism and to the (misleading, when exaggerated) perspective from which there are no facts, but only interpretations of facts. Actually, if we take Nietzsche's *On Truth and Lies in a Non-moral Sense* (1873), the problem that emerges is that men tend to forget that every linguistic connection is artificial, and thus that every truth – because it is always a connection between a subject and a predicate – must be considered starting from its artificial nature, and not as a transcendental value deriving from a dimension other than the human one. It is not in the very origin of postmodern claims, but perhaps in how they have been used purposefully, that we shall look for when searching for the roots of contemporary post-truth politics.

As a matter of fact, Nietzsche underlines how in a comparison between human mind and nature, lies are always the direct product of language and are thus directly related to human life and activities. He wonders where the drive for truth comes from. And he concludes that is comes from the need to coexist pacifically with other individuals: insofar as the individual wants to maintain himself against other individuals, he or she will employ the intellect mainly and essentially for dissimulation, which is an intrinsically human act. Human beings invent truth, which is nothing but a conventional way to establish connections between language and reality, in order to banish the *bellum omni contra omnes.* After this invention, for Nietzsche, that which shall count as truth is *established.*

Language, according to this picture, is nothing but a

> movable host of metaphors, metonymies, and anthropomorphisms: in short, a sum of human relations which have been poetically and rhetorically intensified, transferred, and embellished, and which, after long usage, seem to a people to be fixed, canonical, and binding. Truths are illusions which we have forgotten are illusions – they are metaphors that have become worn out and have been drained of sensuous force, coins which have lost their embossing and are now considered as metal and no longer as coins.
>
> (Nietzsche, 1873)

Men should look back at how language functions in order to recover the meaning of language, and most importantly its function, which is peaceful coexistence.

What we possess are metaphors or colors, trees, flowers, and of facts; these metaphors, according to Nietzsche, correspond in no way to the original entities. And so, conclusively, if language exists, it must be for a purpose. Law proves this connection with its own purpose . . . everywhere.

Bibliography

Bellucci, Patrizia. *A onor del vero. Fondamenti di linguistica giudiziaria*. Firenze, UTET, 2005.

Ferraris, Maurizio. *Documentalità. Perché è necessario lasciar tracce*. Roma-Bari, Laterza, 2009.

Ferraris, Maurizio. *Postverità e altri enigmi*. Bologna, Il Mulino, 2017.

Fitzpatrick, Peter. *Post-truth: for or against socio-legal studies?*, in the Socio-Legal Review (www.sociolegalreview.com/post-truth-for-or-against-socio-legal-studies/). February 24, 2017.

Foucault, Michel. *Security, Territory, Population: Lectures at the Collège de France 1977–1978*, trans. Graham Burchell. Houndmills, Basingstoke: Palgrave Macmillan, 2007.

Glanzberg, Michael. (ed.). *The Oxford Handbook of Truth*. Oxford, OUP, 2018.

Loschiavo, Luca. *Rothari's Edict. German ancestral Customs and Roman legal Traditions between old Questions and new Discussions*, in B. Salway / S. Corcoran (eds), *PROJECT VOLTERRA. II*. London, in press.

Lynch, Michael P. *How to be a Relativist*, in P. Nehrot (ed.), *Truth and Judgement*. Milano, Franco Angeli, 2008.

Nietzsche, Friedrich. *On Truth and Lies in a Nonmoral Sense*. Createspace Independent Pub, 1873/2015.

Pastore, Baldassarre. *Giudizio, prova, ragion pratica*. Milano, Giuffré, 1996.

Patterson, Dennis. *Law and Truth*. Oxford, OUP, 1996.

Taruffo, Michele. *La semplice verità. Il giudice e la costruzione dei fatti*. Roma-Bari, Laterza, 2009.

Tuzet, Giovanni. *Narrazioni processuali*, in *Aphex* n. 7, 2013.

Viola, Francesco. *Judicial truth*, "Persona y derecho", 32, 1995, pp. 249–266.

Viola, Francesco and Zaccaria, Giuseppe. *Diritto e interpretazione. Lineamenti di teoria ermeneutica del diritto*. Roma-Bari, Laterza, 1999.

4 Can we trust *post-truth*? A Trojan Horse in liberal counterspeech[1]

Jacopo Domenicucci

> ...il a été assez naturel de donner [aux démons] le plus d'emploi qu'on pouvait, et de ne les épargner pour les oracles, et les autres miracles païens qui semblaient en avoir besoin. Par-là, on se dispensait d'entrer dans la discussion des faits qui eût été longue et difficile, et tout ce qu'ils avaient de surprenant et d'extraordinaire, on l'attribuait à ces Démons que l'on avait en main. Il semblait qu'en leur rapportant ces événements on confirmât leur existence et la religion même qui nous la révèle.[2]

"Post-truth" is a pervasive trope in media coverage, public speech, public expertise, cultural initiatives and policy agendas these days. This term and its cognates are increasingly setting the frame of our discussions in domains of private and public interest. Its vocabulary is sprawling across all sorts of conversations—from public health to elections, journalism, research, international relations, technology and business. Terms like "post-truth" and "fake news" (and you could add "alternative facts", "post-facts" and "truthy") are featured in political debates and talk shows, in documentaries and pop songs. Journalists use them to describe the impact of social networking on information. They are put to work as an insult against certain media outlets (*which* outlets depending on the speaker). They are taken up by the "Trust and Safety" departments of the tech sector (e.g. Facebook's *Fake news is not our friend* campaign). Policy projects are formulated in these terms all around the world.[3] This makes post-truth arguably one of the

1 I thank for comments Enrico Terrone, Jennifer Cobbe, Stephen John, Pierre Lauret, Mathias Girel, Daisy Dixon, Victor Parchment and Pauline Boyer. I thank audiences at the University of Turin, Maison Sciences de l'Homme, EHESS, and Peterhouse, as well as Milad Doueihi, Maurizio Ferraris, Bridget Kendall, Sankalp Bhatnagar, Tobias Cremer and Ephraim Levinson for helpful conversations. I am grateful to Tiziana Andina and Angela Condello for generously prompting me to gather my thoughts around these issues, first for a conference and then for this volume.

2 Fontenelle (1908/1687) *Histoire des miracles* (Dissertation I, Chapter II, Seconde raison des Anciens Chrétiens pour croire les oracles surnaturels. Convenance de cette opinion avec le système du Christianisme).

3 The word "post-truth" loudly entered in 2016 the *English Oxford Dictionary* as word of the year. Its cognate notion of "fake news", a noun, made its way through the *Collins Dictionary* in 2017. "Alternative facts", which seems an ironic and cynical turn on a postmodern trope, was introduced by White House press secretary K. Conway to

leading narratives of our times:[4] a narrative so pervasive that it seems transparent. But what are you doing when you label a statement, or a speaker "post-truth" or "fake news"? What is this narrative doing to our conversations? What are the pragmatics of post-truth laments and post-truth accusations? What can be achieved through them? Who can use these terms safely and effectively? These are under-discussed questions I start spelling out here.

Most of the debate around the idea that *we may live in a post-truth era* has been an attempt at getting more clear on the actual epistemological state of our societies. Here I don't take a stand on the social epistemology of our times—on whether there is anything exceptional about our current relation to truth norms and collective beliefs. Independently of the actual epistemic and doxastic state of our societies, I want to assess the discursive tools this idea is supposed to provide. I don't take issue either with the current social science agendas devoted to post-truth issues. In social scientific contexts, "post-truth" is mainly a term of the art tagging a variety of research areas. It's a theoretical tool to spotlight worries about our societies—from the dangers of misinformation, to the rise of populism, the state of free speech, the crisis of expertise and the challenge of tech-regulation. As opposed to such high theorizing around *post-truth*, I am just interested in "post-truth" as a (relatively new) term in our everyday language. I look at it as a *meme* featured in ordinary conversations. I take it as a frame that shapes the lay understanding of our times and structures folk debates about politics, society and information (here *folk* is broadly contrasted with social scientific uses of these terms, and includes politicians, journalists and a variety of public experts). Certain

defend the President's spokesperson's inaccurate statement about the size of the crowd at inauguration day. Searching "post truth", Google gives more than 703 million results (783 million for "truth") and Amazon.uk gives 3000 (while 1000 for "populism"). Just to name a few wide audience books on the subject: *Post-truth: the new war on truth and how to fight back*, by Matthew d'Ancona (London: Ebury Press, 2017), *Post-truth: how bullshit conquered the world*, by James Ball (London: Biteback Publishing, 2017), *Post-truth: why we have reached peak bullshit and what we can do about it*, by Evan Davis (London: Little, Brown, 2017), *The invention of Russia: the rise of Putin and the age of fake news*, by Arkady Ostrovsky (London: Penguin Books, 2017), *Weaponized lies: how to think critically in the post-truth era*, by Daniel Levitin (Penguin, 2017). For business, see *The post-truth business: how to rebuild brand authenticity in a distrusting world*, by Sean Pillot de Chenecey (Kogan Page, 2018). For a documentary, see Adam Curtis' 2016 *HyperNormalisation* (I thank Ella Mcpherson for that) and for pop songs Francesco Gabbani's *Pachidermi e Pappagalli* and *La mia versione dei ricordi*. Legal frameworks to tackle post-truth and fake news have been or are being discussed in Belgium, Brazil, Cambodia, Croatia, Denmark, Egypt, France, India, Indonesia, Ireland, Italy, Kenya, Malaysia, Nigeria, the Philippines, Russia, Singapore, South Korea, Spain, Sweden, Taiwan, Tanzania, Uganda, the United Kingdom, the United States... (See www.poynter.org/news/guide-anti-misinformation-actions-around-world).

4 According to the qualitative study conducted by IpsosMori in 27 countries, "60% think other people don't care about facts anymore, they just believe what they want" IpsosMori "Fake News, Post-truth and Filter Bubbles Report" (www.ipsos.com/sites/default/files/ct/news/documents/2018-09/fake-news-filter-bubbles-post-truth-and-trust.pdf).

uses of these tropes have already proved effective in ways that seem disruptive of our public spheres and detrimental to the development of open societies. So-called populists, supporters of illiberal policies, anti-vax, climate sceptics, conspiracists, demagogues and rulers with authoritarian tendencies are making a strategic use of post-truth accusations and laments. And it would be interesting to see why exactly these tools are so effective in their hands.[5] But here I don't explore that. I want to see whether these tools can be harnessed to defend and advance a liberal public sphere. After all, liberal attempts at "reclaiming" this vocabulary are all around us, from academics writing public open-letters[6], to American satirists (e.g. Saturday Night Live), high-profile media outlets (e.g. *Le Monde, The Guardian, The New York Times, La Repubblica*, CNN, BBC...) and public experts. Is there any prospect of success? Should speakers (and citizens) supportive of a liberal, political and social debate welcome this new vocabulary? These are questions about the sort of *liberal counterspeech* which can be produced to counter attacks to an open discursive sphere. Is it appropriate for this vocabulary to feed in forms of liberal counterspeech? Can you advance the defence of an open society by forms of counterspeech that label your opponents or their statements as "post-truth" and "fake news"?

Liberal counterspeech can resort to post-truth tropes in at least two ways: as *hammers* of critique (to borrow Nietzsche's famous image) and as *weapons* of polemic (*ad hominem* counterspeech).

As *hammers*, post-truth tropes are meant to serve the interest we can have in a critical stance. This critical stance is embodied in a folk critical understanding of our times—of the political landscape, of electoral results, of information ecosystems, of public health campaigns... We use it to look at the society we live in and to understand it, as when Brexit commentators *blame it* on fake news. If it is a good hammer, it should help us spot *what* is to be criticized and *who* is to be blamed for it. This is what we do when we criticize public officials for being post-truth or for producing fake news.

As *weapons*, post-truth tropes are polemic, *ad hominem*, responses to one's (actual or potential) interlocutors. Are these weapons a "safe" form of counterspeech when liberal speakers try to use them? What are their collateral damages? Can speakers committed to a liberal public debate afford this move?

This chapter falls in two parts and follows the two functions—critique and counterspeech—or, if you want, the two tools: (1) the *critical hammer* and (2) the *weapon of polemic*. The first part argues that the post-truth hammer is an imprecise critical tool and an ineffective vehicle of blame. The second submits that

5 See Faulkner (2018) for a study of Trump's use of post-truth tropes, e.g. "Fake news items and fake news media exist. However, this paper is not interested in this fact so much as the fact that President Trump regularly calls real news items fake, and calls the established news media the fake news media. These aspersions are intended to discredit news items and media."

6 See e.g. an open-letter to *Science* written by academics using the term "fake news" to voice their worries (Lazer et al. 2018). See also Gewin (2017) reporting in terms of "post-truth" the worries scientists have about their engagement with a broader public.

counterspeech resorting to the post-truth weaponry structurally backfires against certain speakers—the ones committed to a liberal debate.

4.1 A weak hammer: the critique is vague and the blame ineffective

4.1.1 A folk critical theory?

Taken as critical counterspeech, post-truth has the ambition to sketch the spirit of our times. Three questions come to mind:

1 What does the property ascribed to our times amount to?
2 Why does this property apply to our times, why does our age fit the description of post-truth?
3 How did we acquire this property? (Where is the discontinuity with our predecessors? Is this a new step in a longer-term process? Has there ever been anything similar in the past?).

Post-truth does not just neutrally qualify the spirit of our times, though. It clearly differs from, say, "postmodern", which qualified the spirit of another time and might have been used to convey a variety of expressive contents. No surprise if *getting rid of truth* seems a bigger deal than getting past modernity. Truth is something humans seem to care about, a precious good, perhaps a norm for certain actions (e.g. enquiry), attitudes (e.g. belief) and dealings (e.g. testimony, communication). Saying that these actions, attitudes and dealings have abandoned their reference to truth is to flag a serious predicament about them. *O tempora, o mores*, we got post-truth! This triggers two more questions:

1 What's wrong with and what's distinctively bad about this property?
2 How do behaviours instantiating it differ from classic violations of truth-related norms (e.g. lie, pretence and bullshit)?

No need to wait for social scientists, lay liberal counterspeech has ready-made answers. In the order: (1) to be post-truth is not to care about the truth, or to behave in a way that shows disrespect for the truth; (2) this applies to our times insofar as some major public figures do not mind being caught lying and contradicting their previous statements[7], insofar as technical and scientific experts are distrusted[8], and insofar as irrational beliefs are widely held and

7 You can contrast this with G.W. Bush lying at the UN. Strictly speaking, this does not qualify as post-truth. By bringing (alleged) evidence and citing (deceptive) investigations, Bush manifested a form of allegiance to the truth-norm (and misused it of course). In contrast, as noted by Ferraris (2018), a better precursor of straight-out post-truth may be Bush's advisor, who was reported by the NYT Magazine saying "We're an empire now, and when we act, we create our own reality" (Suskind 2004).

8 A widespread contention, the idea of a crisis of expertise, deference and authority is a delicate point. And not only because the very definition of expertise is too broad

shared[9]; (3) the explanation of how we got there lies in the disruption of our informational environment brought about by social media and the subsequent spread of *fake news* [10]; (4) this is pretty bad in many ways, the most salient being that it threatens informed democratic participation; (5) being post-truth is not just to eventually convey deceitful information on the background of a truth-norm, it is rather to act in a way that blurs this very norm.

Summing up, "post-truth" qualifies the (bad) state of the collective relation to truth in our societies, it has techno-cultural roots in the widespread use of ICTs, and it is of political significance. With variations, this seems a widely shared picture of post-truth.

4.1.2 What is criticized?

For something to be a critical tool, it needs at least to make it clear *what* you criticize and *who* you blame for that (if anyone). *What* is being criticized is the target of the critique.

The Oxford English Dictionary (2016) definition of post-truth—which has been eagerly and extensively quoted by journalists and public intellectuals—

brushed. It is unclear whether it tracks any actual tendency of our societies to rely less on experts or simply what people say about such reliance—which seems more likely, since we've rarely relied as much on sophisticated networks of experts.

9 The idea that superstitious, unfounded, irrational beliefs are statistically more widely held. I am not sure we can come with a nice way to measure that. There is further disagreement about where to locate the source of irrationality in conspiracy theories and about what is psychologically and cognitively salient about subjects holding them.

10 "Fake news: (noun) false, often sensational, information disseminated under the guise of news reporting" (*Collins Dictionary* 2017). Fake news are not just false news, inaccurate, incomplete news, e.g. with insufficient sources. Fake news are fake in the sense that they are not, strictly speaking, news—not even imprecise news. They are rather postiche, seeming information, phony news, rotten news. They circulate under the guise of news reporting. Their character may be linked to a deliberate faking, and may be part of a strategy of intentional misinformation, such as forms of propaganda by political lies, for example. But we can also consider that there are fake news by accident, hoaxes that a non-ironic reception ranks as fake news. If the former are a form of deception, the second comes from a misunderstanding. The aetiology behind fake news is not necessarily that of a planned campaign of misinformation. It may result from a prank. Nevertheless, it seems essential to the notion of fake news that the content be presented as factual, or at least received and discussed as such. On the other hand, a joke received as such—circulating as a form of entertainment rather than as a source of information—does not constitute a piece of fake news. Similarly, a simple photo faking is not a piece of fake news per se. A fake photo or a joke can become fake news once they are presented, shared, discussed, commented, as if they represented facts. On the other hand, an elaborate lie supported by a system of so-called evidence does not necessarily belong to fake news. It is thus obvious that fake news is a generic term that awaits a number of distinctions, namely on the basis of who is liable for the utterance (a private individual, an institution, a bot), the domain (health, geopolitics, public administration, finance, show), the circumstances (pre-electoral situation, protected categories), the effects (on the circulation of knowledge, on the representation of minorities, on democratic life…).

already gives a sense of the vagueness of the critique: "*Post-truth*: (adjective) Relating to or denoting circumstances in which objective facts are less influential in shaping public opinion than appeals to emotion and personal belief". A post-truth era is meant to be an era that *no longer* gives truth and rationality their appropriate value. Can you circumscribe situations where emotion prevails over reason, to label them "post-truth"? When would reason prevail over emotions? In this sense, the age of post-truth reminds us of the Ancients' Bronze Age, supposed to follow a fantasized Golden Age we have never actually known. To say we live in an era of post-truth seems a nostalgic complaint about the irrationality of our times: has there ever been a Truth era, though?

The central claim of post-truth is also the most contentious: that truth-telling would be a declining norm. This is unstable between two extremes. On the one hand, the idea of a society where truthfulness is no longer the norm may just be self-effacing: could we engage in any joint venture, in any shared action, or even talk to each other, i.e. could there be a human society that doesn't rely on truthfulness? (It is widely held that the notion of such society is self-defeating—as defended on different grounds by philosophers as diverse as E. Kant, D. Lewis, B. Williams and P. Winch). On the other hand, if you take this idea *less* seriously, it is just as hard to point at empirical parameters to be fulfilled. Even the idea that *fake news* are more widespread, and more widely believed than ever, is far from obvious.[11] This is not to say that the folk-theory of post-truth is empty, but that, if we wanted to take it seriously, we would face an overly complex and contentious picture.

It is hard to use the post-truth vocabulary to target a specific predicament, to articulate a distinct criticism. "The dangers of a post-truth society" is unarticulated and doesn't help pinpoint what needs amended, reformed or improved.[12] Rather than providing a critical synthesis, this frame blurs what is at issue. Electoral lies, pseudoscience, data theft, officials' lies, social network filter bubbles, foreign propaganda and scientific struggle for credibility are put in the same basket. ... These are all features attributed to a post-truth age. Unrefined post-truth descriptions may further offer unhelpful explanatory short-circuits. They often provide too easy an explanation for phenomena that should be more thoroughly investigated. Blaming it on post-truth, we forget more specific, more causally stringent explanations—as in the post-Brexit debate, in discussions around 2016 American elections or in various "Russia-gates". Easy appeal to "post-truth" may distract from

11 For doubts about the actual volume, share (in the overall quantity of news) and impact of fake news, see Fletcher and Nielsen (2018), Watts and Rothschild (2018) and Benkler et al. (2017). Moreover, even if there was evidence of the importance of the share of *fake news* in the overall number of news around, it would still be a question whether the share of such news which is actually believed and taken at face value is significant, or if, overall, *fake news* can be understood as another social practice closer to entertainment.

12 Compare with report for the Council of Europe "Information Disorder: Towards an Interdisciplinary Framework for Research and Policymaking" by MIT TechLab researcher Hossein Derakhshan and fact-checker Claire Wardle.

urgent political, institutional and technological issues. This is all the more worrying when folk-theories of post-truth are cited to support or justify dubious regulatory initiatives from policymakers or the tech sector. By its grand appeal to "truth", the post-truth narrative easily trumps safeguards of transparency and accountability in the area of content-moderation and free speech regulation. This makes it ready for misuse in simplistic, *façade* or even oppressive campaigns.

4.1.3 Who is blamed?

A candidate critical tool that doesn't spot the feature to-be-criticized is already on the wrong track. But it could still help when it comes to *blaming* someone. For that, it would need to be clear on *who* is targeted. But finely targeted blame does not seem available to the post-truth hammer. Do you want to blame Trump, Facebook, anti-vax activists, Cambridge Analytica, Kellyanne Conway, RussiaToday or climate sceptics? For the term "fake news" this ambiguity has been studied in a variety of contexts—lay, academic and policy.[13] It is easy to attack a whole sector and eventually try to erode its credibility—e.g. "mainstream" media, *the* political system. It is easy to make noise with post-truth. It is way less straightforward to call out a specific official for, say, deception, and to put them in front of their responsibilities. This means that the hammers of post-truth are hardly going to improve any form of accountability (public, administrative or legal). Post-truth carries an inherently *temporal* frame: it is ultimately our times that we are blaming when we talk post-truth. And blaming it on our times, rather than on specific contexts, institutions or individuals, may even foster a dilution of responsibility. Everyone does it! (In this sense, a *topographical* notion would do a better job. It would be more fruitful to denounce *where* we risk losing sight of the facts, or which *contexts* are getting immune to rationality.) More fine-grained and contextualized tags, many of which are already available, would carry a better practical purchase in terms of legal responsibility and of political awareness—take "misinformation", "disinformation", "propaganda", "officials' lies", "forgery", "hate speech", "cognitive capitalism"...

4.2 A dangerous weapon: counterspeech that backfires

The discursive tool of post-truth is not only used to criticize, to blame, to propose remedies, to advise and to discuss regulations. It is also used, and crucially so, to

13 See Zuckerman (2017) for fake news: "It's a vague and ambitious term that spans everything from false balance (actual news that doesn't deserve our attention), propaganda (weaponized speech designed to support one party over another), and disinformatzya (information designed to sow doubt and increase mistrust in institutions)." For the term in academic contexts, see Tandoc, Lim and Ling (2018): they examined 34 academic articles using the term "fake news" between 2003 and 2017 and found it used to describe satire, news parody, fabrication, manipulation, advertising and propaganda. See Girel (2008) for a criticism of the use of "fake news" in policymaking in the French context.

silence, to forbid, to attack, to defend, to insult, to threaten and to shame. While not a promising critical hammer, it may still be an effective polemic weapon. As a weapon of polemic, it is trusted by a variety of speakers coming from different social and political horizons. Trump *vs* journalists, journalists *vs* Trump, conspiracists *vs* experts, experts *vs* conspiracists, anti-vax and climate sceptics *vs* scientists, scientists *vs* climate sceptics and anti-vax—just to simplistically name a few.

These means of *ad hominem* counterspeech proved effective at least for certain speakers. They have a strategic payoff, for instance, for supporters of illiberal policies and so-called populist leaders who use them to shut down and silence opponents. As the *meme* circulates the weapon is also increasingly used by speakers from other horizons. Once you have identified a weapon of polemic, and once you have realized how effective it seems in your opponents' hands, it is tempting to add it to your own rhetorical repertoire. This is what speakers committed to an open public sphere seem to be doing. They want to use post-truth accusations in a way that is symmetric and adversarial to, say, the way Trump is using them. Is this weaponry really available for them? Or do they actually get hurt when they try to use it? Does post-truth polemic backfire against liberal speakers who try to harness it in defence of an open public debate? I suspect they may have not exercise enough care in handling this weaponry.

For that, we need some grip on the speech-acts associated with this weaponry: what are you *doing* when you label a claim "fake news" or "post-truth"? And, as the conversation heats up, what are you doing when you call "fake news" or "post-truth" to the speakers themselves? (This would be a complement to the detailed pragmatics of post-truth sketched by Ferraris (2018): Ferraris analysed the distinctive conversational properties of speech actually producing post-truth. He focused on post-truth speakers—speakers producing bullshit, hoaxes, fake news and lies. It would be misleading to say I focus on their respondents. I just look at speakers who advertise themselves as responding to post-truth utterances and who accuse their interlocutors of producing fake news. And among these speakers, I focus on the ones who think of themselves as committed to living in a civil society with an open public space.)

A full speech-act analysis of "fake news" accusations would be overambitious here. Let me just point at a *cluster* of speech activities. I don't unpack the structure of this cluster, that is, I don't take a stand on whether each layer is a distinct speech act or whether there is a single act with a baggage of presuppositions, implicatures and backdoor moves. Some of these effects are plausibly core; others are just triggered under the right circumstances (a broad sense of the priorities should be given by the order in which I present the layers of the cluster). Beyond that, you shouldn't need assumptions about *intentions* of the speaker at hand to make sense of the conversational *effects* I highlight. Finally, I leave aside questions about the complex *felicity* conditions of this counterspeech, even if I raise the problem of the authority these moves assume.

4.2.1 An epistemological diagnosis

Imagine you are talking to your climate-sceptic neighbours. They come up with some absurd figure to support their contention that humans have no responsibility in climate change. You just reply "this is fake news". Instead of addressing the content of their claim to challenge it, you are shifting the focus from the *content* to the *status* of their utterance. You are not even providing an assessment in terms of true or false, such as when you flag inaccuracy in a belief or in a source. Rather than just saying that the statement is factually wrong, you are saying that it is wrong to believe it (endorse it, support it, circulate it, spread it…). The very epistemological status of the statement is denounced: phony, rotten, forged, postiche, manipulated… The utterance is not discussed for its content: it is ranked as epistemologically indecent. Which suggests there is something pathologic about the aetiology of the belief manifested, something that casts it out of the space of reasons. When you say "it's fake news", you are assuming to have the authority of a speech doctor and you are issuing an *epistemological diagnosis.* [14]

4.2.2 Speaker's subordination

This diagnosis is not easily bracketed. There is a natural *spill over* effect from the utterance to the speaker. Disregard for the speaker is already conveyed by the shift from the at-issue discussion to the evaluation of their speech as pathologic. A shift from "It's fake news" to "*You're* fake news" shows a shift from the *epistemological diagnosis* to a form of *subordination*—"you/they are [fake news]" fill in with "post-truth", "(a) populist(s)", "(a) conspiracist(s)" etc. (To a certain extent, we can think of this as just making explicit a move that was already there in "it's fake news".) In this (attempted?) subordination the targeted speakers are disqualified from their discursive status—of rational speakers on a par with you. Doubt is cast on their entitlement to take part in the same conversational game as you. This suggests that fake news accusations are not mere moves to score within a language game. They also affect the very rules of membership in the game.[15] The specific forms of speaker subordination by "fake news" accusations are context-relative. For instance, if you have enough authority you may *silence* the speakers you target. If bystanders are there, targeted speakers may be *shamed*. And if the reference group is sufficiently stable, this may count as a *slur*—e.g. "Brexiteers", a group that exhibits sufficient stability in its socio-economic demographics and whose members are being consistently called "fake news".[16] (Accusations of "heresy" are sometimes identified as an infamous precursor of "fake news" accusations (Coady n.d.). While there are clear analogies here, I wouldn't put too much weight on them. And not only because flagging something or someone as heretic was

14 Compare with Basham (2017) who argues that post-truth accusations *pathologize* our societies, in his reply to *Le Monde* social scientists.

15 For the notion of conversational score and the different ways to score in a language game, see Langton (2009, Chapter 8) and Lewis (1979).

16 I thank Lucy McDonald for this.

integral to a legal and social procedure of actual exclusion, but also because these accusations somehow point at different directions. Heretics may have been accused of abandoning doctrinal truth for a variety of reasons. An epistemic devil-may-care attitude, however, doesn't seem their central charge. They were arguably accused of caring about it, just the wrong way.)

4.2.3 A doxastic imperative

This subordination comes to the fore when you realize that targeted speakers are not just ranked (as in, say, "you're a liar"); they also receive a *directive.* The negative diagnosis and the subsequent subordination of the speaker pave the way for a more active—action-oriented—dimension of this speech activity. What kind of directive is that? You are neither advising your interlocutor to believe something else, nor inviting them to consider appropriate evidence. Don't believe that, don't say that, sounds exactly like an *imperative.* On top of refusing to argue with your interlocutor, on top of disqualifying them, you also fire at them a *doxastic imperative.* Note that is not simply ineffective to change the views of targeted speakers; it is also problematic from the point of view of an audience you may want to convince—whether this is a broadcasted debate, a *café* conversation or a web forum. Giving doxastic orders is hard to reconcile with the form of rationality liberal speakers would otherwise herald.[17]

4.2.4 Tribal self-assertion

When one is (dis)qualified as post-truth and given orders, one is posited as someone *we* can't have a conversation with. This *we* takes me to another layer of speech activity: a form of *self-assertion based on group-identity.* In-group belonging is indirectly rejuvenated, and reasserted, through the moves I spelled out. When you entrust your counterspeech to post-truth tropes, you risk ending up invoking the bonds of in-group, communitarian trust. You would seem to buy in the idea that *these* are the appropriate bonds of trust for political relations. This way you would be giving up on forms of *civic* trust that are crucial to any debate within liberal institutions. You would be reneging on civic trust mediated by institutions and structured by a shared rationality. As a liberal speaker, you are undermining your own aspirations when you have recourse to similar weapons which render the confrontation tribal.[18] *Tribal self-assertions* back a division between communities of

17 Compare with Coady (n.d.) about "epistemic policing" and Habgood-Coote (2018, 22). The latter, while raising similar worries, concludes the paragraph "If you use weaponized terms, you run the risk of hurting people." This is not what I'm pointing at. It is an open question whether liberal citizens can in general be required never to (rhetorically) hurt their anti-democratic, anti-liberal opponents. The problem, as I see it, is that the pragmatics of their speech may undermine their very political commitments, and, perhaps, even fulfil those of their opponents.

18 There are asymmetries in the *we* between the liberal speakers I am focusing on and, say, Trump. So, my picture is severe with liberals. After all, only one camp can be thought

speakers—a division in their references, their modes of information, their patterns of argument, their criteria of justification and their norms of legitimacy. This results in the development of distinct, insulated, discursive ecosystems. This way, calling people fake news doesn't just carry a divisive narrative, it may enact it by echoing tribal self-assertions. (Note that this self-assertive layer seems to have a subtle role—too complex to be unpacked here—in creating the conditions of *assumed authority* which allow you to play the speech doctor, to subordinate your interlocutors and to give them orders. For example, we could think that the more or less salient reference to a group you identify with is actually a vehicle bootstrapping you into an authoritative position. And this fits the ambiguities of the imperative, which seems ambivalent between an *admonition* supported by norms of rationality and a proper *command* based on personal authority.[19])

We've seen why each layer of speakers' activity is problematic for liberal speakers and how they add up. Liberal polemic meets in post-truth accusations its Trojan Horse.[20] Liberal speakers should be wary of post-truth tropes, since their pragmatics structurally undermine the sort of public sphere these speakers/citizens want to support. I am not saying that this weapon is unavailable to liberal speakers because the latter should as a matter of principle never shut down a conversation. I am not saying that they can't afford this weapon because they can't afford to rhetorically *hurt* their interlocutor. I am not saying either that the move should be abandoned just because it is tainted by association with prominent forms of oppressive use. The danger for liberal speakers lies in each of the five levels of speech activity—that can be more or less activated by an actual instance of fake news accusation. And it builds up. Overall, the attempted discursive policing is not only self-effacing but leaves the discussion worse off. It has divisive effects on the community of speakers. It contributes to undermining the minimal conditions for a civil society. On top of direct and indirect damages to the discursive landscape,

of as fully stressing the importance of such *we*. Also, one *we* is self-professed more inclusive and less communitarian than the other. Could you leverage these asymmetries to rescue a liberal reclamation? The other layers of speech activity I spelled out suggest that you can't.

19 For a discussion of the authority of subordinating speech, see Langton (2009, Chapter 4 "Pornography's Authority? Response to Leslie Green").

20 For other—distinct, but plausibly convergent—worries about the dangers in attempts to reclaim post-truth vocabulary, see Habgood-Coote (2018, 18–26) drawing on Jason Stanley's notions of *(bad) ideology* and *propaganda*. The author frames the post-truth vocabulary as "seemingly innocuous speech cue[ing] up" ideology (p.21). Note that Habgood-Coote is explicitly interested in reclamation by "the establishment". There is, however, some slippage in the text between establishment defenders and democracy defenders, as he goes on to consider post-truth terms as "honeypots for defenders of democratic values." I take it that these two sorts of speakers, and citizens, should not be confused (and are often, purposively, identified by antidemocratic propaganda). I further disagree with systematic attributions of *bad faith* to speakers resorting to post-truth tropes: "what fake news is to the right-wing demagogue, post-truth is to the centrist dad" (p.22). As a cultural meme, post-truth travels through our discursive practices and does not need bad faith to prosper. This is why I would rather compare this vocabulary to a Trojan Horse.

fake news accusations affect liberal speakers themselves. First, in their own ethics of communication, which, after reflection, is incompatible with this move. Second, in their reputation since they lose credibility by this compromising shot.

4.3 Conclusion

I argued that if you are committed to a liberal public sphere you should distrust post-truth/fake news laments and accusations; both as hammers of critique and as weapons of polemic. What should liberal speakers/citizens do? They should probably give up on the post-truth framework and try other strategies rather than simply dismiss the claims of their interlocutors with "it's fake news", "you're post-truth", "they're fake news". But one cannot always argue. For citizens committed to an open and inclusive public sphere this ultimately opens up questions about the challenge of liberal counterspeech.[21]

An important *caveat* is that this is not providing an argument for free speech and, further, that this doesn't carry any clear takeaway for the free speech debate. There is a difference between, on the one hand, *shutting down a conversation*, and, on the other hand, *not letting certain conversations* happen. Liberal speakers within a conversation that is taking place would be wrong in shutting down their interlocutor by the distinctive speech activity I just fleshed out. But, as a society, we may think that certain conversations should simply not take place. And the challenges of liberal counterspeech remind us of the importance of upstream intervention on the discursive landscape by various means—e.g. regulation by democratically accountable institutions of, say, the use of *botnets*, tech-regulation by platform curation and eventually de-platforming, promotion of media literacy and "fake news vaccination".[22]

Now, this volume implicitly calls for philosophers and legal scholars to do something about post-truth. What could and should we do? I stressed the importance of handling with caution the readymade notions of post-truth, of being suspicious of this cultural *meme*. I obviously don't think this is *all* philosophers can do about post-truth. A brief assessment of our ordinary language is definitely not the only way to engage with the social, epistemological and political worries that lurk in the background of such lay talk. And I don't think that what I said has a bearing for scientific uses of post-truth narratives in designing research programmes or constructing theoretical tools to analyse the epistemic and political shortcomings of our societies.[23] A reflection on the social distribution of epistemic credit and the new social infrastructures of trust in digital societies is developing and *post-truth* theoretical worries naturally have a place in it.

As citizens, we should bear in mind that this vocabulary is limited and dangerous. We could not be too cautious when tempted to shut down our interlocutors

21 For the philosophy and pragmatics of *counterspeech*, see Rae Langton's current work on counterspeech—e.g. Langton 2018, and forthcoming monograph.

22 For the possibility of "active inoculation" against fake news, see Roozenbeek and van der Linden (2018).

23 For the opposite view, see Habgood-Coote (2018, 26).

with a "that's post-truth" rebuttal. Short-sighted deployment of this weaponry may hide a Trojan Horse.

References

Basham, L. 2017. "Pathologizing Open Societies: A reply to the Le Monde Social Scientists." *Social Epistemology Review and Reply Collective*, 6, n° 2, pp. 59–68.

Benkler, Y., Hal, R., Robert, F., Etling, B., Zuckerman, E., and Bourassa, N. 2017. "Partisanship, Propaganda, and Disinformation: Online media and the 2016 U.S. Presidential election." Berkman Klein Center for Internet & Society Research Paper.

Coady, D.n.d. Talk at the Fake Knowledge conference at the University of Cologne, CONCEPT – Cologne Center for Contemporary Epistemology and the Kantian Tradition (http://concept.phil-fak.uni-koeln.de/36447.html, to watch the talk: https://youtu.be/Lum5nJHm3fA).

Faulkner, P. 2018. "Fake Barns, Fake News." *Social Epistemology Review and Reply Collective*, 7, n° 6, pp. 16–21.

Ferraris, M. 2018. "Le défi de la défiance", in Doueihi, J. and Domenicucci, M. (eds.), *La confiance à l'ère numérique*, Paris: Editions Berger-Levrault and Editions Rue d'Ulm, pp. 215–249.

Fletcher, R. and Nielsen, R. K. 2018. "People don't trust News Media – and this is key to the global Misinformation Debate", in *Understanding and Addressing the Disinformation Ecosystem*, FirstDraft-Knight Foundation-University of Pennsylvania.

Fontenelle, B. de. 1908/1687. *Histoire des oracles*, éd. L. Maigron, Paris: Hachette.

Gewin, Virginia. 2017. "Communication: Post-Truth Predicaments." *Nature*, 541, n° 763, pp. 425–427.

Girel, M. 2018. "De quoi parle le projet de loi sur les Fake News?", on AOC, 04/06/18https://aoc.media/analyse/2018/06/04/de-quoi-parle-projet-de-loi-fake-news/.

Habgood-Coote, J. 2018. "Stop Talking about Fake News!" *Inquiry*, pp. 1–33. doi:10.1080/0020174X.2018.1508363.

Langton, R. 2009. *Sexual Solipsism*, Oxford: Oxford University Press.

Langton, R. 2018. "Blocking as counterspeech", in Fogal, D., Harris, D. W. and Moss, M. (eds.), *New Work on Speech Acts*, Oxford: Oxford University Press, pp. 144–165.

Lazer, D.M.J., Baum, M.A., Benkler, Y., Berinsky, A.J., Greenhill, K.M., Menczer, F., Metzger, M.J., Nyhan, B., Pennycook, G., Rothschild, D., Schudson, M., Sloman, S.A., Sunstein, C.R., Thorson, E.A., Watts, D.J., and Zittrain, J.L. 2018. "The Science of Fake News", *Science*, 359 (6380), pp. 1094–1096. doi:10.1126/science.aao2998

Lewis, D. 1979. "Scorekeeping in a Language Game", *Journal of Philosophical Logic*, 8, pp. 339–359.

Roozenbeek, J. and van der Linden, S. 2018. "The Fake News Game: Actively Inoculating against the Risk of Misinformation", *Journal of Risk Research*, doi:10.1080/13669877.2018.1443491.

Suskind, R. 2004. "Faith, Certainty and the Presidency of George W. Bush", *The New York Times Magazine*, www.nytimes.com/2004/10/17/magazine/faith-certainty-and-the-presidency-of-george-w-bush.html.

Tandoc, E. C. Jr., Lim, Z. W. and Ling, R. 2018. "Defining Fake News". *Digital Journalism*, vol. 6, n° 2, pp. 137–153. doi:10.1080/21670811.2017.1360143.

Watts, Duncan J. and Rothschild, D. M. 2018. "The Minority Report on the Fake News Crisis: (Spoiler Alert: It's the real News)", in *Understanding and Addressing the Disinformation Ecosystem*, FirstDraft-Knight Foundation-University of Pennsylvania.

Zuckerman, E. 2017. *Stop Saying Fake News, It's not Helping*, My Heart is in Accra, www.ethanzuckerman.com/blog/2017/01/30/stop-saying-fake-news-its-not-helping/

Reports

Derakhshan, H. and Wardle, C. 2017. "Information Disorder: Towards an Interdisciplinary Framework for Research and Policymaking", report for the Council of Europe (https://rm.coe.int/information-disorder-toward-an-interdisciplinary-framework-for-researc/168076277c).

Report by IpsosMori "Fake News, Post-truth and Filter Bubbles Report" (www.ipsos.com/sites/default/files/ct/news/documents/2018-09/fake-news-filter-bubbles-post-truth-and-trust.pdf).

The Poynter Institute, www.poynter.org/news/guide-anti-misinformation-actions-around-world

5 Who cares about privacy?

The documedia surplus value

Maurizio Ferraris

5.1 Privacy, post-truth, and documedia surplus value

Ninety-two percent of young people do not read privacy terms and conditions, but maintain that it is important to do so.[1] I do not know how many old people like me do *not* read the terms and conditions nor believe it's important to do so, but I wouldn't be surprised if the percentage was even higher. Not only because many people are willing to give up their privacy to share their thoughts, words, and works for free on social networks, but also (and above all) because the centrality of privacy is a thing of the past: it belongs to the world of bourgeois freedoms and civil rights.

We have excellent reasons to regret the intrinsic values of that world, the values of Max Weber and Thomas Mann, but that world is no longer ours, and hasn't been for a long time: totalitarianisms, world wars, and especially the mass media have generated a different world, one where the relationship between people and their public image, as well as the concept of "privacy", has completely changed. Privacy is obviously the least of problems for those (over half of the world) who post content on social networks, and those (almost all of the world) who give their consent to the use of cookies, eager to get on with it and access the given service. It is not a question of bourgeois confidentiality, of decorum, of minding one's own business with due discretion; it is a question of labor.

In the same way, the relationship with the truth has also changed. The fact that one is willing to accept the existence of "alternative facts" is the result of multiple circumstances: ideological ones, like the postmodern critique of objectivity; sociological ones, like the formation of the "society of the spectacle"; and above all technological ones, which have determined what I call "documedia revolution". The latter is the boom of recording that has determined an unprecedented multiplication of documents – the so-called "big data" – and a horizontalization of the media through social networks. Now, instead of focusing on the phenomenon itself, I think it is important to look at its context and at what has made it possible.

The real problem, in the perspective I propose, is neither privacy nor truth, but the disproportion (which I define "documedia surplus value") between the data

1 M. Ainis, *Il regno dell'Uroboro*, Milano, La Nave di Teseo 2018.

available to the general users (the "mobilized") and the companies that manage the web platforms (the "mobilizers"). As we carelessly give up our privacy and navigate in the waters of post-truth, we produce wealth. This, in my opinion, is the essential core and the preliminary condition to focus on, in order to have a correct understanding of epiphenomena such as the transformations of privacy and post-truth. How much does an unemployed person care about their privacy? Consider the many smartphone-owning beggars we see today: would they be happier if their privacy were protected, or if their mobilization was recognized as work, and paid, recognizing the documedia surplus value? Or think of those who see the web as the space in which to vent their dissatisfactions, most often motivated, but blamed on often imaginary causes: what do they care about post-truth?

Now, privacy is priceless, even in the sense that it does not necessarily matter to many, and it is not clear how it can be protected; the same goes for truth, which is certainly a great good, but only for the few (usually scientists) who care about it, while for most of humanity post-truth (the current version of myth) works just fine. But the value produced by our mobilization on the web, which involves the renunciation of privacy as well as production and distribution of post-truth, does have a price, which can be quantified and must be paid by the platforms without weighing on national budgets. This would decrease social discontent, and perhaps make politics easier, making it more honorable, feasible, and rewarding to serve a less scared and angry people.

5.2 From the superstructure to the structure

With a move that Karl Marx would have defined typical of bourgeois economics, the debate on the ongoing revolution is concentrating on its superstructures, but its structure has remained in the shadows. Now, what does it consist of? In Europe, in the United States, and progressively around the world (with a huge competitive advantage of China, which has one billion and three hundred and seventy million inhabitants, but one billion mobile phones) daily acts that until a very recent past would have disappeared into thin air today are recorded and therefore capitalized upon. Social objects (i.e. those objects that would not exist in the absence of society: money, titles, status…) require recording, that is, they follow the rule Object = Recorded Act. A social object is the result of a social act (such as to involve at least two people, or a person and a delegated machine, or two delegated machines) that has the characteristic of being recorded. The boom of recording involves a proportional growth in social objects, thus generating the most ubiquitous and informed capital in history. Every byte, for the few who currently have the means to interpret it (i.e. web platform managers and web analysts) is a bearer of knowledge and generates value.

Even assigning a very low value, for example a thousandth of a euro, to every byte generated every day, we would still face the total value of €4 billion per day. Because of this enormous data production, our world is not liquid and elusive, as postmodernists claimed. It is perhaps the most solid world that history has ever known, since everything is kept track of, therefore everything can be taken into account and everyone can be asked to account for it. And everything ultimately goes to the account of Documedia Capital, the heir of financial capital and industrial capital, which replaced goods and finance with a richer and more manageable asset – documents.

Documedia capital does not provide the means of production, but the means of interpretation, that is, the correlations and the meaning of the data, which it keeps for itself and resells or reuses. Today's workers are not subjected to monotonous or tiring tasks, as was the case in the age of industry, but they must pay for the means of production, i.e. the web terminals. Production is at the bottom, knowledge at the top, although obviously the mobilized can access knowledge (for example, books or encyclopaedias), except that in so doing they produce further and much more precious knowledge about themselves, to which they do not have access. This unprecedented and largely unforeseen way of producing wealth through documents needs to be recognized and understood. This is necessary in order to establish a new social contract, the lack of which is felt dramatically especially in Europe and the United States, with the advancement of populism triggered by a formal unemployment that is as extensive as real mobilization is capillary.

This gap in the access to data is the fundamental point to understand the present. In theory, in fact, the relationship between mobilizer and mobilized is fair: the first offers services, the second pays with information. In fact, however, this is not the case: between what the mobilizer gives and what the mobilized does there is a crucial asymmetry, which can also be represented in terms of truth and post-truth. The mobilized has much post-truth, the mobilizer much hyper-truth. By "hyper-truth" I mean the quality of the knowledge that the mobilizer can acquire about the mobilized. From this point of view, the difference between the data available to the mobilizer (who owns the platforms) and the mobilized (who simply has access to it) could not be more astounding.

From the point of view of the mobilized, documedia surplus value produces a monadization of knowledge. Each of us is a monad in the sense that we see the world, the World Wide Web, from our own very personal perspective, determined by the coordinates that the web algorithms have attached to us. So, that World Wide Web becomes the description of our home, and universal communication becomes the interlocution with the unhappy few with whom we share prejudices and preferences. We all live in different worlds – as sleepwalkers, it would seem, if we follow Heraclitus, since "The awake share a common world, but the asleep turn aside into private worlds".[2]

The image of the world available to the mobilizers, the managers of the platforms, is completely different. If we want to follow the Kantian categorization, in terms of quantity the data on the platform are enormous, while those of the mobilized are comparatively poor (although we may have the impression of being inundated with information); in terms of quality the data of the platforms are rich, because they are individual and consist of very detailed profilings, while those

2 Heraclitus, DK 22B 89.

available to the mobilized are general-generic, referring not to individuals but to general notions; in terms of relation the data of the mobilizers are secret, while those of the mobilized are blatant and in the public domain; finally, in terms of modality, the data of the mobilizers are real, in the sense that they record actual behaviors on the net, while those accessible to the mobilized are a mixture of real information and fake news.

So, let's proceed to an analysis of this disproportion, in order to highlight the documedia surplus value.

5.3 Quantity: big data

Let's start from quantity. For every information of the mobilized there are several recordings on part of the mobilizer. Google translate has capitalized on all the existing texts on the web, and Tesla cars improve their software through the data collection offered by Autopilot, Tesla's semi-automatic driving system. While providing a service, you acquire information (which does not happen in the simple passive documentation of commodities: the label of a wine informs only us, while an online purchase informs us as well as others, about us). The power of Google or Amazon lies in an innovative scheme, based on the development of old things (the register, in the case of Google; the postalmarket, in the case of Amazon), but in a new context that has exponentially increased the possibility of recording, and therefore of capitalization. *It may not be immediately clear to what extent the accumulation of data, regardless of the knowledge it provides (which I will discuss in relation to quality), constitutes capitalization* per se, *but this will be perfectly evident if we consider that money itself is data.*

In fact, if money is a commodity like any other, as economists remind us about, it is primarily because it is a document like any other: it is like a passport, for example, of which it shares the complicated doodles and characteristic colors. With a passport, a state authorizes a citizen to leave the country (as it originally used to be) and with a banknote it authorizes him to buy things. Since the citizens who want to buy are much more numerous than those who want to leave, banknotes are more numerous than passports. Also, since money changes hands, banknotes are not nominal, and – since the exchanges are done quickly and may involve illiterate agents – to prevent misunderstandings about their value, in most States (albeit with the significant exception of the United States) banknotes have different sizes and colors, so that money could be defined as the documents of those

Table 5.1 A way of conceptualizing Documedia Capital

Kantian Categories	*Mobilizers*	*Mobilized*
Quantity	Big data	Small data
Quality	Rich data	Poor data
Relation	Secret data	Public data
Modality	Real data	Virtual data

who cannot read. Moreover, both with passports and with banknotes, the state did not come up with anything new, but simply gave a paper form to ways of fixing acts and quantifying value that originate in our animal past, and whose evolution coincides with the evolution of human cultures.

Many economists have noted that money is a recording system (although they often speak of "information")[3]– namely a low-cost means to keep track of previous resource allocations[4]– and that money is superfluous when agents have access to all their previous mutual interactions,[5] because ultimately money is nothing but memory. This thesis has been developed in particular by American economist Narayana Kocherlakota.[6] The memory is an agent's knowledge of the acts of all the agents with whom he has had direct or indirect contacts in the past; money is an object that, unlike commodities, you cannot manufacture yourself and is available in fixed quantities; and yet, these amounts of money somehow make up for the limits of human memory, representing an artificial informational deposit and ultimately resulting in a form of primitive memory: instead of taking note of a given or rendered service, a universally accepted document is created that sums up the annotation in an anonymous form (this is particularly interesting for the narcos and the mafia).

In an environment where money is replaced by memory, every social actor has an imaginary account. When an actor gives assets to another actor, his account increases, along with his future ability to receive assets. When an actor receives assets from another actor, her account decreases, and this decreases her ability to receive assets in the future. In an environment endowed with memory, an agent's account does not only depend on her transfers. If Tom gives something to Dick, and Dick's account is empty, Tom's account does not increase. So Tom's account is not only based on his actions, but also on those of the actors he is in contact with and on those of the contacts of the latter. This environment is the web. The environment in which money is replaced by memory also has the advantage of being able to account for finer transactions: favors, reputation, physical pleasures (intellectual assets, on the other hand, are an exception to this exchange system, in agreement with Franklyn's principle that sharing an idea does not mean losing it). At this point, big data are the absolute memory and the absolute currency, and the exchanges that take place on the web are exchanges in the strictest sense of the term (that is, they produce value by being recorded in the great worldwide calculation of give and take).

In fact, between traditional currency and documedia money – documoney if you will – there is no match. The credit guarantee and the facilitation of the exchange can be implemented in a much more effective way through the collection of data, which

3 J. Ostroy, *The Informational Efficiency of Monetary Exchange*, in *American Economic Review*, 63, 1973, pp. 597–610.

4 R. Lucas, *Equilibrium in a Pure Currency Economy, Models of Monetary Economics*, in J. H. Kareken and N. Wallace (ed. by), MN, Federal Reserve Bank of Minneapolis, Minneapolis 1980.

5 S. R. Aiyagari, N. Wallace, *Existence of Steady-states with Positive Consumption in the Kiyotaki-Wright Model*, in *Review of Economic Studies*, 58, 1991, pp. 901–916.

6 N. N. Kocherlakota, *Money is Memory*, Federal Reserve Bank of Minneapolis, Research Department Staff Report 218, 1996 October.

inform about the state of the market (not only economic, but political, demographic...) incomparably better than currency may do. In fact, the latter only provides economic information through a rough summary of the price of products. As for the value reserve, it is still left to currency, for now, though in the context of a growing marginalization of banks (which are increasingly becoming value deposits and must renounce their consulting functions). The progress of cryptocurrencies suggests, however, that in the near future even the credit guarantee will cease to be a privilege of the banks (that is, in the last instance, of the sovereign states). But here we are already moving from the realm of quantity to that of quality.

5.4 Quality: rich data

So, let's come to quality. Currency is a datum. But, more importantly, data are qualitatively much richer than money; or, more accurately, the data of the mobilizer are rich data, since they hold information about the individual's details, while the data available to the mobilized are general information, the kind that can be obtained on the web, on the labels of products, on price tags. The rise of data as knowledge of the individual is an event that has far greater social and political repercussions than those related to the mere protection of privacy – which, moreover, from a formal point of view, is preserved by the fact that big data say everything about us, except our name. True transformations do not take place on the level of privacy, but on that of industry and capital.

In fact, under the profile of industry, rich data entail a decisive transformation.[7] A world that for centuries had resigned itself to the idea that the individual was unknowable, and that only types, classes, and species could be known – just as modern industrial production embraced the standard, renouncing the manufacture of individualized products – has now discovered that the individual is not ineffable, and that the production of the individual is not unfeasible. On the one hand, we now know individuals up to their heartbeats and musical preferences (perhaps the only thing that remains unknown is their name: but what does it matter at this point?). On the other hand, the production of individualized commodities has returned to being economically sustainable, as in pre-industrial times; this is true both in traditional industries and for digital artisans (makers) that produce items with 3D printers using individualized parameters. This encounter between producibility and knowability of the individual, once again, makes documents much more powerful than money.

But above all, rich data entail a radical transformation of the economy. Traditionally, documents had a commemorative value: they kept track of an agreement, maintaining a social object in existence. But in the case of big data, the point of interest shifts from the past to the future. The value of documents is now predictive, with a potentiality that is multiplied now that machine learning methods use data not only to transform them into predictions, but to verify previous predictions, precisely by learning on their own. The data that documents contain can provide general information on large sections of society and on the market, as in the case of big data,

7 M. Carpo, *The Second Digital Turn*, MIT Press, Cambridge (MA)-London 2017.

or specific information on the behavior of the individual consumer (that, note well, is also a producer), and this is the case with rich data.

In short, documents as commodities allow for unprecedented individual profiling, knowledge and production – just think of the homepage of large online sites that cater to the consumer by providing individualized suggestions, decreeing the end of the standardized market. The phenomenon appears to be the opposite of the shadow economy. The shadow economy is a commodity production that secures a hidden profit to the producer and is not quantified in the nation's gross domestic product. Here instead we have a production of commodities that are even more profitable than money itself, that is – as we have seen when talking about big data – highly informative and individualized documents generated through the mobilization of users on the web. This mobilization, though, does not bring economic benefits to the producer, whose activity is not even conceptualized as labor.

This process has a definite impact on the market as a whole. Classic industry has a pyramidal structure, and this makes it unsuitable to compete with the new internet giants, which not only have very few employees (since we are the ones who do the work), but are much more suited to a situation where companies seems to lose weight in favor of the market, that is, the wide sphere of intermediation provided by the web. This has been realized by traditional but forward-looking industries such as Daimler, in Germany, which will integrate the hierarchical management pyramid with interdisciplinary and cross-functional groups – that is, transversal groups endowed with humanistic skills – which will gradually form the new core of the company.[8] On the production side, which is more closely related to the passage from commodities to documents, there has been a transition from company to market. The latter, in fact, constantly increases its self-awareness (whereas before it was short of information compared to companies), and therefore becomes increasingly efficient while companies have to run after it.

5.5 Relation: secret data

Once again, the violation of privacy appears as a secondary problem compared to a more general framework, which has to do much more with the production of value than with the protection of secrecy. This circumstance appears particularly evident precisely when one examines the category of the relation, which is the one that has more to do with privacy. From the point of view of relation, the mobilizer has secret or at least exclusive data, in the sense that only he has them, while the mobilized accesses data in the public domain, which from a strategic point of view are infinitely less relevant. Indeed, one can distinguish two levels of recording that account for the asymmetry of web exchanges in terms of secrecy[9]: the infrastructure recording, accessible to

8 V. Mayer-Schönberger and T. Ramge, *Reinventing Capitalism in the Age of Big Data*, Basic Books, New York 2018.

9 J. Domenicucci, *Trust, Extended Memories and Social Media*, in *Towards a Philosophy of Digital Media*, A. Romele and E. Terrone (ed. by), Palgrave Macmillan, Basingstoke 2018, pp. 119–142.

a hacker or to the police but also, note well, to the companies that manage the web platforms; and conversational recording, explicit and accessible to the mobilized.

The latter is therefore the only recording with respect to which the mobilized are aware of dealing with privacy issues, as it is the extension of classical communication contexts. But already at this level the mobilizers tend to underestimate the advantages that come from owning a continuous, centralized, and always active archive. To make an example, an Austrian law student, resorting to a European law, has asked Facebook for all the material collected on him and received a CD with 1200 PDF pages, including the comments he had deleted. And even in the case of IM services where the message disappears once it has been read by the recipient, the content remains accessible to the company that manages the platform; another obvious case of asymmetry between mobilizers and mobilized. Even in the competition between companies, digital technologies create a huge cognitive asymmetry that allows capital to first destroy existing forms of business and then manage entire sectors of the economy in a monopolistic way.

But it is infrastructural recording that provides the mobilizers with the greatest benefits. Thanks to it, they accumulate data about the mobilized of which the latter are not even aware, such as (just to give an example) the brightness of the place they happen to be, not to mention all the bodily data that are recorded by devices like the Apple Watch which, again, is bought by the mobilized and has the obvious effect of giving a huge amount of free data to the mobilizers. Whether we are awake or asleep, the gigantic archive that we familiarly call web is always growing and producing. If we think that 90% of all data currently stored in the world has been generated only in the last two years, it will be clear that the digital transformation has had an impact that will soon be equivalent, if not superior, to the industrial revolution. In that case, the driving force was given by steam and mechanical devices; here the revolution makes no noise: it leaves *traces* and creates *documents.*

These documents are secret in many ways, but in a different form from those involved in conversational recording. The latter, so to speak, were "plain" secrets, expressed in natural language, whereas here we are dealing with secrets that are often not even recognized as such, and which constitute knowledge only if we have the tools to interpret them. Once again, more than the violation of privacy (can privacy really be unknown to those directly involved? Of course this does not correspond to the traditional concept of privacy, and most likely to no concept of privacy in general). Rather than a violation of the private sphere, therefore, we are dealing with a new form of capitalization (and labor) whose dimensions have not yet been acknowledged.

5.6 Modality: real data

So, let's come to the last category, that of modality, which is the most directly concerned with post-truth. From the point of view of modality, in fact, the mobilizer has real data, because they reflect the actual behaviors of the mobilized; obviously you could create algorithms to confuse the results, and maybe you do, but quantitatively speaking most of the documents would remain truthful. On the other hand, the mobilized navigate in a sea of true, false, or purely verisimilar information. This is the world of post-truth.

This circumstance suggests once again that the web space is a document rather than an information context[10]: a docusphere rather than an infosphere. According to the theoreticians of the infosphere,[11] information is essentially made up of well-formed, true, and meaningful data, so that false information is not really information. However, on the web there is also post-truth, which is anything but true; recording can explain it (it is a written act, although it refers to things that are not true),[12] information cannot. So, even in this case we are dealing with a phenomenon that finds its condition of possibility in the unprecedented formation of documedia capital, and we must bear this in mind to understand the profound nature of post-truth.

Post-truth, in other words, is explained by the documedia revolution and is one of the side effects of the formation of documedia capital, just like the mobilization on the web. As for the way it works, I propose to outline it once again using the Kantian categories, but this time, this being a communicative sphere, I will use them in the version offered by the four "conversational maxims" enunciated 40 years ago by English philosopher Paul Grice.[13]

The principle of quality says: Be genuine, and provide truthful information to the best of your knowledge. Trump says that Obama spied on him, but it is not true. A simpleton would say that Trump is a liar; a man of the world would say that what Trump expresses is an alternative truth. The term "alternative truth" is the tribute that vice pays to virtue, but it is also a formally radical chic construct, which raises the suspicion that the truth is fascist and dogmatic, and claims to emancipate while deceiving. The man of the world might very well have learned this trick in some good university in which liberal and naive professors like the professor of *The Blue Angel* preached the farewell to the truth in the name of justice: solidarity is more important than objectivity, democracy is more important than truth. There are at least two weaknesses to this idealistic defense of lies in democracy, or, if you will, two precious lessons that can be drawn from post-truth. The first is that the audience addressed by the philosophers is already trained to worship the truth, but must be sensitized to respecting solidarity and otherness. The second is that, after having offered an involuntary ideological assist to populists and having deprived the intellectuals of their only weapon (the pride, if not the courage, of the truth), postmodernists did not consider that a democracy without truth is not a democracy, and that if solidarity prevails over objectivity, this produces an uncontrollable drift (after all, the mafia or amoral familism are notable examples of the prevalence of solidarity over objectivity).

Grice's maxim of quantity recites: Do not be reticent or redundant. Aware of the fact that the best reticence is redundancy, post-truth engages in the industrial production of bullshit. In terms of quantity, post-truth is favored by technology: there is a ceaseless

10 M. Ferraris, *Documentality. Why It Is Necessary to Leave Traces*, Fordham UP, New York 2013.

11 L. Floridi, *The Fourth Revolution. How the Infosphere is Reshaping Human Reality*, Oxford UP, Oxford 2014.

12 M. Ferraris, *Postverità e altrienigmi*, il Mulino, Bologna 2017.

13 H. P. Grice, *Logic and Conversation* in P. Cole e J. Morgan (ed. by), *Syntax and Semantics*, vol. 3: *Speech acts*, New York, Academic Press 1975.

production of documents on the web, and each receiver can in turn become their transmitter and the re-transmitter (the bullshit reaches its critical mass thanks to the re-tweet, the forwarding that inaugurates virality). Is this production systematic and intentional, as claimed by the Marxist doctrine of ideology, according to which those who control the means of production control the ideas? No: behind bullshit there is no great puppeteer, no intelligent and strategic capital. What we inadequately call "capital" is precisely a documedia system, that is, I repeat, the union between the constitutive power of documents ("documentality") and the mobilizing power of the media, generating behaviors that are difficult to explain with age-old categories belonging to a different world. Hence a second teaching of post-truth: let's try to explain what happens with different criteria, in particular by seeing the convergence (very accidental and not very intelligent) between a technological organization and a natural human weakness: we might understand something more about the world we live in.

The maxim of relation is: Be pertinent. But pertinence is a rare, burdensome, and obnoxious quality, whereas the hoax is mediagenic and viral. It is gossip, heir of the fairy-tale, the fantastic, and the futurist words in freedom. But once again, postmodernism contributed too, by claiming that the world depends on our language and our conceptual schemes. Which, if said in a seminar, can make you smile or think (do dinosaurs really depend on the word "dinosaur"?), but outside the classroom can justify the idea that things are the docile subordinates of words: if you say that there are weapons of mass destruction in Iraq, then there are weapons of mass destruction in Iraq, and if you say, on May 1, 2003, that the war in Iraq is over, then it's over. These hoaxes are much more demanding than the claim that a restaurant in Padua serves human flesh, but at the same time they manifest the human lordship over language that philosophers and non-philosophers were so passionate about in the twentieth century, and of which now (the third teaching of post-truth) we recognize the vanity.

Finally, the maxim of modality is: "Avoid ambiguity" and *fashionable nonsense*. However, people like nonsense – this is an unquestionable truth. It is neither true nor post-true that humans naturally seek knowledge, as Aristotle claimed: rather, they hate the potential consequences of their lack of knowledge, which is a very different thing. In short, although the truth sooner or later comes out, the search for truth can hardly be carried out with bare hands and with no cultural training. Augustine says so in his Confessions: I want to *do* the truth, not only in my heart, but also in writing and in front of many witnesses. What does he mean? Can you do the truth like you do a sport? No. I would propose we interpret this sentence as follows: truth is not granted, and requires technical training as well as a good dose of goodwill and sometimes even personal courage. In short, while post-truth can be constructed by means of nonsense and illogicality, the truth asks for more but also has much more to offer. And if we really cannot give up post-truth, and maybe are very attached, say, to the concept of "bad hombre", it is better to submit it, rather than to a minimal fact checking, to the challenging test proposed by William James: "True ideas are those that we can assimilate, validate, corroborate, and verify. False ideas are those that we cannot".[14]

14 W. James, *Pragmatism*, 1907, New York, Dover 1995, Lecture VI.

5.7 The unfair exchange

Let's return to our general goal: to understand the determination of the documedia surplus value. As pre-Marxian economists did not see that workers were only paid for part of their work, so today we tend not to consider that the mobilization is paid only in part by the free services offered by the web. It is difficult not to grasp the asymmetry between give and take here. The documents that the archives provide to the mobilized are general and accessible to everyone, by definition: therefore, they do not offer competitive advantages. The information that the mobilized offer to the archives are individual and accessible only to the archives: therefore, they offer enormous competitive advantages. Of this advantage I only get the negative part, the one that pushes me to spend due to the probabilistic prediction of my habits. Add to this that, as I recalled, the mobilized also pay for the means of production: devices and internet provider subscriptions (not unlike what happens for the house in Airbnb or the car in Uber). Trying to draw a general law from the various categorizations proposed so far, I have obtained a law on the formation of documedia surplus value that can be formulated as follows:

Let's call the documedia value v, the amount of generic data received from the mobilized Q and the amount of specific data provided by the mobilized X.

(1) The way things appear to the mobilized: receiving a free amount of Q seems to coincide with the documedia value
$v^* = Q$

(2) What actually happens: the mobilized receives Q in exchange for X (whether they know it or not), therefore the true documedia profit is:
$v = Q - X$

(3) We can quantify X as quantitatively and qualitatively superior to Q, therefore expressed by the formula
$X = (1 + k)Q$ (with $k>0$)
Therefore the true documedia profit is
$v = Q - X = Q - (1 + k)Q = -kQ$

And consequently the surplus value obtained by the system (social network or else):
$p = X - Q = - v = kQ$

In particular, if we say that the mobilized receives 50 from the platform in generic data and gives 100, this is equivalent to saying $k = 1$, which means that $X = 2Q$

Therefore the documedia profit is
$v = -Q$

And consequently the surplus value is
$p = -v = Q$

In short, we have $v = -Q = -v^*$, i.e. the mobilized person believes they have a documedia profit v^*, instead they face a documedia loss of the same value. On the contrary, the surplus value of the system is equal to the data that it has apparently given to the mobilized user.

Until this law is clear, I fear that we will continue to operate with inadequate categories and to nurture social hatred – which is the most serious problem of an age that, in many ways, is the richest and most evolved in human history.

References

Ainis, M. *Il regno dell'Uroboro*, Milano, La Nave di Teseo 2018.

Aiyagari, S. R. and Wallace, N. "Existence of Steady-states with Positive Consumption in the Kiyotaki-Wright Model", in *Review of Economic Studies*, 58, 1991, pp. 901–916.

Carpo, M. *The Second Digital Turn*, MIT Press, Cambridge (MA)-London 2017.

Domenicucci, J. *Trust, Extended Memories and Social Media*, in *Towards a Philosophy of Digital Media*, A. Romele and E. Terrone (ed. by), Palgrave Macmillan, Basingstoke 2018, pp. 119–142.

Ferraris, M. Documentality. *Why It Is Necessary to Leave Traces*, Fordham UP, New York 2013.

Ferraris, M. *Postverità e altri enigmi*, il Mulino, Bologna 2017.

Floridi, L. *The Fourth Revolution. How the Infosphere is Reshaping Human Reality*, Oxford UP, Oxford 2014.

Grice, H. P. "Logic and Conversation" in Peter Cole e J. Morgan (ed. by), *Syntax and Semantics, vol. 3: Speech acts*, New York, Academic Press 1975.

Heraclitus, DK 22B 89.

James, W. *Pragmatism*, New York, Dover 1995.

Kocherlakota, N. N. *Money is Memory*, Federal Reserve Bank of Minneapolis, Research Department Staff Report 218, 1996 October.

Lucas, R. *Equilibrium in a Pure Currency Economy, Models of Monetary Economics*, in J. H. Kareken and N. Wallace (ed. by), MN, Federal Reserve Bank of Minneapolis, Minneapolis 1980.

Mayer-Schönberger, V. and Ramge, T. *Reinventing Capitalism in the Age of Big Data, Basic Books*, New York 2018.

Ostroy, J. "The Informational Efficiency of Monetary Exchange", in *American Economic Review*, 63, 1973, pp. 597–610.

6 Believing fake news

Anna Elisabetta Galeotti

6.1 Introductory remarks

The proliferation of misinformation, inaccuracy in data processing, twisted scientific findings through the web and social media, in a word the proliferation of "fake news", has raised worries concerning their alleged impact on democratic processes. For example, events such as Brexit and Trump's election are ascribed to the effects of "fake news" on citizens' choices, as well as the xenophobic attitudes against refugees and the mistrust of scientific research. Deception, self-deception, misreading of evidence, biased interpretations of facts, mixed with propaganda and spin have always been present in democratic politics and society. At first sight, what is new is the multiplying effect of web dissemination as well as a diffuse sense of danger and threat induced by the denunciation of the unstoppable spreading of false information among citizens and governments of Western democracy. Despite these worries, which have monopolized media's attention in the past couple of years, research on this subject, though growing, is still in an early stage and mainly focused on web communications. Yet, the nature of fake news and the reasons why it is so massively and virally believed require much more digging and theorizing.

In this chapter, I want to tackle this phenomenon by raising two questions. The first concerns what fake news is, or, to put it differently, whether it is a specific form compared to traditional public disinformation and deception. More precisely, I shall ask whether the novelty of fake news lies just in the multiplying effect of the web and in the speed of dissemination, or if there is something more specific to it, linked to the information selection allowed by the web platform and to the cognitive traps triggered by this means of communication. Incidentally, even if the fake news phenomenon were only quantitative, the mass of misinformation disseminated by the new media is such to engender a different scale of risk for democratic and open society. Therefore, even the mere quantitative dimension of the phenomenon creates a specific new issue for our society.

The second question addresses the issue of fake news from the viewpoint of the recipient or consumer, and asks on the basis of which cognitive traps and mechanisms cognizers end up believing fake news at a higher and faster rate than true news (Vosoughi et al. 2018). Is fake news believed in the same ways as lies or are there more complex cognitive and motivational elements factoring into coming to believe in fake news? A first immediately visible difference between someone duped by a lie and someone duped by fake news is that the latter usually becomes an active propagator of the false information to large audiences through social media, contributing to the deception of many other users.

In the first section of this chapter I shall thus take up the discussion on what fake news is and see whether a specific account can be provided that marks it specifically off compared to traditional forms of public deception. The relevant deception here is public for fake news typically affects large audiences and constitutes a public concern for a healthy democracy. In the second section of this chapter, I shall try to map the cognitive and motivational traps making people victims of this form of disinformation and deception. Finally, in the third section, I shall take up the discussion about possible remedies, focusing on the ones directed at improving individual epistemic responses to fake news exposure. There is a lot of discussion about institutional remedies, whether through the web providers or through political institutions, as well as a significant resistance to forms of political control and censure of the web. The issue of institutional control, however, must preliminarily consider what political values are at stake and whether political intervention can defend them effectively without endangering others. But this work goes beyond the scope of this chapter. Meanwhile, on the issue of cognitive countermeasures, as we shall see, the research is still to be developed. While there are a number of studies focused on new media communications, and while there is an important literature on cognitive and motivational distortions and bias and on the epistemology of testimony, there is little work connecting the two and seeing how the findings in cognitive psychology and in epistemology bear on the fake news belief formation, persistence and dissemination. I shall try to connect the two literatures and see whether some hints for counteracting the effect of fake news can be found.

6.2 What is fake news?

The expression "fake news" was introduced more than a decade ago to connote a special genre of popular television entertainment, such as the *Daily Show*, where political satire is embedded in the humorous reviews of daily news (Holbert 2005). It is a form of reality-based television, since the content of the satire is taken from current political news. The satirized reporting, though, often create ambiguity concerning what is factual and what is fictional, so that the audience must play an active role in determining the true meaning of the satire. The original sense of the expression, then, relates to a style of news presentation, uncorrelated to truth, highlighting inconsistencies in political rhetoric, which might make it difficult for viewers to separate satire from facts, truth from fiction. Fake is more precisely the form in which satire is presented as (inverted) news, while it is up to the audience to decipher the satirical and fictional nature of the show. Some researchers still use "fake news" in reference to either political satire (Balmas 2014) or, by extension, to the "tabloidization" of news as means of attention grabbing and sharable reporting, epitomized by clickbait headlines (Chen et al. 2015). In this latter sense, the sensationalist form is responsible for blurring the line between fact and fiction. More specifically, in the case of clickbait headlines, the indifference towards the truth leads to information whose only purpose is to induce people to click on a link to a webpage to increase the page views. The content of the message is not necessarily fiction, but often misleading, unverified and seldom corrected. Fake here is referred to the fact that clickbait headlines are exaggerated, suggestive, easily misleading, hence represent one important source of fake news and of its spread.

In sum, originally, fake news meant something quite different from lies, namely messages whose fictional nature was wrapped up in a form mimicking reality, leaving the job of drawing the boundaries and decoding it in an appropriate way to the individual recipient. The very categorization of this genre of satirical news as "fake" exploits a line of reflection in experimental psychology on the effect of (explicit) fiction in inducing beliefs in subjects (Gerrig, Prentice 1991; Gilbert et al. 1990; Marsh, Fazio 2006). Even if authors of fiction do not aim at producing an accurate account of the world, there is a lot of information that readers acquire from fiction. Some of this information is accurate, and some is instead made up in the fictional story. Experiments have shown that some of the fictional inaccuracies about the real world go undetected by readers and come to be encoded in subsequent beliefs, as if the compartmentalization of fiction vs. real world information were blurred. The integration of fiction and real world sources into self-ascribed beliefs is apparently less significant when fiction deals with fantastic world remote from daily and familiar experience. By contrast, when fiction deals with familiar events in a realistic world similar to ours, the integration is eased, resulting in inaccurate reports of state of facts by the readers (Rapp, Hinze 2014). Hence, a satirical content presented in a form similar to news reportage may well induce confusion between fiction and reality.

If the original meaning of fake news thus referred to forms of communication blurring the boundaries between fiction and real world, and did not mean the spread of false information, the prevalent meaning of fake news is now rather different. Especially after the 2016 American election, the term has come to mean false stories describing events in the real world by mimicking the forms of traditional media reportages, fabricated and promoted on social media either for ideological reasons or for financial gain (Rubin et al. 2015; Silverman 2016; Mustafaraj, Taxis Metaxas 2017; Allcott, Gentzkow 2017; Rini 2017; Jang, Kim 2018). In this new definition, the following features characterize fake news:

(1) News occurrences are *false*, being explicitly *fabricated* by their producers, and are not simply the result of mistakes.
(2) They are propagated through *social media*, implying that they are targeted on *large audiences.*
(3) They are usually *motivated* either by the wish to manipulate people's beliefs in a polarized political context or by the wish to grab attention in order to increase the clicks on certain links and pages for financial gain.

In the latter case, there is no interest in the doxastic states of the social media consumers, only in inducing a certain behavior advantageous for the producers.

This definition covers both intentionally fabricated news articles, large scale hoaxes and humorous fakes, i.e. articles originated in satirical websites that can be misunderstood as factual, especially if viewed out of context on Twitter or Facebook. Moreover, it is agnostic concerning the intentional deception component in fake news. Some authors in fact hold that intentional deception is one of its characterizing features (Rini 2017; Jang, Kim 2018; Mustafaraj, Taxis Metaxas 2017), while others do not take a side on the matter (Allcott, Gentzkow 2017; Vosoughi et al. 2018). I think that the intentional deception component is neither a necessary nor a sufficient condition for fake news. We have seen that some fake news is motivated by financial gain, while some others depend on the consumer's inability to understand humorous jokes as such. Hence, not all instances of fake news are prompted by the intention to deceive the social media users into believing something that is false but in the interest of the liar to have them believe. Moreover, I suspect that those scholars who underline the intention to deceive conflate the fact that the information passed on is false and the producer is aware of this fact with the explicit intention of deceiving others. The two things must be set apart for in the first case the deception usually occurs but simply as a by-product of passing on false information for other reasons, while in the second case the deception of others is the outcome of a deliberate strategy of lying. True, some fake news information, notably the ones with political content, are deliberately created and disseminated aiming at the manipulation of beliefs and behavior of citizens. In this respect, political manipulation by fake news seems to be no different from traditional political manipulation via politicians' statements, apart from the social media effect of multiplying and speeding up dissemination. But this similarity concerns only a section of fake news and, even in this section, evidence coming from current research shows that there are specific features setting political fake news apart from old propaganda and manipulation. On the one hand, as many scholars hold, internet and social media seem to affect the selection process of the information one is exposed to (Sunstein 2007; Pariser 2011; Mustafaraj, Taxis Metaxas 2017), and, on the other hand, cognitive traps, heuristics and motivational interference are more easily triggered in social media contexts (Levy 2017). Moreover, there are consequences of the spreading of fake news, such as their agenda setting power on traditional media and public discourse (Vargo 2018).

In other words, current research has successfully shown that there are some specific features of the platform's algorithms allowing producers of fake news to find the people likely to disseminate the false news, and, at the same time, that the dissemination is parasitic on cognitive features of users. Fake news producers exploit technological possibility of the platforms to reach potentially sensitive users (Mustafaraj, Taxis Metaxas 2017), while clickbait headlines exploit the proneness to attention-grabbing cues of human minds (Chen et al. 2015). Moreover, once a fake news story has become viral, it is discussed in the public forum (Vargo 2018).

So far, we have seen that "fake news" can be characterized as something specific compared to traditional political deception and propaganda, with reference to: (1) how the false news is fabricated, posted and disseminated through social media and research engines; (2) how the dimension of misinformation, due to the size of the affected audiences and to the speed of the dissemination, is incomparable with traditional forms; (3) how it comes to be believed by the social media users; and (4) how it powerfully affects the agenda setting in the public discourse of a society.

Despite the possibility of a specific characterization of fake news, some researchers doubt that the expression represents a useful notion for analytical purpose. The ideological use of the concept, now habitually used polemically to criticize and reject unfavorable political information, seems to discourage its adoption in a more analytical context. Whatever negative information comes about in the public forum about any politician or party is now commonly rejected as fake news, as intentionally planted falsehood to discredit him or her, apparently without need to provide evidence for the allegation. This partisan and symmetrical use of fake news to reject critical information about oneself or one's party has the effect of enwrapping political discourse in a fog where truths and fabrications are mixed together, leading some commentators to speak about the present as a regime of post-truth (Manjoo 2008). For this reason, some researchers have grown suspicious of using the expression in scholarly analysis, and now they prefer to substitute the expression with *false* news and information vs. *true* news and information (Vosoughi et al. 2018). While I understand their qualms, I think that fake news better conveys the specificity of this novel form of misinformation compared to traditional false information. Hence, I shall stick to the expression fake news, aware of the misuse in partisan politics, but also confident that conceptual analysis can dispel the fog.

6.3 Why do we believe fake news?

The question of why we believe in fake news may appear otiose, for we believe fake news in the same ways as we believe true information. Experimental psychology has actually validated an intuition by Baruch Spinoza concerning belief formation while understanding a message: as Spinoza claimed, evidence supports that while understanding a piece of information we accept it as true, and maybe later we come to disbelieve it (Gilbert et al. 1990). This experiment gives primacy to believing information as true rather than suspending judgment. One usual way of getting information is through testimony and, as a rule, we believe information by testimony, if there are no reasons either to mistrust the testifier or to doubt the content of the information that is either incoherent or at odds with our system of beliefs.[1] A recent paper has actually argued that from the point of view of the epistemology of testimony, believing in fake news is often individually reasonable (Rini 2017). Despite the fact that the relationship between testifier and testimony in the case of social media is more ambiguous, nevertheless people mainly treat

1 The evaluation of the truth of a statement can count on five criteria: (1) general acceptance by other people; (2) gauging of the available evidence; (3) compatibility of the other beliefs; (4) general coherence of the statement; (5) credibility of the source (Schwarz et al. 2016). In case of belief by testimony, criterion (2) does not apply, but the other four are actually available.

social media transmission as if it were a normal form of testimony. Even though, according to Rini, social media transmission is a form of *bent* testimony that should make us more cautious before accepting the information as true; nevertheless, certain conditions in the use of social media make the acceptance of testimony through them subjectively reasonable. That is because social media news often concerns political matters and, to be precise, highly polarized political messages. If, as Rini claims, partisanship in not epistemically unreasonable, then it follows that accepting partisan testimony transmission is compatible with epistemic virtues. For this reason, she concludes that believing fake news with a political partisan content, all in all, is not subjectively unreasonable. I shall not discuss this claim now. I only refer to this argument in order to show that the question of why we believe in fake news may appear otiose prima facie, given that not only do we believe in testimony as a default, but also that there are good subjective reasons to believe in the form of bent testimony represented by social media.

Yet, despite the fact that accepting fake news may be judged in line with the epistemology of testimony, the question of why we believe in fake news is not otiose, given that recent research has established that fake news is spread on social media more broadly, rapidly and deeply than true news (Vosoughi et al. 2018). This work, based on the analysis of Twitter from its beginning to 2017, confirms the finding of another research, which instead examined Facebook news during the final three months of the US presidential campaign in 2016: "The analysis shows how viral fake election news stories outperformed real ones on Facebook" (Silverman 2016). Both researches actually measure the *spread* of fake news, and not the *beliefs* resulting from it, but, as we shall see more properly later, beliefs are a function of their diffusion and, even if not all re-tweeters are in fact believers in the news content, a good number of them supposedly are. If we are to infer, then, that the social media induce false beliefs at a higher rate than true beliefs, why we believe in fake news is far from being an otiose question.

Going back to the findings of the Vosoughi research, the authors looked for an explanation of the superior capacity of penetration of falsehoods; hence, they firstly tested the conventional wisdom according to which the spreading of fake news is explained by the structure of communication and by individual variances. In other words, the conventional wisdom attributes these results on the different—longer or shorter—presence of people on Twitter, on their being more or less active, having more or less contacts and so on. But Vosoughi and his colleagues found that this explanation has no grounds. For alternative answers, they subsequently looked at information theory and Bayesian decision theory, and hypothesized that novelty might be an important key factor for news spreading. Novelty has not only an attention-grabbing power, but it is more valuable for it provides new information and grounds for decision making, as well as for social factors. The provider of new information acquires a higher social status as the one who is "in the know". Since fake news usually contain new and striking information, given their attention-grabbing nature, novelty could represent the relevant cue. The novelty hypothesis was in fact confirmed by a check on subjects' previous exposure to fake vs. true information, as well as by a check on the emotion displayed in the retweeting. For fake news, the prevalent emotions were surprise and then disgust, which corroborate the hypothesis that fake news typically transmits new and surprising information. Thus, the cue priming retweeting has nothing to do with the truth credentials of the news. As said earlier, this very important research concerns the diffusion of news on social media, and more specifically on Twitter, by checking the rumor cascades from any original tweet, whether true or false. It does not advance any claim about beliefs. Retweeting is not equivalent to endorsing and believing the information one is transmitting. The difference between the two has to do with the uncertainty of the norms of communication governing social media, even if, despite ambiguity in testimonial intentions, it seems that above a certain threshold of sharing, any ambiguity seems to be washed away and people take the sharing as a form of endorsing the transmitted claim (Rini 2017).

The relationship between news spreading and correspondent beliefs formation deserves to be analyzed more closely for it may help to respond to our question. In general, a precondition for a piece of news to be believed is to reach out to people, and, in that sense, the broader and faster spreading of fake news increases the probability of its being believed. Yet, given that retweeting does not imply believing the news, we can speculate here that the reasons or causes for retweeting can be different from the reasons or causes of coming to believe the news. The novelty of the message, as suggested in the research earlier, grabs the attention and surprises the user, which, in turn, motivates him/her to retweet the message. The correspondent belief can at this point more easily be formed, even if at the beginning the subject was unsure about the truth of the message, on the basis of two different mechanisms described by cognitive psychology. One is predicted by perception theory, that is the tendency to infer belief from behavior, or, to put it differently, to use behavior as a sign of the correspondent belief, justifying the behavior ex post (Bem 1967; Bem, McConnell 1970). In this sense, retweeting may be taken as revealing the correspondent belief justifying the action of spreading the message. The second consists of the effect on fluency processing of information, so that a more easily retrievable stimulus affects what people come to believe (Alter et al. 2007; Rapp et al. 2014). Suppose that the retweeting user is originally agnostic about the claim of the message. Yet retweeting exposes the user twice to the same message, and if the dissemination proceeds, there is a good chance that the same claim may reach the user by a different cascade, and furthermore by the claim being reported on traditional media. Repeated exposure facilitates familiarity and the fluency processing, which, in turn, induces the correspondent belief, just because the retrieval of the information is easier and more readily available (fluent). The fluency effect strikes automatically, even if, originally, one had doubts about that piece of information, and it may be activated by the salience and simplicity of the message, as well as by repetition and familiarity. It may seem that novelty and familiarity are going in opposite directions concerning their effect on belief, and that the one should limit the effect of the other. In fact, in the dissemination of fake news, the two, apparently opposite, cues for fluency processing are likely to work together. The novelty arouses attention and emotion of surprise, which make the message salient and the subjects prone to suggestibility (Eslik et al. 2011). Then, retweeting is a repetition, which is likely to be only the first, for the message can reach the user through other cascades and from traditional media commenting on it. This increases familiarity as well as the perception that the information is shared and held by others, reinforcing the belief in it being true.

Both self-perception and fluency processing work below the radar of awareness and analytical reasoning, and strike anyone, in the appropriate context. I like to stress the difference between the two mechanisms. Self-perception is a distorted form of self-attribution of beliefs ex post based on actual behavior, which has been interpreted as a form of reduction of cognitive dissonance (Festinger 1957); by contrast, fluency processing is a heuristics, a process speeding our cognitive process bypassing epistemic rules, which, under the appropriate circumstances, produces reliable judgments open to epistemic justification (Reber, Unkelbach 2014).[2] Yet, heuristics can as well lead to wrong conclusion in the unfavorable circumstances. The consideration of fluency processing shows that, even if the media user is relatively sophisticated epistemically, and not immediately duped by the fake news, the latter may automatically affect his doxastic state, at a later time, just because of the repeated exposition and to the action of retweeting (Levy 2017). In sum, even though the researches by Silverman and by Vosoughi and colleagues concern the spreading of fake news, the broader and faster rate of spreading is likely to induce an increase of correspondent false beliefs, given certain cognitive mechanisms.

The reason why fake news stories are believed is thus firstly correlated to certain cognitive features, amply analyzed by cognitive psychology, which are displayed in all sorts of acquisition and retrieval of knowledge, but which are especially triggered by the working of social media. That is because not only the news on social media is presented in a simplified, but attention-grabbing form, but also because it tends to spread rapidly and to come back from multiple paths to social media users so as to induce familiarity, hence enhancing fluency processing. Beside these two features of news circulation online and on social media, another factor affecting the credibility of information is its general acceptance by others. The larger the number of people believing that P affects the tendency to acquire and share the belief that P. Now it is unclear whether the influence of a popular view on our

2 I shall refer to heuristic and implicit modes of belief acquisition without taking sides in the controversy over the dual process of reasoning or the unified process of reasoning. The supporters of the dual process envisage two different strategies of learning, one based on intuition, making use of heuristics, fast and often unreliable; the second, based on analytical thinking, much slower, but under control, and epistemically adequate (Alter et al. 2007; Schwarz et al. 2016). The supporters of a unified process of learning think of a continuum of different strategies in knowledge acquisition and retrieval, some of which are implicit and quick, some are slower and explicit, and some are automated after many repetitions (Osman 2004). For the purpose of this chapter, the relevant fact is that the supports of either theory acknowledge that acquisition and retrieval of knowledge can proceed by implicit or automated processes, below the radar of awareness, and by explicit analytical thinking modules.

doxastic system belongs to the same kind of automated mechanisms described earlier or not, for the fact that a belief is shared among other people is often a reasonable corroboration of its truth (Schwarz et al. 2016). If, however, other grounds justifying the belief are lacking, accepting a belief as true because it is largely popular may be a display of conformity bias. Clearly, the multiplying effect of social media largely amplifies this tendency, contributing in making falsehoods believable as true facts. Evidence shows that especially when a view is held by people with whom we identify, the influence on our doxastic system is especially powerful (Del Vicario et al. 2015; Levy 2017).

This phenomenon leads me to consider the motivational interference in the acquisition of information, as a relevant cause of misinformation, and the effect of partisanship and ideology, as sources of specific forms of motivated false beliefs. I define partisan viewpoints as "ideological", if they work as screens for selecting information, blocking out the adverse news and prompting the acceptance of favorable ones. Much research done on political misinformation either through politicians and old media or through new media confirms the effect of partisanship in accepting or rejecting certain news, according to whether its source is one's party or more generally one's side or not (Cohen 2003; Uhlmann et al. 2009; Silverman 2016; Piacenza 2018). However, relatively little reflection is available on the different components contributing to the effect of ideological views on beliefs. I argue that relying on ideology as selector of information embodies: (1) a reasonable component; (2) a fluency processing component and (3) a motivational component influencing the belief formation. The reasonable component has been argued for by Rini (2017) in the article previously discussed. If someone holds a comprehensive view of politics and society, and is genuinely convinced it is true, he/she shares a special bond and trust with the people sharing the same world-view. As much as one trusts the testimony of a trustworthy friend, similarly, one tends to trust information coming from the party or the group sharing the same comprehensive view, for that makes them trustworthy. In that respect, believing information coming from the party or group that one trusts is in general reasonable, at least if the content of the news fits with what one knows about the world and is consistent with one's other beliefs. However, and that is precisely one of the fake news features, the content of the information passed on via social media is often outrageous and striking, has sometimes the character of a hoax, or of satire. Think of the infamous news spread during the last US presidential campaign against Hillary Clinton, concerning the use of the basement of a pizza parlor in Washington, for pedophile activities (Cush 2016). This is typically the kind of information that should make anyone who has previous information about Hillary Clinton be dubious of its veracity, no matter whether one liked her politically or not and whether the news source is from one's party. Nevertheless, the news was widely believed by Trump's supporters who willingly contributed to its spread on social media. In such a case, which is far from being isolated in the dissemination of political falsehoods on social media, there is no reasonable justification to believe the information, even from the subjective viewpoint of a partisan. Lacking reasonable justification, external cues may perhaps explain the belief formation.

Such information is new, surprising and attention grabbing: such features contribute to make it salient, and, in turn, salience triggers fluency processing. This kind of news arouses attention and emotional responses of both surprise and disgust, as reported by Vosoughi's research, and sticks to one's memory much more than mundane pieces of facts. Partisan misinformation through social media are especially fit to elicit such cognitive responses. However, if the reason of believing such an incredible story was just fluency processing, that is, a "cold" cognitive mechanism, how come the believers were all Trump's supporters? Fluency should strike indiscriminately either conservatives or liberals. This consideration leads me to consider the motivational component as crucial, which, may in case trigger the fluency processing component. Evidence of the motivational component is abundant in all studies on political polarization. Motivated irrationality is a well-known area of study in epistemology and philosophy of mind. It has mostly concentrated on two specimens, namely self-deception and wishful thinking. The analysis of motivated irrationality has also been applied to ideology, under the strictly Marxian notion of false consciousness (Elster 1983). Now I propose to extend the motivated irrationality analysis to ideological convictions in a broader sense, as comprehensive worldviews, which people not only believe as true, but with which they also identify themselves. In general, if we firmly hold a worldview, we are inclined to believe any news consistent and fitting into that view. The "consistency push" is neither irrational nor necessarily motivational: actually, among the criteria for evaluating whether a belief can be accepted as true, one is precisely its consistency with the other beliefs one holds, and another is the coherence of the content of the information (Schwarz et al. 2016). Yet, we have seen that in the case of fake news, such checks are usually suspended when the misinformation comes from the group or party sharing our worldview, despite the fact that its content is unfitting the world as we know it. In front of a preposterous news, such as the pizzagate and Hillary Clinton, what makes people believe it cannot be the consistency push. We must rather presuppose a wish to believe information favorable to one's party as the push for partisans to believe something without warrant and despite good sense. Obviously, ideology has always worked in this way much before fake news was circulating online, and contributed to people's holding falsehoods. What is new now is the quantity of partisan information spread through social media and coming back to research engines on the web and on traditional media and the preposterous nature of fake news claims. In turn, the false beliefs seem to be immune from correction and new evidence.

This observation leads me to a final issue, which represents a major concern for the effect of fake news, that is, the resistance to corrections: even in case of subsequent exposure to new and compelling evidence against the fake news, subjects tend to retain their false belief in line with their ideological views, despite debunking. When a subject believes that P according to her wish but against available evidence, this is precisely a case of self-deception. The fact that once-formed beliefs seem immunized to new evidence and new arguments is widely reported in many researches in experimental psychology and political psychology (Gilbert et al. 1990; Marsh, Fazio 2006; Nyhan, Reifler 2010; Eslik et al. 2011;

Lewandowsky et al. 2012; Peter, Koch 2016). Furthermore, some experiments have proved that the attempt of debunking fake news with evidence and arguments often have the backfire effect of reinforcing the false belief. Strangely enough, this kind of research has never considered the work done in the area of self-deception by epistemologists, philosophers of mind and experimental psychologists, for I think that it might have helped to make a clearer sense not only of the resistance to corrections but also of the backfire effect.

The backfire effect has been especially investigated by Nyhan and Reifler (2010). They precisely tested participants by exposing them to information contradicting their political beliefs and opinions, for example exposing them to negative information relative to their preferred candidate. This is a case where, in order to preserve one's political conviction, it is not sufficient a careful selective search of information, to the effect of filtering out all data contradicting one's convictions. The biased search strategy is actually one of the typical mental activity displayed by self-deceivers to defend their favorite belief that P against threatening evidence. In this case, though, the negative evidence has been put in front of the participants' eyes, and in order to defend that P is not sufficient to look away and filter out the evidence for ~P. The account of persisting in a false belief cannot simply refer to the fact that people believe what they want to believe, as the authors of this research pointed out. On the one hand, we cannot believe by fiat, and, on the other, if that were possible, humans would live in a delusional world and that would be extremely dangerous for their own survival. In fact, most of the time we hold beliefs appropriately, whether formed by heuristics or by expressed reasoning. This is what makes so puzzling the phenomenon of self-deceptive beliefs, that is, false motivated beliefs held in the teeth of evidence. Thus, how come the participants of the experiment were directly exposed to information contrary to their belief, and nevertheless, not only retained their belief, but also became firmer in their conviction? In this case, in order to defend the belief that P, the subjects must either explain away the contrary evidence or block the inference from the contrary evidence to ~P. Either way, the subjects must engage in sophisticated counterarguments to avoid concluding that ~P, either questioning the credibility of the information, or its relevance for the judgment on their preferred candidate. Since the negative evidence does not directly compel one to believe ~P, there is always a little latitude for engaging in arguments, twisted and yet sophisticated, leading to the self-deceptive belief that P. This finding actually confirms researches and studies on self-deception (Wentura, Greve 2003; Wentura, Greve 2005; Michel, Newen 2010) where it is apparent that the persistence of a counter-evidential belief according to one's wish is brought about by a whole host of arguments displaying a quasi-rationality. As a result of such argumentative activity, subjects end up even firmer in their convictions.

In sum, not only ideological convictions contribute to make fake news believed in accordance with one's ideological outlook, but they motivate partisan people to hold on to their preferred beliefs even when contrary evidence becomes available, and may even induce backfire effect. Making use of the work on motivated irrationality, we can say that ideological motivations lower accuracy, manipulating the acceptance threshold in processing information concerning one's ideological outlook (Mele 2001). The positive information is therefore immediately and fluently processed to form the favorable belief that P. In case of welcoming stimuli, the ideological motivation triggers subintentional mechanisms directly producing the belief that P thanks to a lowered acceptance threshold. This is usually how wishful thinking, that is believing beyond evidence and in accordance with one's wishes, comes about. The negative information, by contrast, primes a self-deceptive process, for self-deception is precisely believing something according to one's wish and against the evidence. But, while wishful thinking is brought about directly by the working of subintentional cognitive mechanisms triggered by the wish, self-deception is set in motion by the threatening negative evidence and the emotionally loaded wish to believe that P, in case of costs of accuracy sinking or discounting (Galeotti 2018). The last condition is important to sort out the selectivity issue of self-deception, namely the fact that self-deception does not strike all the times reality frustrates our desires (Talbot 1995; Bermudez 2000). Incidentally, Nyhan and Reifler indirectly referred to selectivity when they pointed out that the backfire effect cannot be explained by the fact that people believe what they want. Self-deception cannot be the default response whenever information runs counter to our preferences. In front of the negative evidence, the rational response would be to act so as to counteract the threat and bring about the desired state of the world. However, sometimes action is precisely foreclosed by the circumstances, or it is too costly, or, in any case, the consequences do not befall on the agent. This circumstance leads to sinking or discounting the costs of inaccuracy, lowering the threshold of evidence for believing something true and heightening the threshold for disbelieving it. Let us apply this model to the ideological backfire effect in front of debunking. The person holding certain ideological convictions is actually powerless to counteract the negative information she is exposed to; the discomfort induced by the bad news cannot be undone with an accurate processing of data. In a word, for her there is nothing to gain by epistemic accuracy, only to increase her discomfort and uneasiness. Thus, the circumstances favorable for a self-deception process are all in place. The subject at this point starts thinking about how to reject the negative evidence and to go on holding one's cherished conviction. The motivated reasoning is affected by biases in data treatment, so that when the subject has found an explanation washing away the negative evidence, she can stop and go on holding what accords with her favored view. Since the subject must produce arguments to dismiss the negative data, the process embodies explicit reasoning that, though twisted, biased and below standards, does not proceed randomly.

One of the reasons why the reference to the motivated irrationality literature is important concerns the understanding of the motivation underlying the stickiness of ideological convictions. To be sure, lots of research has been done on the persistence of errors in experimental and political psychology, mostly testing interference of inaccurate information with memory retrieval. However, these experiments are designed to highlight the effect of external cues, fluency processing and other subintentional mechanisms in the difficulty of correction of mistakes, clearly not considering the very possibility of motivational interference. I argue, however, that the motivational influence is crucial to make sense of cognitive phenomena which otherwise would look contradictory, for example the phenomenon of "Blind choice" which seems to go opposite to the stickiness of erroneous beliefs. The blind choice phenomenon emerges in experimental contexts where the participants are asked to express their agreement with certain statements, and then, through a subtle manipulation of the experiment sheets, are asked to justify their own answers, some of which have been reversed by the experimenters (Hall et al. 2012) Many participants do not realize the manipulation, and take the answers written down as their own, hence proceed in justifying them. The blind choice experiments are deliberately designed to test self-perception theory, namely the tendency to infer beliefs from behavior ex post, and the interpretation of the irrational shift in beliefs is provided by the reduction of cognitive dissonance, in the direction of internal consistency. This experiment, however, must be considered in a larger context to be realigned with the findings on the persistence of mistaken belief and the difficulty of correction. It is doubtful that the drive to consistency is purely cognitive and has nothing to do with the sense of self and the desire to save face. The strange behavior of people who argue in favor of viewpoints that earlier on they have explicitly rejected, more than proving that they self-attribute certain beliefs from their written responses, to my mind, proves that they want to avoid embarrassment. My interpretation finds confirmation in another experiment on the phenomenon of blind choice reported by Neil Levy (2017): the experiment asks participants to write an essay supporting a view running counter to their preferences, namely that university fees should be raised. The participants were divided into three groups: one was given financial incentives, one was asked to volunteer to do the task and the third was the control group left free to support either views on the issue. As expected, the control group wrote against the raise of university fees; the others instead followed the instruction. Yet, when asked to expand on their essay, the group who received financial incentives had no difficulty in saying that they wrote the essay for money without believing what they argued. The group of volunteers instead defended their essay and endorsed the argument they wrote following the instruction but against their preference. The explanation in terms of self-ascription theory does not seem completely convincing. To my mind, it was not that they inferred their preferences from what they wrote, driven by the need of internal consistency, but rather, they felt uneasy and ashamed about having volunteered to switch their positions, and in order to defend their integrity they ended up endorsing the disliked thesis. This irrational shift of positions concerned more their moral consistency, the integrity of their own self, rather than merely their logical or epistemic consistency. Such a problem did not affect the group paid to write the essay, for they had an external reason to sustain a thesis contrary to their conviction and their moral integrity was not stained by their response to the task. The defense of one's image and identity is the same motivation underlying the motivated irrationality induced by ideological convictions: the endorsement of an ideology defines people's identity and self-image. The negative information threatening the robustness of ideology is at the same time a threat on one's self-image as sharing that view and on the group with which one identifies himself: no one likes to be associated with political corruption and illicit behavior. Hence, the resistance to corrections, though it may well be eased by the presence of implicit or automated cognitive mechanisms, is triggered by the desire to defend one's image and the image of the group with which one identifies. In this respect, the motivational and the cognitive component are integrated: desires are triggers of cognitive implicit and subintentional mechanisms leading to believing or persisting to believing that P. When the subject is confronted with negative evidence, the subintentional mechanisms are supplemented by explicit, though biased, reasoning arguing against the negative evidence.

Such cognitive distortions, motivated and non-motivated alike, are actually spread in all forms of communication, interpersonal, public, through old or new social media. As already mentioned, the specificity of fake news spread on social media concerns: (1) the quantity of messages and information one is exposed to; (2) the way news on social media is fabricated to convey simple, striking, even outrageous messages leading people to disseminate; (3) the enhancement of fluency, given the form of the message and its repetition. Concerning specifically political news, then, many scholars have advanced the worry on the increase of polarization. As effect of social media, citizens not only come to hold more false beliefs in line with their ideology, not only resist correction, but tend to be more ideologically segregated and more polarized, making bleaker the chances for a healthy democracy (Abramowitz, Saunders 2008). The effect of new media on polarization had first been denounced by Cass Sunstein at the beginning of the millennium (Sunstein 2001; Sunstein 2007). He was especially worried by the unlimited filtering of information allowed by the web, which would virtually produce the echo-chambers effect where consumers only listen to themselves. The segregation effect is further increased by the working of web-platforms, which propose users' contents of their liking, based on previous choices (Del Vicario et al. 2015; Flaxman et al. 2016). A healthy democracy would instead require that citizens were exposed to a large range of opinions in order to form political views through a balanced and informed inquiry of issues and candidates. Much subsequent research, however, have shown that the worries about political segregation via the web and especially social media are largely exaggerated (Gentzkow, Shapiro 2011; Bakshy et al. 2015). These researches pointed out that internet and social media are far less segregated than networks of trusted friends. To my knowledge, there is, however, no research on polarization specifically, hence so far, the hypothesis that news passed on social media and the internet induce a greater polarization is reasonable, given the nature of the messages. Moreover, the repeated effect at debunking certain fakes by general media may induce in partisans the backfire effect analyzed earlier, contributing to strengthen increasingly polarized positions.

6.4 What is to be done?

Neil Levy, in his article "The Bad News about Fake News" (Levy 2017), projects a very bleak view on the possibility of changing the communicative landscape so as to free our society and polity from fake news. We usually tend to think that fake news dupes unsophisticated people, typically "others" with respect to the groups we identify with. This third-person effect of fake news has actually been detected and analyzed: people perceive the effect of fake news as being greater on outer political groups than on themselves or on their own group (Jang, Kim 2018). Clearly, such perception is deceptive, yet it is reasonable to think that fake news does not affect everyone in the same way. Levy's argument is instead meant to counter the common idea that sophisticated social agents may be immunized against fake news. He claims that the danger implicit in fake news stories is not just caused by the difficulty to detect and debunk them, but also by the mere fact of being exposed to them. Experimental psychological work on fiction (Gerrig, Prentice 1991; Marsh, Fazio 2006; Rapp, Hinze 2014), as we have mentioned, shows that even when people know that they are reading or viewing fictional works, the latter leave representations in their mind, subsequently retrievable by memory and often giving rise to beliefs, in case related beliefs are not stable and clear. In sum, there is no way to escape from fake news and the related dangers, according to Levy. If one is easily taken in by them, then, as we have seen, she is likely to resist corrections and to become more convinced as a result of the backfire effect. If one is sophisticated and epistemically cautious so that she is not easily duped by misinformation, she is in any case exposed and repeatedly, given the fake news agenda power in traditional media and the public forum. Such repeated exposures increase the chances to end up believing what she knew from the start as being false. In a word, Levy precisely projects a world of post-truth where our reasoning capability and epistemic virtues are at a loss in the fight against misinformation. Similar conclusion is reached by a different argument by Rini (2017): if believing fake news is subjectively reasonable in many circumstances, then, she argues that we cannot rely on epistemic virtues to fight falsehood. That is why she advocates institutional measures, which seem the only possible conclusion from Levy's view. However, as said, I do not intend to open the Pandora box of the institutional measures, whether concerning web-platform or politics, because, to start, we should preliminarily clarify what are the values and rights worth protection here. Assuming we have epistemic rights (Watson 2018), how can such rights be enforced, and does not the enforcement risk infringing on other rights? These complex questions deserve to be dealt with at length. For this reason, I shall now confine myself to consider measures at the level of the individual epistemic subject.

In this respect, I would start by saying that the danger of mere exposition to fake news has been greatly exaggerated by Levy: exposition may facilitate the formation of a correspondent belief, but only in a second time and only in case the subject is not certain about his beliefs on that matter. Otherwise, all of us would believe anything that comes in our way and, as a result, we would all share the same beliefs, instead of being polarized on controversial information. Moreover, despite the emphasis on automated and implicit processes in bringing about false beliefs, on the base of suggestibility, repetition, familiarity and fluency memory retrieval, cognitive psychology also provides some guidelines to counter the misinformation effect on beliefs. A first interesting suggestion comes from a research aimed at blocking the fluency effect in belief formation (Alter et al. 2007). The authors have found that when subjects experience metacognitive difficulty in activating fluency processing, they instead activate analytic forms of reasoning that assess, and in some cases correct, the output of more intuitive forms of processing information. In other words, facilitating disfluency helps set in motion explicit forms of reasoning leading to a more critical validation of the received information. The finding is undoubtedly interesting, yet the problem is how such disfluency can be induced outside the lab, and especially in users of social media. A different kind of suggestion derives from a research specifically on validation of information (Richter et al. 2009). This research tested the hypothesis of a fast-track validation system interacting with comprehension, and activated in early stages of information processing, based on background knowledge. Contrary to the thesis according to which the acceptance of information is primary and implicit in comprehension while the epistemic validation, if at all, comes later (Gilbert et al. 1990), and is slow and costly, the researchers provide evidence that the validation takes place at the same time as comprehension, and is a fast, routinized process relying on the cognizer's background knowledge. This validation modality, called epistemic monitor, actually checks the inconsistencies in the incoming information vis-à-vis what we know of the world, and represents an efficient filter to detect falsehoods and deception. Thus, we are in principle endowed with a system allowing us to believe only what is in line with epistemic validation: how come then are we so easily duped by fake news? The experiment shows that the epistemic monitor works efficiently only if the cognizer has the relevant background knowledge: in the opposite case, as it happens with medical information, the subject is not able to detect falsity and is actually prone to believe the information. Here we have an important hint, namely that the more people are educated and knowledgeable, the less they can be victim of misinformation. This consideration actually correlates with findings in political psychology (Rapp 2008; Rapp et al. 2014): the more background knowledge the people have, the less prone they are to believe in fake news (*pace* Levy). The finding is not unexpected, however some less general suggestions may be inferred concerning the areas where misinformation is especially widespread and publicly dangerous, namely politics and science. Some researches on political polarization have actually found that more worrisome than polarization is the widespread ignorance among citizens about political facts (Bullock et al. 2015).

In conclusion, we seem to know quite a lot about how we are duped by fake news, but relatively little about how to fortify our epistemic capacities, though knowing that we are endowed with an epistemic monitor is reassuring. A different path to avoid cognitive traps is to adopt strategies of pre-commitment, that is, strategies providing external constraints compelling us to be more accurate cognizers.[3] In a way, such strategies implement the idea to create disfluency in order

3 Pre-commitment has been analyzed by Jon Elster (1979), as the strategy to counter weakness of the will by binding oneself at a time t^2, in condition of cognitive lucidity, to avoid at time t^1, under emotional pressure, to fall prey of a behavior against one's better judgment. Pre-commitment is symbolized in the story of Ulysses who made himself bound to the ship mast before being exposed to the siren's fatal singing, hence avoiding to jump off the board.

to provide a warning flag activating explicit and analytical reasoning. For example, the symbols used by Facebook to alert of the possible inaccurate claim of a certain news can be seen as a form of pre-commitment. It is clear though that in order to work such kind of strategy presupposes the acknowledgement of the problem and the willingness to overcome it. And, in that respect, cultivating epistemic virtues and being convinced of one's epistemic rights may be the first crucial step.

References

Abramowitz, A.I., Saunders, K.L. (2008) Is Polarization a Myth? *The Journal of Politics*, 70: 542–555.

Allcott, H., Gentzkow, M. (2017) Social Media and Fake News in 2016 Election, *Journal of Economic Perspectives*, 31: 211–236.

Alter, A.L., Oppenheimer, D.M., Epley, N., Eyre, R. (2007) Overcoming Intuition: Metacognitive Difficulty Activates Analytic Reasoning, *Journal of Experimental Psychology*, 136: 569–576.

Bakshy, E., Messing, S., Adamic, L. (2015) Exposure to Ideologically Diverse News and opinion on Facebook, *Science*, 348: 1130–1132.

Balmas, B. (2014) When Fake News Becomes Real: Combined Exposure to Multiple Sources and Political Attitudes of Inefficacy, Alienation and Cynicism, *Communication Research*, 41: 430–454.

Bem, D.J. (1967) Self-Perception: An Alternative Interpretation of Cognitive Dissonance Phenomena, *Psychological Review*, 74: 183–200.

Bem, D.J., McConnell, H.K. (1970) Testing the Self-Perception Explanation of Dissonance Phenomena: On the Salience of Pre manipulation Attitudes, *Journal of Personality and Social Psychology*, 14: 23–31.

Bermudez, J.L. (2000) Self-Deception, Intention and Contradictory Beliefs, *Analysis*, 60 (4): 309–319.

Bullock, J., Gerber, A., Hill, S.J., Huber, G. (2015) Partisan Bias in Factual Beliefs about Politics, *Quarterly Journal of Political Science*, 10: 519–578.

Chen, Y., Conroy, N., Rubin, V. (2015) Misleading Online Content: Recognizing Clickbait as "Fake News", *WMDD '15 Proceedings of the 2015 ACM on Workshop on Multimodal Deception Detection*, Seattle, Washington, USA (November 13), 15–19.

Cohen, G.L. (2003) Party over Policy: The Dominating Impact of Group Influence on Political Beliefs, *Journal of Personality and Social Psychology*, 85: 808–822.

Cush, A. (2016) What is Pizzagate? The Insane Child Sex Conspiracy Theory that Led a Man to Fire a Rifle in a Restaurant Explained, *Spin.archive*, www.spin.com/2016/12/what-is-pizzagate-the-insane-child-sex-conspiracy-theory-that-led-a-man-to-fire-a -rifle-in-a-restaurant- explained/.

Del Vicario, M., Bessi, A., Zollo, F., Petroni, F., Scala, A., Caldareali, G., Stanley, H.E., Quattrociocchi, W. (2015) The Spreading of Misisnformation Online, *Pnas*, www.pnas.org/doi/10173/pnas151744113

Elster, J. (1979) *Ulysses and the Sirens*, Cambridge: Cambridge University Press.

Elster, J. (1983) *Sour Grapes*, Cambridge: Cambridge University Press.

Enikolopov, R., Petrova, M., Zhuravskaya, E. (2011) Media and Political Persuasion. Evidence from Russia, *American Economic Review*, 101: 3253–3285.

Eslik, A.N., Fazio, L.K., Marsh, E. (2011) Ironic Effect of Drawing Attention to Story Errors, *Memory*, 9: 184–191.

Festinger, L. (1957) *A Theory of Cognitive Dissonance*, Stanford: Stanford University Press.

Flaxman, S., Goal, S., Rao, J.M. (2016) Filter Bubbles, Echo Chambers and Online News Consumption, *Public Opinion Quarterly*, 80: 298–320.

Galeotti, A.E. (2018) *Political Self-Deception*, Cambridge: Cambridge University Press.

Gentzkow, M., Shapiro, J. (2011) Ideological Segregation Online and Offline, *Quarterly Journal of Economics*, 126: 1798–1839.

Gerrig, R.J., Prentice, D. (1991) The Representation of Fictional Information, *Psychological Science*, 2: 336–340.

Gilbert, D.T., Krull, D.S., Malone, P.S. (1990) Unbelieving the Unbelievable. Some Problems with the Rejection of False Information, *Journal of Personality and Social Psychology*, 59: 601–613.

Hall, L., Johannson, P., Stroundberg, T. (2012) Lifting the Veil of Morality: Choice Blindness and Attitude Reversal on a Self-Transforming Survey, *Plos-one*, 7(9): e 45457.

Holbert, R.H. (2005) A Typology for the Study of Politics and Entertainment Television, *American Behavioral Scientist*, 49: 436–453.

Jang, S.M., Kim, J.K. (2018) Third Person Effect of Fake News: Fake News and Media literacy Interventions, *Computers in Human Behavior*, 80: 295–302.

Levy, N. (2017) The Bad News about Fake News, *Social Epistemology Review and Reply Collective*, 6: 20–36.

Lewandowsky, S., Ecker, U.K.H., Seifert, C.M., Schwarz, N., Cook, J. (2012) Misinformation and its Correction: Continued Influence and Successful Debiasing, *Psychological Science in the Public Interest*, 13: 106–131.

Manjoo, F. (2008) *True Enough. Learning to Live in a Post-Truth Society*, Hoboken, N.J.: Wiley.

Marsh, E., Fazio, L. (2006) Learning Error from Fiction: Difficulties in Reducing Reliance on Fictional Stories, *Memory and Cognition*, 34: 1140–1149.

Mele, A. (2001) *Self-Deception Unmasked*, Princeton: Princeton University Press.

Michel, C., Newen, A. (2010) Self-Deception as Pseudo-Rational Regulation of Beliefs, *Consciousness and Cognition*, 19: 731–744.

Mustafaraj, E., Taxis Metaxas, P. (2017) The Fake News Spreading Plague: Was it Preventable? https://arxiv.org/pdf/1703.06988.pdf.

Nyhan, B., Reifler, J. (2010) When Corrections Fail: The Persistence of Political Misperception, *Political Behavior*, 32: 303–330.

Osman, M. (2004) An Evaluation of Dual Process Theories of Reasoning, *Psychonomic Bulletin and Review*, 11: 988–1010.

Pariser, E. (2011) *The Filter Bubble: How the Personalized Is Changing What We Read and How We Think*, London: Penguin.

Peter, C., Koch, T. (2016) When Debunking Scientific Myths Fails (And When It does Not): The Backfire Effect in the Context of Journalistic Coverage and Immediate Judgment as Preventive Strategy, *Science Communication*, 38: 3–25.

Piacenza, J. (2018) How Perceptions of News Accuracy Shift with Outlet and Topic, *Morning Consult*, https://morningconsult.com/2018/08/16/how-perceptions-news-accuracy-shift-with-outlet-topic/

Rapp, D.N. (2008) How Do Readers Handle Incorrect Information During Reading? *Memory and Cognition*, 36: 688–701.

Rapp, D., Hinze, S. (2014) Amazing Stories: Acquiring and Avoiding Inaccurate Information from Fiction, *Discursive Process*, 51: 50–74.

Rapp, D.N., Hinze, S., Kohlhepp, K., Ryskin, R.A. (2014) Reducing Reliance on Inaccurate Information, *Memory and Cognition*, 42: 11–26.

Reber, R., Unkelbach, C. (2014) The Epistemic Status of Processing Fluency as a Source of Judgment of Truth, *Review of Philosophy and Psychology*, 1: 563–581.

Richter, T., Schroeder, S., Wörhman, B. (2009) You Don't Have to Believe Everything You Read: Background Knowledge Permits Fast and Efficient Validation of Information, *Journal of Personality and Social Psychology*, 96: 538–558.

Rini, R. (2017) Fake News and Partisan Epistemology, *Kennedy Institute of Ethics Journal*, 27: E-43-E-64.

Rubin, V., Chen, Y., Conroy, N. (2015) Deception Detection for News. Three Types of Fakes, *Information Science with Impact: Research in and for the Community*, November 6-10, St Louis.

Schwarz, N., Newman, E., Leach, W. (2016) Making the Truth Stick and the Myth Fade: Lessons from Cognitive Psychology, *Behavioral Science and Policy*, 2: 85–95.

Silverman, C. (2016) This Analysis Shows How Viral Fake Election News Stories Outperformed Real News on Facebook, *Buzzfeed*, www.buzzfeednews.com/article/craigsilverman/viral-fake-election-news-outperformed-real-news-on-facebook.

Sunstein, C. (2001) *Echo-Chambers: Bush vs. Gore Impeachment and Beyond*, Princeton: Princeton University Press.

Sunstein, C. (2007) *Republic.com.2.0*, Princeton: Princeton University Press.

Talbott, W.J. (1995) Intentional Self-Deception in a Single, Coherent Self, *Philosophy and Phenomenological Research*, 55, 27–74.

Uhlmann, E.L., Pizarro, D.A., Tannembaum, D., Ditto, D.H. (2009) The Motivated Use of Moral Principles, *Judgment and Decision*, 4: 476–491.

Vargo, C. (2018) Agenda Setting Power for Fake News: A Big Data Analysis on the Online Landscape from 2014 to 2016, *New Media and Society*, 20: 2028–2049.

Vosoughi, S., Roy, D., Aral, S. (2018) The Spread of True and False News Online, *Science*, 359: 1146–1151.

Watson, L. (2018) Systematic Epistemic Rights Violations in the Media: A Brexit Case Study, *Social Epistemology*, 32: 2, 88–102.

Wentura, D., Greve, W. (2003) Who Wants to Be Erudite? Everyone! Evidence for Automatic Adaptations of Trait Definition, *Social Cognition*, 22: 30–53.

Wentura, D., Greve, W. (2005) Evidence for Self-Defensive Processes By Using a Sentence Priming Task, *Self and Identity*, 4: 193–211.

7 From transparency to "Trumparency"

Sara Guindani

The current political and social discourse seems to be all about "more transparency" in the natural relationship that transparency is supposed to have with truth.

The latest French political elections have gone against all expectations due to the discreditation of the initially favored candidate and his lack of transparency. Transparency is also the focus of a social revolution that is going on all over the world in the wake of the Weinstein case under the name "metoo": that is, the revelation of the violence and abuse undergone by many women in the workplace. The unspeakable suddenly comes to light often thanks to the "transparency" offered by technology. The problem is not that this "praise" of transparency has meant that we now have Emmanuel Macron rather than François Fillon, or that because of it some people have been condemned.

What seems to me interesting and symptomatic to consider is the paradoxical relationship between the continuous calls for transparency – in a society that seems to be increasingly able to realize this desire thanks to new technologies and our being hyperconnected – and the emergence of a phenomenon on the contrary so muddy and opaque as that of post-truth. What is the relationship between this imperative of transparency and the phenomenon of the so called "post-truth"?

In order to do this, I will first of all analyze some philosophical aspects of the concept of transparency in its relationship to truth, secondly see how they apply in contemporary political philosophy, and finally use these tools to analyze a concrete case study related to the Trump administration and to his speech about transparency and truth.

Transparency is a *Leitmotif* that runs through the whole of Western philosophy. Before becoming a metaphor, transparency was a concept related to the optical field. As noted by Emmanuel Alloa[1], *transparentia* is the Latin translation of the Greek *diaphanes*, and refers to the aesthetic quality of a material that transmits light without deviating it. Then the notion of transparency gradually filtered into the domain of epistemology where – in analogy with light – it may sometimes indicate the intuition of the mental gaze, or the self-evident nature of certain truths.

1 E. Alloa, *Das durchscheinende Bild* (Zürich: Diaphanes, 2011), pp. 123–178.

One could say transparency is the engine of philosophy itself, considering the latter's yearning for an idea that transcends sensible contingency. The sensible medium should dissolve – becoming transparent – and leave room for an idea. The more the medium is dematerialized and matter is spiritualized the closer we get to the truth. In short, the truth is reached when the sensible loses its opacity and resistance and acquires transparency. This is Jacques Derrida's diagnosis of metaphysics and its tendency towards logocentrism. Writing has been devalued as opposed to orality, just like the body and matter have been devalued as opposed to an immaterial principle (be it the soul or the idea).

Transparency brings other associated terms with it: spirit, truth … The semantic network of this term shows that it does not simply indicate the quality of visibility, but also has significant moral connotations. In the European tradition, transparency alludes to the phantom of a pure presence, which can only appear by dissolving its material medium. The Greek notion of *aletheia*, meaning truth as unveiling, is strongly linked to that of transparency. The notion of transparency, though, is also related to two other terms that define its moral and temporal implications: innocence and immediacy. Jean Starobinski, in *La transparence et l'obstacle*, speaks about the dream of transparency made real by the technique of vitrification: "The technique of vitrification is inseparable from a dream of innocence and substantial immortality. Transforming a corpse into translucent glass is a victory over death and over the decomposition of bodies. It is already a step towards eternal life."[2]

Another important term to understand the notion of transparency is "pure-visibility", namely the idea that what is transparent "places no filters, no barriers to the gaze: the inside is never visually separated from the outside, and the two spaces are entirely visually permeable."[3]

In this sense, transparency has significant political weight as it plays a role in defining the "inside" and the "outside", the "public" and the "private" of social life. Plato already expressed worry about the fact that citizens should hide aspects of their lives. In *Laws*, when discussing what makes a good administration, Plato makes the Athenian say:

> ATH: (…) As to the walls, Megillus, I agree with Sparta in thinking that they should be allowed to sleep in the earth, and that we should not attempt to disinter them; there is a poetical saying, which is finely expressed, that "walls ought to be of steel and iron, and not of earth"; besides, how ridiculous of us to be sending out our young men annually into the country to dig and to trench, and to keep off the enemy by fortifications, under the idea that they are not to be allowed to set foot in our territory, and then, that we should surround ourselves with a wall, which, in the first place, is by no means conducive to the health of cities, and is also apt to produce a certain effeminacy in

2 J. Starobinski, *Jean-Jacques Rousseau. La transparence et l'obstacle* (Paris: Gallimard, 2003 [1971]), p. 203.

3 R. Donati, *Critica della Trasparenza* (Turin: Rosenberg & Sellier, 2016), p. 11.

> the minds of the inhabitants, inviting men to run thither instead of repelling their enemies, and leading them to imagine that their safety is due not to their keeping guard day and night, but that when they are protected by walls and gates, then they may sleep in safety; as if they were not meant to labour, and did not know that true repose comes from labour, and that disgraceful indolence and a careless temper of mind is only the renewal of trouble.[4]

Transparency in the social space is good if not necessary for the morality of the citizens. Walls weaken their spirit, make them lose their fighting spirit and resourcefulness. Transparency is therefore crucial to the constitution of the *polis* and is therefore central to the virtue of a good citizen.

If the spectre of dematerialization is ancient, the possibility of its realization is a specific attribute of modernity. The dematerialization process of our cities and our daily lives is to be read in parallel with the advent of electricity and telecommunications:

> Electricity marks the end of the idea of reality as a continuum of solid and compact bodies, while at the same time generating the aesthetic and political dream of the penetrability of matter, if not of its complete dissolution into pure energy.[5]

The modern world has always broken into bodies and minds, using technology to go as deep as possible into the cosmos and into matter, into the human body and its psyche.

The prophetic list McLuhan made in 1964 seems to make it clear that technology aims precisely at this dematerialization and openness:

The telephone: speech without walls.
The phonograph: music hall without walls.
The photograph: museum without walls.
The electric light: space without walls.
The movie, radio and TV: classroom without walls.[6]

At a socio-political level, this dematerialization translates into the crisis of enclosure institutions ("milieux d'enfermement" according to the Michel Foucault expression).

Gilles Deleuze talks about this in his *Post-scriptum sur les sociétés de contrôle* (1990):

> We are in a generalized crisis in relation to all the environments of enclosure—prison, hospital, factory, school, family. The family is an "interior," in crisis like all other interiors—scholarly, professional, etc. (...) everyone knows

4 Plato, *Laws*, VI, 778 a - 779 b. I am grateful to Ernesto Sferrazza-Papa for pointing this passage out to me.
5 R. Donati, *Critica della Trasparenza* (cit), p. 12.
6 M. McLuhan, *Understanding Media* (New York: McGraw-Hill, 1964).

> that these institutions are finished, whatever the length of their expiration periods. It's only a matter of administering their last rites and of keeping people employed until the installation of the new forces knocking at the door. These are the societies of control, which are in the process of replacing the disciplinary societies.[7]

But what is a society of control? Deleuze defines it as a very fast mode of control that no longer takes place by means of enclosure but through constant control and instant communication. In 1990, at the dawn of the digital age, when people still did not imagine how ubiquitous the Web would become, Deleuze managed to grasp how it would transform individuals and institutions. He makes the example of hospitals, with the increasing cases of day-hospital interventions and home health care, which he sees as the sign of a potential ambivalence of freedom and control.

In addition to remarking the metamorphosis of space, Deleuze notes that the society of control also changes time: "In the disciplinary societies one was always starting again (from school to the barracks, from the barracks to the factory), while in the societies of control one is never finished with anything" – and our everyday experience of email seems to support this thesis. The temporality of this new regime is that of urgency and immediacy, in both senses of the term: the lack of a medium implies an acceleration. This phenomenon was first mentioned by Virilio; recently the German sociologist Hartmut Rosa has analyzed the relationship between acceleration and alienation[8], and the French philosopher Bernard Stiegler has investigated the "madness" of this "disruption."[9]

In 1990, Deleuze wrote:

> The conception of a control mechanism, giving the position of any element within an open environment at any given instant (whether animal in a reserve or human in a corporation, as with an electronic collar), is not necessarily one of science fiction.

With a tremendous imagination (also in the ethical sense of the term, noted by Hannah Arendt), Gilles Deleuze has succeeded in interpreting the symptoms of his society so as to envision the possible evils of a society to come:

> In the prison system: the attempt to find penalties of "substitution," at least for petty crimes, and the use of electronic collars that force the convicted person to stay at home during certain hours. For the school system:

7 G. Deleuze, « Post-scriptum sur les sociétés de contrôle », in *Pourparlers 1972–1990* (Paris: Les éditions de Minuit, 1990). English translation available at: https://cidadeinseguranca.files.wordpress.com/2012/02/deleuze_control.pdf

8 H. Rosa, *Alienation and Acceleration: Towards a Critical Theory of Late-modern Temporality* (Aarhus: Aarhus University Press, 2010).

9 B. Stiegler, *Dans la disruption, comment ne pas devenir fous?* (Paris: Les liens qui libèrent, 2016).

> continuous forms of control, and the effect on the school of perpetual training, the corresponding abandonment of all university research, the introduction of the "corporation" at all levels of schooling. For the hospital system: the new medicine "without doctor or patient" that singles out potential sick people and subjects at risk, which in no way attests to individuation—as they say—but substitutes for the individual or numerical body the code of a "dividual" material to be controlled. In the corporate system: new ways of handling money, profits, and humans that no longer pass through the old factory form. These are very small examples, but ones that will allow for better understanding of what is meant by the crisis of the institutions, which is to say, the progressive and dispersed installation of a new system of domination.[10]

Indeed, for Deleuze, power is mainly a "form of visibility" – a view shared by Foucault who, in *Surveiller et punir*, argues that the stability and legitimacy of political power rely on a model of vision. This model, for Foucault, is the panopticon: a *transparent* and *circular* prison imagined by philosopher Jeremy Bentham in the late 18th century. In it, the institution's representative, the guardian, housed in a central tower, has an absolute scopic power that allows him to observe all the prisoners without them knowing if they are being watched. "Seeing without being seen" is the abstract formula of the panopticon. "Being seen without seeing," instead, is the formula from the point of view of the dominated.

The panopticon is the model that reflects, but also overcomes, the disciplinary society. In fact, it replaces a much more "concrete" surveillance system based on quarantines and enclosures, supervisors and controls. With the panopticon, one supervisor is enough, as all information is available to him through the visual device. Foucault writes: "Full lighting and the eye of a supervisor capture better than darkness, which ultimately protected. Visibility is a trap."[11] Hence the most important function of the panopticon: "to induce in the inmate a state of conscious and permanent visibility that assures the automatic functioning of power."[12]

The panopticon is a "machine for dissociating the see/being seen dyad: in the peripheric ring, one is totally seen, without ever seeing; in the central tower, one sees everything without ever being seen".[13] It is a device aimed at improving the exercise of power by making it faster, lighter, more effective. If, then, the society of enclosure has a vision model that anticipates the society of control, the latter has "surviving elements" of the former. But Deleuze was already very lucid on this point: "It may be that older methods, borrowed from the former societies of sovereignty, will return to the fore, but with the necessary modifications."[14]

10 G. Deleuze, « Post-scriptum sur les sociétés de contrôle » (cit).
11 M. Foucault, *Discipline and Punish* (New York: Vintage Books, 1995), p. 200.
12 Ibid., p. 201.
13 Ibid., p. 202.
14 G. Deleuze, « Post-scriptum sur les sociétés de contrôle », (cit).

7.1 From transparency to "Trumparency"

And this is what, after this long conceptual premise, brings me to Trump and to his relationship to truth in its link with transparency. How to explain Donald Trump's obsession with the wall between the United States and Mexico? How to interpret this will to "close" space when the "open", transparent and fluid society of global control has come to its peak?

In an interview with *The New York Times* on July 13, 2017, Donald Trump made remarkable and significant statements about the construction of this wall, which I am here taking as a symbolic or symptomatic figure of his exercise of power. When the journalist asked him whether he was joking about building a solar wall, the President of the United States said:

> No, not joking, no. There is a chance that we can do a solar wall. We have major companies looking at that. Look, there's no better place for solar than the Mexico border — the southern border. And there is a very good chance we can do a solar wall, which would actually look good. But there is a very good chance we could do a solar wall.

But the most interesting thing is that this wall should have particular visual qualities. Trump in fact continued as follows:

> One of the things with the wall is you need *transparency*. You have to be able to see through it. In other words, if you can't see through that wall — so it could be a steel wall with openings, but you have to have openings because you have to see what's on the other side of the wall.

To explain the reasons for this transparency, Trump has used moral and legal reasons:

> And I'll give you an example. As horrible as it sounds, when they throw the large sacks of drugs over, and if you have people on the other side of the wall, you don't see them — they hit you on the head with 60 pounds of stuff? It's over. As crazy as that sounds, you need transparency through that wall. But we have some incredible designs.[15]

Why should transparency deter "those" who throw sacks of drugs over the wall? The transparency invoked here seems to imply the self-regulatory functioning Foucault said would operate through the panopticon, that is, the ability "to induce in the inmate a state of conscious and permanent visibility that assures the automatic functioning of power."

This is a paradigmatic example of the paradoxical nature of Trump's power. The manifest discourse is that of a reactionary, closed, nationalist and xenophobic

15 Interview in *The New York Times*, July 13, 2017.

society, implying enclosures and the multiplication of barriers. However, these proclamations clash against the reality of the society of control. The wall separates and hides, whereas the new barriers are dematerialized and light. They look more like the electronic gates at airports or stations (but now also museums and schools, after the recent terrorist revival). The new barriers are light, penetrable, transparent, mobile and are everywhere[16]; and they also have the ability to extract information about us, to intrude into us up to making us transparent. This is Foucault's intuition come true: full light shows more than the shade, visibility is a trap.

Trump's call to make the wall between the United States and Mexico transparent seems to me as a sort of symptom or latent meaning in his own political discourse. This image claims to fall under the interests of the global system, despite its protectionist and nationalist façade. Transparency is used here as the main instrument of control of the globalized world, where what is transparent is only such from a certain position of power.

Indeed, transparency has never been simply given, it is *manufactured*, and what is interesting is that these manufacturing techniques are then denied and made invisible. This is the kind of power that, in *Mémoires d'aveugle*, Jacques Derrida attributes to lenses: they allow us to see only insofar as they are themselves unseen.

In this sense, truth as perfect transparency (*aletheia*) becomes problematic. Truth is always manufactured, in the sense that it always emerges in connection with a certain technicality of appearance.

On this point, and in a more direct relation with the question of post-truth, we agree with what Maurizio Ferraris, in his book on post-truth, defines as "meso-verità" ("mesotruth"). "Mesoverità", far from being a "middle truth", is rather a truth indissociable from "media" (technical), "a technological result of the relationship between ontology and epistemology".[17] It is opposed by Ferraris at the same time to the "ipoverità" (hypotruth) of hermeneutic philosophy and to the "iperverità" (hypertruth) of analytic philosophy, guilty respectively of having overestimated ontology or epistemology without having considered the question of the technique.

However, this position seems incompatible with the hypothesis of a direct genealogy between post-modern and post-truth that Ferraris supports. In fact, for the post-truist, the truth is always whole and absolute, no doubt comes to crack it, no point of view of the other can be contemplated, no mediality is considered. It is the phenomenon produced by the so called "filter bubbles", a system of personalized filtering of information used by the algoritimic functioning of the Internet, that remains unseen by the user but that is capable of creating an intellectual and cultural isolation letting him find only information that meets his potential agreement and then suppress, on the duration, any critical capacity.

16 This aspect of the society of control has been discussed at a seminar of the Collège d'études mondiales/Fondation Maison des Sciences de l'Homme in Paris with Olivier Bouin, Françoise Vergès, Bernard Stiegler, Maurizio Ferraris, Ernesto Sferrazza Papa and many other colleagues, to whom I am grateful.

17 M. Ferraris, *Post-verità e altri enigmi* (Bologne: Il Mulino, 2017), p. 129.

For the hermeneutic philosopher it was quite the opposite: the thing is not denied but multiple points of view can be given on it. Furthermore the etymology of the word itself, "hermeneutics", seems to be very close to the meaning of that "mesoverità" indicated by Ferraris: the hermeneutic wants to be the heir of Hermes, god of communication and mediality.

Any uncritical call for transparency means to forget (or make us forget) the role of medias, of technology and therefore of power in conveying information.

Now, in his wish to build a transparent wall, Trump is precisely enacting the dream of paranoid transparency of the panopticon. However, one should note that this transparency is only possible if there is a *punctum caecum* lying outside this transparency: the formula of the panopticon is "seeing without being seen", after all.

The position of the Trump administration should be read in the light of this paranoid visibility: even in the campaign, the transparency invoked for others implied significant opacity when it came to the means to obtain it.[18]

In this context, rather than transparency, we should talk about *Trumparency* – like we talk about a politics of "Trump-l'oeil", as Joan Wallach Scott pointed out in her article about the concept of "Trump"[19].

I am thinking of course about the emails stolen from the Democratic party during Hillary Clinton's campaign and published by Wikileaks in the name of "transparency"; whereas the means to obtain such emails have not been subject to the same requirements. Not to mention the links with Putin's criminal politics, the paradox of an alliance with Julian Assange – who is officially under an international arrest warrant – and an organization like Wikileaks, which American institutions officially regard as a criminal association. In short, the mechanism of transparency seems to work only if all the conditions that determine it are invisible – meaning out of any transparency.

I wish to conclude with a passage in which Jacques Derrida, talking about his own philosophical writing, warns us about an acritical call for transparency:

> My own experience of writing leads me to think that one does not always write with a desire to be understood – that there is a paradoxical desire not to be understood. It's not simple, but there is a certain "I hope that not everyone understands everything about this text", because if such a *transparency* of intelligibility were ensured it would destroy the text, it would show that the text has no future [avenir], that it does not overflow the present, that it is consumed immediately.[20]

This desire for non-transparency, as Derrida clearly says responding to Searle's criticism, is not a lack of clarity, but a "need of excess", a desire "to leave a kind of

18 For an interesting analysis of the relationships between transparency, conspiracy and post-truth in Trump's era see the article by C. Birchall "Interrupting Transparency", in E. Alloa & D. Thomä (eds) *Transparency, Society and Subjectivity. Critical Perspectives* (London, Palgrave Macmillan, 2018), pp. 365–394.

19 www.politicalconcepts.org/trump-joan-wallach-scott/

20 J. Derrida, M. Ferraris, *A Taste for the Secret* (Cambridge: Polity Press, 2001), p. 30.

openness … which leaves room for the future". For Derrida, going against transparency means leaving space in the text for what has not yet happened, for those who have not yet come, for those who will arrive, for the other as someone that cannot be expected.

Derrida's thought and work, his reflections on transparency and secret, warn us against considering accessible documents as straightforward and transparent. The presupposition of such transparency, as Derrida suggests, would mean the very destruction of the given text or document, the annihilation of its potential to have a future outside of immediate consumption. Every document must be respected in its ability to be read and interpreted differently, in its ability to give space to the other witness, to the witness of the other order, in its unpredictability, and in its being the bearer of a secret to come.

Bibliography

E. Alloa, *Das durchscheinende Bild* (Zürich: Diaphanes, 2011).

E. Alloa, D. Thomä (eds) *Transparency, Society and Subjectivity. Critical Perspectives* (London: Palgrave Macmillan, 2018).

H. Arendt, « Lying in Politics », in *Crisis of the Republic* (New York: Harcourt Brace Jovanovich, 1972).

G. Borradori, « Politiques du secret. Snowden, WikiLeaks, et Derrida », in *Jacques Derrida, la dissemination à l'œuvre* (Paris: Editions Maison des Sciences de l'Homme, 2019).

G. Deleuze, « Post-scriptum sur les sociétés de contrôle », in *Pourparlers 1972–1990*, (Paris: Les éditions de Minuit, 1990). English translation available at: https://cidadeinseguranca.files.wordpress.com/2012/02/deleuze_control.pdf

J. Derrida, M. Ferraris, *A Taste for the Secret* (Cambridge: Polity Press, 2001).

J. Derrida, *Histoire du mensonge* (Paris: L'Herne, 2004).

R. Donati, *Critica della Trasparenza* (Turin: Rosenberg & Sellier, 2016).

M. Ferraris, *Post-verità e altri enigmi* (Bologne: Il Mulino, 2017).

M. Foucault, *Discipline and Punish* (New York: Vintage Books, 1995).

M. McLuhan, *Understanding Media* (New York: McGraw-Hill, 1964).

G. Michaud, *Tenir au secret (Derrida, Blanchot)* (Paris: Galilée, 2006).

Plato, *Laws* (Cambridge: Cambridge University Press, 2013).

H. Rosa, *Alienation and Acceleration: Towards a Critical Theory of Late-modern Temporality* (Aarhus: Aarhus University Press, 2010).

J. Starobinski, *Jean-Jacques Rousseau. La transparence et l'obstacle* (Paris: Gallimard, 2003 [1971]).

B. Stiegler, *Dans la disruption, comment ne pas devenir fous?* (Paris: Les liens qui libèrent, 2016).

J. Wallach Scott, Trump, in *Political Concepts. A critical Lexicon*, available at: www.politicalconcepts.org/trump-joan-wallach-scott/

8 Fake news, the crisis of deference, and epistemic democracy

Diego Marconi

Fake news has been with us since the beginning, if not of history, of history writing. According to Thucydides (II, 48), at the time of the "plague" (probably a hemorrhagic fever like Ebola) that hit Athens in 430 b.C. during the Peloponnesian war the rumor spread that the Spartans had poisoned the wells in Piraeus. The ground for the rumor was that the epidemics had started there, not in Athens proper, and Piraeus at the time had no fountains of drinking water, only wells. In fact, the epidemics was coming from Africa, so that it would naturally hit the port city of Piraeus before reaching Athens.

Many centuries later, the Great Fear of Summer 1789 and the ensuing violence that devastated many regions of Eastern France was caused by rumors of forthcoming attacks by invading Austrian troops, or by British marines having landed at Brest, or by a regiment of Swedes led by the count of Artois (king Louis XVI's fiercely reactionary brother), or, most commonly, by "brigands". Sometimes, crowds of farmers in arms against the alleged brigands were themselves mistaken for the brigands they were chasing (Shama 1989, p.428 ff.). Though the Great Fear vanished with the end of the summer, the paranoid attitudes that had developed were there to stay, until the Terror and later.

That such "news" was widely believed does not require an explanation: we tend to believe *any* news, for we tend to rely on testimony—*any* testimony. As David Lewis argued, use of any language L—i.e., communication in L—is based on "a convention of *truthfulness* and *trust*" in L (Lewis 1975). I.e., (1) we trust other people to be trying to tell the truth most of the time, (2) we believe to be trying to tell the truth ourselves most of the time, and (3) we believe other people to share such trust and beliefs. Moreover, we are *right* to entertain such beliefs and trust, for indeed most people, including ourselves, do try to tell the truth most of the time. Otherwise, there would be no language (as a vehicle of communication, as distinct from an abstract object); for a sign system that were used in such a way that it could not be trusted to provide truthful information (most of the time) would be of no interest for communication.

As, *ceteris paribus*, we tend to believe everything we are told, we tend to believe fake news as well. Of course, to be believed, fake news must be communicated. Nowadays, the web takes care of that, reaching unprecedented audiences: as of June 2017, about 51% of the world population, or about 3,2 billion people. No communication system in human history ever approximated such efficacy. However, for bad quality information to effectively reach an audience, filters on entrance must be inoperative or ineffective. This is indeed the case, often enough, with information that is communicated through the web as contrasted with traditional media. First, much alleged information is not subject to checking on entrance: "There are no longer any gatekeepers: the journals and op-ed pages that were once strictly edited have been drowned under the weight of self-publishable blogs" (Nichols 2014); "The Internet lets a billion flowers bloom, and most of them stink" (Nichols 2017, p.108). Secondly, motivation for self-checking is weakened by the frequent possibility of anonymous (or, equivalently, pseudonymous) contribution. Anonymous contributors avoid the risk of being held responsible for spreading misleading or utterly false information. Thirdly, the very form of many contributions (think of Twitter) creates habituation to lack of justification. We get used to taking seriously assertions for which no justification is provided. *Ungrounded opinion* tends to be legitimized as a contribution—indeed, the typical contribution—to public debate.

Post-hoc checking—However, what I would like to focus on is the lack or inefficacy of *post-hoc* controls. An assumption of democratic theory is that the "informed citizen" should be in the position to check the quality of publicly available information.[1] Probably, this was never entirely the case. However, it is plausible to suppose that, until a few decades ago and limited to developed societies, a significant proportion of citizens who had access to public discourse also possessed enough education and information to discard at least the most blatant pseudo-scientific or pseudo-historical nonsense. But now, hyperfragmentation of knowledge has made most disciplinary sub-languages so arcane as to be only intelligible to sub-disciplinary experts. Factual considerations that are relevant to public issues are only accessible to and can only be checked by such experts. It is not just that the "informed citizen" is unable to judge whether an antitumoral therapy is or isn't viable all things considered; she cannot even understand, let alone assess, positive or negative arguments concerning the therapy; indeed, she does not really understand what the therapy consists in. Clearly, fragmentation of knowledge has deeply affected the relation between knowledge and democracy, by drastically reducing (perhaps destroying) the checking power of that minority of citizens ("informed citizens") who had been able to mediate, somehow, between experts and "the people".

A few years ago—before the "web revolution"—the philosopher Stephen Toulmin drew from an analysis of the politically catastrophic consequences of hyperspecialization the conclusion that we ought to move towards a different intellectual world: one that would realize that theoretical physics should not be a model for knowledge in general, and make more room for empirical observation,

1 E.g., the assumption could be seen as a necessary prerequisite of Rawls' prescription that liberty of conscience and freedom of association should guarantee that citizens make "an informed and effective use" of their powers of deliberative reason (Rawls 1993, VIII, §9).

everyday practice, and middle-range theories (Toulmin 2001). This, I believe, is utopian. It is utterly unlikely that specialization will recede and that we go back to more generalist competences and a better communication between the knowledge community and ordinary citizens. On the one hand, scientific subcommunities are jealous custodians of the fragmentation of knowledge, for their power is based on it (as Toulmin himself shows). On the other hand, hyperspecialization has generated an immense amount of knowledge, much of which is useful and some of which is vital: giving it up would be hard and managing it without relying on mechanisms based on specialization would be impossible.

Hence, the only viable option for ordinary citizens, "informed" or not, is *deferring* to experts: i.e., in matters involving knowledge that is not widely available they ought to (1) systematically side with expert over non-expert opinion, (2) when experts disagree, side with the socially established experts rather than with heterodox, self-proclaimed "experts", (3) when there is serious disagreement among established experts, wait until some majoritarian consensus is reached.[2]

The crisis of deference—However, as many have remarked and Tom Nichols (2017) has shown in some detail, it seems that nowadays the experts' authority is systematically challenged, often on no particular ground:

> Tackle a complex policy issue with a layman today, and you will get snippy and sophistic demands to show ever increasing amounts of "proof" or "evidence" for your case, even though the ordinary interlocutor in such debates isn't really equipped to decide what constitutes "evidence" or to know it when it's presented.
>
> (Nichols 2014)

In Franca D'Agostini's apt phrase, the experts' "alethic right" to be "acknowledged as reliable sources of truth" goes unrecognized (D'Agostini 2017, p.18). Why? What are the reasons of such crisis of deference?

Perhaps experts themselves are to be blamed to some extent. John Ioannidis, a professor of both Medicine and Statistics at Stanford, has specialized in showing (based on a vast amount of research) that published scientific research is often flawed—mostly, statistically flawed—so that its results are utterly unreliable. Considering only top medical journals, Ioannidis found that two out of three studies were—in a matter of months, or a few years at best—effectively refuted by further research, and, consequently, abandoned and forgotten. Looking at other fields such as chemistry and physics he found much the same situation (see Freedman 2010). Such refutations of apparently "respectable" scientific results should not be described as a normal aspect of "the advancement of science" (we all know that no science is purely cumulative: some research is superseded by better research, new

2 A case in point has been the debate on climate change and human responsibility for it: consensus was reached (in 2001) through a long and at times conflict-ridden process that eventually involved about 1500 researchers, including every prominent climatologist in the world. See Marconi 2001.

experiments make older hypotheses less plausible, previous research is re-contextualized and re-interpreted, etc.). Here we are talking about research that was flawed from the beginning, and that—if Ioannidis is right—ought never to have been published in the first place. It is hard to say whether such a situation is to be brought back to the "publish or perish" craze due to competition on the job market, or to the pressure of funding interests, or to personal ambition, or to a combination of all such factors. In any case, it doesn't speak for the reliability of much scientific research and the intellectual honesty of many researchers. If one adds to that the perverse synergy of self-advertising by scientists and the journalists' frequent lack of understanding of the science they are reporting, one can see that the layman has many reasons to be wary of the scientific results that eventually reach him.

However, such serious reasons for mistrusting both alleged scientific results and vulgarization of them may not be the real ground of widespread lack of confidence in scientific experts. It can be safely assumed that not many people are aware of how precarious scientific research really is, and how misleadingly it is often presented. Instead, many choose to believe what is in fact rather infrequent, i.e., that scientific research is deliberately distorted to favor the interests of Big Pharma or some other economic Moloch. We'll go back to that. But first, let us consider the most time-honored explanation of mistrust of experts, namely Plato's. According to the father of philosophy, expert knowledge is often unpleasant, whereas people, as a rule, choose to believe what they would like to be true:

> If the physician and the cook had to enter into a competition in which children were the judges, or men who had no more sense than children, as to which of them best understands the goodness or badness of food, the physician would be starved to death.
>
> (*Gorgias* 464d, tr. Jowett 1937)

Assuming, as the aristocratic Plato did, that most people "have no more sense than children", they will be prone to choose agreeable fake news over disagreeable (or neutral) truth. But why should fake news be agreeable? I.e., why would people *like* it to be true that vaccines or chemtrails (really, contrails) are dangerous, or that 9/11 was masterminded by the Mossad or the CIA?

Here, social psychology may help. Some research has shown that conspiracy-prone commentators on the web are particularly fond of beliefs that can be characterized as *anti-establishment*: i.e., beliefs which, if true, would show the perversity of this or that sector of the establishment (politicians, big corporations, official science, or "the rich and powerful" in general), and which, therefore, the establishment is trying to keep from being publicly known. They are so fond of such beliefs that they may even accept inconsistent propositions at the same time, provided they both have establishment-damaging implications (Wood & Douglas 2013). So, this may be one reason why people choose to believe (at least some) fake news. If true, they prove the establishment's wickedness on several grounds: because of what they do (e.g., enforcing dangerous vaccines or GMOs on regular, innocent people), because they do it to make even more money, and because they hide such truths from "the people". It makes sense to suppose that a great economic crisis would stimulate mistrust of the establishment and authorities in general (of which experts are perceived as both part of and spokespersons for). So, Plato's explanation can be rescued (in part) by assuming that many people "love to hate" the establishment: therefore, they are happy to believe anything that casts a sinister light on some segment of it, whether or not experts endorse such beliefs (if they don't, that is because they are themselves part of the establishment, or on its payroll).

Epistemic democracy—However, such social and political factors and the ensuing attitudes are only part of the explanation. Another part is belief in *epistemic democracy*; i.e., the belief that every opinion is not just as legitimate as any other, but as *authoritative* as any other. Freedom of the expression of opinions is a constitutive principle of liberal democracy. However, it does not carry with it the corollary that all opinions are equally valuable. Freedom of expression is compatible with the notion that there are socially grounded *entitlements* that make some opinions more authoritative than others, depending on subject matter. A trained physicist is not necessarily more authoritative than me in matters of politics, or morals, or cooking, or biking, etc., but she is more authoritative than me in matters of physics (including "chemtrails"). In a liberal-democratic society, such epistemic entitlements are not based on birth, or wealth, or political allegiance: they are based on socially established educational processes and the judgment of socially acknowledged communities of experts.

Yet, somehow, a different view has prevailed. Expert opinion is challenged on several, non-exclusive grounds: (1) based on alternative opinions, often from heretical "experts" that lack the customary entitlements or represent a tiny minority of the relevant scientific community; (2) because experts are perceived as biased in favor of established interests (e.g., they are suspected of being on someone's "payroll"); (3) or simply because the customary entitlements are seen as no valid ground for epistemic authority. The last reason to challenge expert authority is often based, albeit implicitly, on the claim of epistemic democracy: in principle, all citizens are epistemic equals; public choices should be the outcome of a democratic process in which "everyone counts for one",[3] independently of his or her *a priori* epistemic credentials.

However, as we know since Plato's time, there is no such thing as epistemic democracy. As far as justification of beliefs goes, we are not all on a par: different people have different epistemic credentials (hence different authority) in different areas, nobody is universally authoritative, and most people have very little authority in most areas. These I take to be truisms. Nevertheless, they are widely rejected.

3 "Uno vale uno" (one counts for one) has been a slogan of the Italian "Five stars" movement, which won a relative majority in the national parliamentary election of 2018.

Epistemic democracy, seen as a semi-conscious attitude, is part of the general anti-élitism that inspires present-day populism in the Western world: it is anti-élitism aimed at the knowledge establishment. However, it has a somewhat "highbrow" antecedent in the late Richard Rorty's opposition of solidarity to objectivity (and reduction of the latter to the former). Philosophical realists, Rorty argued, want to ground solidarity on objectivity (i.e., they want public choices to be based on respect of objective truth), hence they must construe truth as correspondence to reality. By contrast, pragmatists—in Rorty's sense—wish to reduce objectivity to solidarity: for them, truth is what is good for *us* to believe ("us" is italicized). *Prima facie*, this looks like a vindication of Plato's cook against the doctor: truth is whatever we would like to be true. However, in the same context, Rorty goes on to argue for a more respectable view, i.e., antirealism about truth: "There is nothing to be said about either truth or rationality apart from descriptions of the familiar procedures of justification which a given society -*ours*- uses in one or another area of inquiry" (Rorty 1991, p.23).

In other words, "what is good for us to believe" should be understood as "what our community (with its familiar procedures of justification, etc.) regards as fit to believe". Now this sort of antirealism, radical as Rorty intends it to be, surely does not legitimize belief in a causal connection between vaccines and autism or in the dangerous nature of "chemtrails": indeed, such beliefs are inconsistent with "our familiar procedures of justification" in the relevant areas of inquiry.

However, Rorty has had less cautious followers. The Italian philosopher Gianni Vattimo offered a more radical interpretation of the reduction of objectivity to solidarity. E.g., he wrote that he didn't mind (George W.) Bush's and Tony Blair's lies, provided they were "justified by a good end, i.e. by an end I share" (Vattimo 2009, p.14); the trouble was *not* their being lies, but that "they were told for the purpose of waging a war that we don't believe we can approve of". Democracy doesn't need truth; indeed, "truth is a danger more than it is a value" (p.25). A farewell to truth (the title of Vattimo's book) "is the beginning and the very base of democracy" as opposed to "a dictatorship of the experts, of Nobel prizes of the several disciplines" (notice disparagement of experts; I'll come back to that in a moment). "Truth of politics is to be found first and foremost in the construction of consensus and civic friendship, of communitarian sharing ... that does not depend on sentences being true rather than false" (pp.26–7). So, Rorty's reduction of objectivity to justification procedures established within our community has turned into the *replacement* of objectivity with "civic friendship" and the sharing of beliefs that are chosen, it seems, independently not just of whether they are true or false, but on whether they are justified or not by Rorty's "familiar procedures". What I would like to emphasize in Vattimo's kind-hearted pragmatism is not his distaste for objective truth but his opposing democracy to competence ("the dictatorship of experts")—an opposition that Rorty, for one, did not share. There is, of course, an issue as to whether we should interpret truth as justification, or replace truth with justification, as different schools of antirealism believe. However, the issue of deference to experts is independent of which stand we take in the realism/antirealism dispute. Neither view has negative implications for the reasonableness of deference: indeed, most antirealists (including a radical antirealist like Rorty) tend to identify justification with *competent* justification, which entails truth's reduction to (or replacement by) the experts' considered opinion. It follows that deference to experts is highly reasonable, for it is not just our best chance of hitting upon truth (as most realists believe): it is our *only* chance of hitting upon epistemically valuable beliefs.

By contrast, basing public choices on pure consensus, with no room left for epistemic authorities and deference (as in Vattimo's view), presupposes epistemic democracy: indeed, it makes epistemic democracy a prerequisite of genuine democracy, as opposed to a "dictatorship of Nobel prizes". I doubt that today's populist politicians, or the No-Vax people, are familiar with Vattimo's recent thought. However, Vattimo himself has always been extremely perceptive of the *Zeitgeist*. So, perhaps a longing for civic friendship is behind all this. Unfortunately, not much in the web debates seems to be permeated with friendly feelings.

References

F. D'Agostini (2017) "Diritti aletici", *Biblioteca della Libertà* 52, n. 218, 5–42.

D. H. Freedman (2010) *Wrong. Why Experts Keep Failing Us – And How to Know When Not to Trust Them*, Little, Brown & Co., New York.

B. Jowett (tr.) (1937) *The Dialogues of Plato*, Random House, New York.

D. Lewis (1975) "Languages and Language", in K. Gunderson (ed.), *Language, Mind and Knowledge*, University of Minnesota Press, Minneapolis, pp. 3–35.

D. Marconi (2001) "Rassegnarsi agli esperti", *Kéiron*, Dec. 2001, 20–31.

T. Nichols (2014) "The Death of Expertise", http://thefederalist.com/2014/01/17/the-death-of-expertise/.

T. Nichols (2017) *The Death of Expertise*, Oxford University Press, Oxford.

J. Rawls (1993) *Political Liberalism*, Columbia University Press, New York.

R. Rorty (1991) "Solidarity or Objectivity?", in *Objectivism, Relativism and Truth*, Cambridge University Press, Cambridge, pp.21–34.

S. Shama (1989) *Citizens*, Vintage Books, New York.

S. Toulmin (2001) *Return to Reason*, Harvard University Press, Cambridge Mass.

G. Vattimo (2009) *Addio alla verità*, Meltemi, Roma.

M. J. Wood, K.M. Douglas (2013), "'What about building 7?' A social psychological study of online discussion of 9/11 conspiracy theories", *Frontiers in Psychology*, July 8, 2013.

9 Idealism, empiricism, pluralism, law

Legal truth after modernity

Luke Mason

9.1 Introduction

Making a connection between 'post-modernism' and post-truth has by now become a standard trope, both within academia and popular discourse, despite post-truth's only recent emergence as a concept. Such claims are often rather vague and fanciful and lack an altogether credible account of either phenomenon in many cases. This Chapter argues, however, that within a legal context, there is the emergence of a *legal* post-truth which is the direct consequence of a concrete form of post-modernity within legal practice and thought. While law may be called upon to engage in judgments of 'truth' in numerous interesting ways, it does not itself have any particular form of privileged access to the truth of statements or allegations, even though it is often treated as doing so. However, the most persistent question which law must deal with, and indeed the most persistent question within legal philosophy, relates to a deeper form of inquiry into truth: the question of legal truth. In simple terms this refers to the correctness of any particular proposition of law. Within legal theory, this expands to the larger question of what makes, in general, any legal proposition valid, or true. Reflecting upon legal scholarship through the lens of truth reveals that theories of law can be broken down into two broad and radically distinct categories. On the one hand, there exist empirical accounts of law which fundamentally understand questions of legal truth as social questions whose answers are empirically demonstrable. On the other hand, there are 'idealist' accounts of law which view legal content, and hence truth, as existing in some way or other in a manner which transcends social practice and which is autonomous from it. Both of these classical accounts, while radically different, share an interesting paradox: they see truth in law as an objective fact, but one which is fleeting and distant, far from the paradigm of legal certainty upon which the ideology of law is partly based.

However, such accounts of legal truth share many other unstated aspects, and are largely based upon ideas which place the *separateness* and *completeness* of legal systems at their heart, providing either a unified ideal or a unified empirically observable social practice. However, they share a common flaw, namely the failure to account for what might be called a *post-modern* phase of development in law, in which ordinary legal questions now regularly require the complex and nonhierarchical interaction of competing legal systems with different 'truths' and different ways of arriving at such truths. Such phenomena are commonly referred to as legal or, at times, constitutional 'pluralism'. This ***post-modern turn*** within law has also produced, therefore, what we might call a form of ***post-truth*** within law. This is particularly significant because it places under great strain both the empirical and ideal accounts of legal truth and require us to re-elaborate an account of what makes a legal proposition true. From certain perspectives, this legal post-truth shares certain important aspects with the cultural phenomenon of post-truth, namely its apparently capricious and deracinated nature.

However, it is argued in this Chapter that, in the legal context at least, post-truth allows for the transcendence of the empirical/ideal divide and the revealing of deeper forms of legal truth and our ability to account for them through theory or, put more simply, explanation. Upon greater reflection, legal truth is ***generated*** by the very forms of argument, or modes, which allow access to it. Such forms of argument exist also to produce legal truths outside and between legal orders where these appear to conflict or collide. While some legal scholars and others claim that such pressures on structures of knowledge reveal the end of the potential for law to generate truth, it is argued here that, on the contrary, they require a more open and more transparent use of the pure methods and modes of reason which both reveal but also generate legal truth in the first place. This is relevant to post-truth more generally in one specific way, despite the numerous idiosyncrasies of legal truth and knowledge: when assertions of truth within structures of power seem to come to embody the perspectivism and relativism used as methods of deconstruction, the post-modern and deconstructionist projects themselves require radical change: they stay true to their goal of deconstructing structures and discourses of power by applying the classical epistemologies which are rejected by those in power. Just as legal outcomes which are asserted rather than reasoned or justified are most convincingly deconstructed through sober legal modes, so can the post-modernist project find purpose in a world where dominant *epistemes* seem to have come to embody a simplistic version of post-modernist critiques.

9.2 The mythologies and truths of law's relationship with the truth

Law has a complex and autonomous relationship with *the truth*, in that it has its own cognitive approaches and communities of practice which seek to arrive at conclusions regarding the veracity of certain propositions. This is true in a least two broad but largely disparate ways, only one of which is the concern of this Chapter. The everyday encounter with the law, whether through legal practice or through observation of the legal system at work in all its guises, reveals a social institution which makes claims about its ability to judge questions of 'truth' or 'fact' outside the law itself, and even change the 'truth', or social ontology, of that outside world. However, this is not the law's most important relationship with the generation or discovery of truth, nor its most controversial. Even a cursory examination of legal argument or legal theory and scholarship reveals that the most fraught, and perhaps most important, question in law is what it is that makes a *legal* proposition true, or, more precisely, *legally true*. In order to focus squarely on that question, it is first necessary to distinguish it from the separate, perhaps instinctively more central, relationship between law and truth.

As is well-known to all people with a passing interest in the law, each legal system has its own procedures which are used to allow the officials of that system to reach decisions regarding the truth and significance and certain propositions of fact. In this way, it could be said that law possess its own philosophy of science or epistemology (Laudan 2006, Ho 2008). Perhaps more precisely, it could be stated that each area of law within each legal system has a complex set of rules constituting its own epistemology for deciding questions of fact in that field, which might, at times, be quite different from other epistemologies within that same legal system. In this manner, legal systems have complex rules of procedure and of evidence regarding how and in what circumstances certain objects, propositions, assertions and arguments may be presented within a legal forum, and how these things are analysed, assessed and rebutted. Such rules often concern the order in which these facts are presented and the ways in which they were obtained. Certain legal systems, and certain areas of law, such as criminal law, have extremely strict rules regarding the consequences of the breach of these procedural requirements, such as the entire exclusion of that purported evidence (Stumer 2010). Equally, the rules will often concern the manner in which evidence is questioned or presented, with important limits on this.

Equally, different legal systems will task different types of person with different types of task in assessing the 'truth' of any such assertion, and the legal consequences of such findings will depend on the purpose and type of legal proceeding in the first place. In some cases, judges are tasked with making such decisions, whereas in other legal systems or types of cases a mixture of judges and laypersons or exclusively non-lawyers will be required to make decisions regarding such questions of fact (Dammer and Albanese 2013). Sweeping typological categories of legal system are often presented to draw general distinctions between types of procedure in this regard. Thus we talk of *inquisitorial* systems versus *adversarial* systems of procedure, regarding whether it is the court or the parties (or their representatives) which are primarily tasked with investigating and presenting such matters. Equally we talk of jury and non-jury based approaches, regarding whether non-legal professionals are required to make certain types of decisions. In this manner we see that law purports to make decisions regarding non-legal states of affairs or events in order to reach conclusions which may have dramatic effects in the real world, such as the incarceration or even execution of the accused in a criminal trial, or the awarding of damages or other remedy in a dispute between private parties. Of course, courts, as we shall see in the remainder of this Chapter, are not only tasked with this form of epistemic task, as they also are required to decide on the truth of propositions of law as well as fact. However, this function of the Court as a forum for the purported resolution of fraught questions of disputed truth is rather curious. Regardless of one's understanding of the nature of truth, to be discussed in detail in the remainder of this Chapter, our treatment of the legal forum as an adjudicator of such matters probably bears little resemblance to other considerations of the truthfulness of propositions. While legal rules of procedure put in place certain safeguards and privileges of access to seek to prioritise the trustworthiness of certain assertions of truth, as well as the rights and interests of the parties concerned (Stumer 2010), it would seem almost axiomatic that the legal process and the courts have no privileged access to 'the truth', *even if* we were to consider 'truth' a complex matter of social convention. There is no requirement, it would seem, for legal decisions to fit with broader social conventions regarding decisions of truthfulness or their findings. Despite the legal process's privileged societal role in resolving questions of 'truth' for the purpose of settling disputes and for questions of liability in a more or less satisfactory or fair manner, such procedures and practices can tell us little about truth or the law's relationship with it more generally.

A more subtle version of this relationship between law and truth is to be found not in the law's adjudicatory role but in its legislative or law-making guise, that is its ability, or at least purported ability, to 're-cast' the world in its own image, forging its own truth in the world in a broadly constructivist manner (Luhmann 2004). This occurs in two connected ways. In a straightforward sense, the law changes the rules regarding behaviour and its consequences (Raz 1975). To the extent that these rules are either followed or enforced, law has a peremptory relationship with certain ontological arrangements, with consequences for the truthfulness of propositions. Slightly more complex is the impact which the law has in creating agents, actors, institutions or pathways for action through its regulatory structures, such as creating the private law 'person' or the 'employee' of labour law, by granting certain rights and responsibilities through their enactment (Sinzheimer 1976a, 1976b). The point here is important but should not be laboured: law has the ability, alongside many other social institutions and phenomena, albeit in an often more deliberate and codified manner, to project a 'truth' about the nature, identity and interaction of people, and thus re-cast social ontology. In a society in which law is effective and possesses this social function, the 'truth' of propositions of social affairs will depend, to some extent, on those same propositions being contained within law, however implicitly.

The concept of truth, as evidenced in this volume more generally, and indeed subsequently in this Chapter, is contested. The respective roles of epistemology and ontology and their relationship with what we consider to be truth are recurrent themes within centuries of debate on this matter. As the preceding paragraphs have demonstrated, the law, in its *adjudicatory* and *legislative* guises, has both an epistemic and ontological 'contribution' to matters of truth and their nature. However, these are rather minor and far from unique, in that major institutions and social phenomena possess similar characteristics, with the law's being more significant and visible due to the law's significance in resolving, for practical purposes, disputed propositions and in arranging states of affairs pre-emptively through a projection of its perspective onto the world through the social function and/or enforcement of its rules. These questions are of minor significance in our discussion of post-truth simply because they are socially and historically contingent. The content of these rules could be different, and their significance and social role could change. They tell us little about law's special relationship with truth itself. This relationship is to be found elsewhere, that is in questions of the truth of legal propositions.

Legal procedure might often appear to be centred around propositions of events or states of affairs outside the law and their truthfulness, however in reality this is not the nature of most legal practice. Legal practice is in fact largely based around propositions *of law*, that is regarding what the law says or what it means. Questions of whether someone 'did it' or is telling the truth are not questions which the law has any privileged way of answering, although it is at times required to do so and is treated as doing so. On the other hand, questions of whether, by way of arbitrarily selected example, Article 11 of the European Convention of Human Rights (ECHR) concerning Freedom of Association grants a right to strike, and if so to whom and in what circumstances, is a matter upon whose truthfulness legal thought and legal practice has some form of privileged access. It is this question which this Chapter seeks to analyse.

9.3 The truth of legal propositions

In common parlance it is often uttered that 'it is the law that…'. This might be followed with a curious anecdote, such as 'it is the law that you cannot take lions into cinemas' in a certain municipality, or something rather more serious or prosaic. Such statements are made as if they were propositions about something with some kind of ontological status in the world, worthy of linguistic formulations that mirror propositions about the natural and social world, such as 'elephants have tusks'. What is it to say that a proposition of law is true therefore, and what can such reflections reveal about the present collection's focus on the phenomenon of post-truth? It is true that *lawyers* also make similar statements about the law, containing propositions of legal truth, although they often leave unsaid the qualifying premise that they are talking about the law. However, much of the discourse among lawyers revolves around disagreement, or at least the search for clarification, about propositions of law (Dworkin 1986). Taking the example given at the end of the previous section, it might be (and indeed is) plausible to disagree in myriad different ways regarding whether and to what extent Article 11 of the ECHR does include a right to strike (Ewing 2013). Such disagreements are not simply incidental to legal practice or discourse. On one view, it is the function of legal practice, and of legal reasoning, to provide for an appropriate forum to arrive at the resolution of such disagreements.

Law's mythology and surrounding political philosophy, such as the notion of the Rule of Law, might be couched in terms which present the law as providing a solid framework of justice based on clear and knowable rules (Fuller 1969, Kramer 2004, Wiener et al. 2012). However, the realities of legal discourse are far removed from this in many ways, revealing the elusiveness of the resolution of questions of the truthfulness of legal propositions (Mason 2014). As well as being seen in the disagreements between practising lawyers and court judgments, this can also be seen in two crucial ways within legal scholarship. Firstly, the great majority of legal scholarship, filling thousands of pages every year on every area of law within every legal system, concerns discussion regarding the content of the law, that is the truthfulness of certain propositions of law. Secondly, and possibly more importantly from the perspective of this discussion, legal scholarship of a more general nature, sometimes called 'jurisprudence' or the philosophy of law, is primarily concerned with the *nature* of law (Hart 2012). While this is a complex question with all manner of component parts, its most central and fundamental aspect, and indeed the elements around which there is most animated disagreement, is the question of truth within law, that is what it is that makes a proposition of law 'true' (Dworkin 1986, chap. 1).

The philosophy of law, or *general jurisprudence* as it is sometimes known, is a surprisingly fraught area of scholarship to those who are unfamiliar with it. It seeks to interrogate the fundamental components of the rather mysterious social practice and/or ideal which we refer to as law. Attempts to characterise even the central tenets of law and legal systems vary wildly, with heated debates regarding the inclusion or exclusion of supposedly central elements. Such debates find their roots in the philosophy of Ancient Greece, in particular Aristotle, and can be traced directly through the work of Aquinas, to enlightenment philosophy of various stripes and all manner of Nineteenth and Twentieth Century philosophical movements. Debates within legal theory have clear links to political philosophy, the philosophy of language, ethics and metaethics and theories of social action and social ontology, among other fields. However, legal philosophy is also a mature field with an identifiable, if internally contested, canon of its own. The major disagreements within legal philosophy tend to focus around the extent to which law can be reduced to an observable social practice, and in which case of what type (Hart 2012). Critics of such perspectives tend to underline the apparently inevitable moral component of law, either within identifying the nature of law itself (as an inherently moral question) (Finnis 1982) or within the content of the law itself (Dworkin 1986). However, this debate, between perspectives which sometimes reductively labelled 'positivist' and 'natural law', in fact hides a far broader and richer discussion within legal scholarship regarding how lawyers go about determining the truth of legal propositions. A small amount of explanation of the complexity of this theme is warranted at this stage, before examining the competing theories of truth, and the importance of ideas of post-truth within law.

Take the question posed earlier, regarding Article 11 of the ECHR. Paragraph 1 of that provision states that 'Everyone has the right to freedom of peaceful assembly and to freedom of association with others, including the right to form and to join trade unions for the protection of his interests.' All, or at least most, lawyers and legal scholars would agree that this provision is what we might call a valid 'ground' of law, at least if it remains in force in a relevant legal system. It is a 'ground' in the sense that it might form the basis of a legal proposition which flows from it. As a written source of law in this respect, Article 11, and the ECHR itself, is neither 'true' nor 'false', although a proposition regarding its validity may be of course. The reason why the truth of legal propositions is fraught is that these are things which are built upon legal grounds, which require additional work to enquire into their *meaning* (Patterson 1999). Propositions of a very general nature do often flow directly from grounds of law in an uncontroversial manner, such as, in the case of Article 11, 'there is a right to freedom of association', but as soon as any detail is added to such a proposition, such as who is the bearer of such a right, for instance individuals or organisations, or both, a large space has emerged between the ground itself and potential propositions of law regarding its content.[1] What might make any proposition of law true in any particular legal system will of course, in the first instance, depend on the rules of interpretation and application within that jurisdiction. This might include the place of certain rules of statutory construction, the role of previously decided cases, and so on. The matter might also require other grounds of law to be taken into account which might provide other assistance in resolving the status of any proposition of law as true or otherwise. Such matters, in particular in legal systems in which 'constitutional' or 'supreme' courts have an important role in interpreting the constitution and setting the limits for legislative action, are of huge political and cultural import, and the controversy around the resolution of such matters is well-known.

In particular legal systems, such matters are debated around the legitimacy of certain approaches to legal reasoning, such as the fraught debate regarding originalist, textualist, purposive and evolutive interpretation of the United States Constitution (Sunstein 2015). Similar such debates are ongoing in most societies, and in all communities of lawyers and legal scholars (Choudhry 1998–1999). However, such issues exist around the content of law in all fields of law, not limited to large constitutional controversies (Dworkin 1986). On this reading, it is perhaps less surprising to learn that the nature of the truth of legal propositions might be said to be the most controversial and indeed central issue within general jurisprudence or the philosophy of law. A general account of law seeks to understand law from outside the perspectives of the snapshot perspective of one given legal order, and instead attempts to understand law in a more universal sense. A general account of law thereby seeks not to understand 'what makes a proposition of law true in legal system *x*' but rather 'what makes a proposition of law true in general'. In this way, legal philosophy can transcend the parochial legal practices of given legal systems and attempt to understand the nature of law more generally and its relationship with other important concepts and institutions, such as the State, politics, economics, morality, justice, coercion and language (Raz 2008, Hart 2012). This is of course a tremendously ambitious project, seeking to overcome the myriad differences between legal systems and their own philosophical quirks. Indeed, some celebrated legal theorists abandon this catholic project to some extent, deliberately seeking to explain a certain form of legal system in order

1 This question has recently been heard before the European Court of Human Rights, and these precise issues were raised, with the Court ruling for the first time that Article 11 did include a limited right to strike. In particular, see *Demir and Baykara v Turkey* (Application no. 34503/97) [2008] ECHR 1345. The same question has been asked within other legal orders in which there exists a legal protection of freedom of association, with sometimes differing results, reflecting differing views of the nature of that right (Fudge 2004, Langille 2009).

to draw out broader lessons from its exemplarity (Dworkin 1986). The following section seeks to locate the dominant themes of general jurisprudence within a broader scholarly discourse about the nature of truth.

9.4 Truth and legal truth

Broadly speaking, philosophical accounts of the nature of truth can be categorised into two categories: those which see questions of truth as questions of *correspondence*, and those which see them as questions of *coherence* (Kirkham 1995, Künne 2003, Burgess and Burgess 2011). While such a distinction would be resisted by many commentators for numerous subtle, and indeed valid, reasons (Strawson 1949, Tarski and Corcoran 1983), this distinction serves our purposes here. On the one hand, therefore, there are accounts of 'truth' which are related to an *ontology* and a *metaphysics* of the world, which exists outside the content of the pronouncement of any proposition which might be said to be true or false. Such accounts can be called the correspondence thesis (Russell 1906, Vision 2009). For instance, to say that the proposition *mice eat cheese* is true would require there to be such things as mice and cheese and for mice to eat cheese, and for this to refer to an action which exists in the world. This presupposes a series of metaphysical assumptions or theses about the world, including that there exist metaphysical facts. The alternative view of truth, which can be labelled the *coherence* thesis, sees accounts such as the correspondence thesis as problematic, in particular due to the atomistic nature of any given 'truth' in its account. The coherence thesis locates truth within a broader, more holistic account of knowledge, understanding truth as stemming from a proposition's coherence with a more overarching understanding of the world or a particular field (Joachim 1906, Walker 1989, David 1994).

While a correspondence thesis therefore sees truth as connected to a series of ontologically extant discrete 'facts' within a myriad of truths and falsehoods, the coherence thesis tends to speak more generally of 'truth' in the singular, that is as an overarching approach to knowledge. And while the correspondence thesis can be understood as linked to an understanding of truth as linked to metaphysics and ontology, the coherence thesis can therefore be seen as connected to viewing truth as an epistemological question. There are all manner of other central controversies within the philosophy of truth which may also help us understand certain questions within legal theory, primarily the centrality and nature of language, however this will not form the basis of the discussion of the remainder of this Chapter. Instead the discussion will focus on the *non-linguistic* analysis of legal reasoning and practice and what this tells us about how propositions of law might be said to be true.

The truth of legal propositions is crucial because of the question of the requirement to find the meaning of the law in any given area, whether to resolve a dispute in an adjudicatory context or to work out the requirements of the law in relation to one's conduct and what the law requires of it. Twentieth Century legal philosophy was most markedly characterised by the distinction between legal theorists who argued that law was essentially a question of man made rules or standards of some kind which had an ultimate source, probably socially generated, and those who argued that, on the contrary, so deliberation regarding the correct content of the law could be reduced to brute empirical facts in this way, and that moral reasoning was ultimately the arbiter of legal content (Dickson 2001). Such questions generated a tremendous amount of rich, detailed scholarship which had a huge influence within the practice of law itself as well as the philosophical and empirical study of other fields, from ethics to anthropology. However, what this debate revealed was the centrality, as discussed in the preceding sections, of the question of the basis for the truth of legal propositions in understanding the more general nature of law. This allows us to open up the question to a far broader range of perspectives than are usually included in those afforded the glamour of being included within 'general' accounts of jurisprudence. Legal analysis from movements such as law and economics, critical legal theory, legal realism and various theories of legal interpretation also qualify, on this basis, as theories of law in this central sense, in that they seek to explain what makes a proposition of law true.

Due to law's status as a social practice which consists of a community of knowledge, i.e. people engaged in identifying and applying valid propositions of law, most theories of law contain elements of both the ontological and epistemic versions of 'truth' discussed earlier in relation to the correspondence and coherence thesis respectively. On the one hand, law is a brute social fact meaning that some aspect of accounting for the facts in the world is usually found within an account of law. On the other hand, that fact is at least partly constituted by shared practices which are used to determine the truth of legal propositions. To this extent, legal accounts of truth therefore cut across the dominant distinction found within general philosophical theories of truth, discussed earlier. However, it is also true that theories of law tend to accentuate one or the other of these to a greater or lesser degree, focusing on the empirically observable fact of the existence of legal systems in the world as the basis of law, or, alternatively, on the structures of reasoning against which legal propositions are measured. Nonetheless, it is argued here that a different dichotomy characterises disagreement about legal truth. This distinction is broadly between those accounts of law which see the truth of legal propositions as dependent on empirically observable facts, and those who view it as based on ideals or values. This distinction might be superficially seen as mapping loosely onto the correspondence/coherence dichotomy discussed earlier, however this would be a misleading assumption in various ways.

The most central instance of the empirical theory of legal truth is that exemplified by HLA Hart's (2012) practice theory of law in which law is understood as a system of rules whose validity (i.e. status as true propositions of law) rests on an ultimate social practice, a conscious convergence of behaviour amongst legal officials. This social practice is, according to Hart, a *social rule* containing the criteria to make, change, interpret and abrogate the other rules of the legal system. Ultimately, Hart's account of law seeks to explain law as an empirically observable (social) fact which is nonetheless *normative*, that is a question of rules and capable of generating obligations and rights, etc. This also gives us a rather general account of what makes legal propositions true for Hart: a legal proposition is true if it meets the criteria contained within the empirically observable social practices of the legal community in that particular space. From a general perspective, therefore, legal truth is simply a matter of observing what people do and the rules they feel under an obligation to follow. In this way, Hart is part of a much broader empiricist 'positivist' tradition within legal philosophy which broadly agrees about the notion of law as an observable practice characterised by certain forms. Positivists of this type might disagree with Hart about what the form and nature of that social practice are, or the form that laws come in, however there is a fundamental agreement regarding the socially located nature of answers to questions of the truth of legal propositions (Bentham 1970, Raz 1980, Austin 1995).

More difficult to place in this tradition is the equally influential work of Hans Kelsen (1960), who refused to locate his theory of law into social practice, considering the content of law, and therefore the truth of legal propositions, to be a matter of legal logic alone rather than its ultimately social nature. However, for Kelsen, the validity of a law was dependent upon its having been passed according to the requirements of a hierarchically superior norm within the legal system, a system whose ultimate validity was ultimate simply 'assumed', as the ultimate norms of the legal system were not authorised by any higher norm within the legal system itself. Despite its rather ethereal nature, Kelsen's theory can also be understood as an empirical one when it comes to the truth of legal propositions, as, regardless of the ultimate validity of a legal system, the question of whether a higher norm has authorised an inferior one is ultimately an observable and therefore empirical question, even if the understanding of this innate structure was a question of something approaching logic, at least an internal, or pure, legal logic for Kelsen. Such accounts as those of Hart and Kelsen were influential in the Twentieth Century, and indeed continue to be so, in that they take legal language and concepts, such as its apparently rule-based nature, seriously, while seeking to separate it from what they saw as entirely separate issues of its specific content and, more specifically, its morality or justice. These were separate questions for Kelsen and Hart. In the end, Hartian and Kelsenian accounts of the nature of law differ regarding law's ultimate source and how we should explain this; however they see legal truth as resting on empirically observable facts.

However, there exists a strong counter current within legal scholarship which rejects this attempt to reconcile the apparently rule-based nature of law with its apparently socially contingent and empirically observable grounding. Such arguments, most commonly associated with a family resemblance concept commonly referred to as *legal realism*, claim that talk of 'rules' or similar concepts within law is misleading, because rules are inherently indeterminate in their real world effects, and that the truth of legal propositions comes through the examination of the application of the law in the real world (Holmes 1897). In its most widely known form, legal realism states that a proposition of law is, at best, a prediction of the application of the law by a legal official (Leiter 1995). Its truth is therefore to be determined by observation of that application. This vision of law embraces in a more holistic manner the atomistic form of truth inherent in the correspondence thesis discussed earlier, rejecting the rule-based components of modern legal positivism as unempirical. Brian Leiter (2007) has recently referred to the legal realist movement as *naturalising* jurisprudence, that is, in the terms of inquiry of this Chapter, seeking to locate the truth of legal propositions in the empirical traditions of the natural sciences. There exist other forms of legal realism which differ in extremely important ways, but which can be understood as seeking to identify the truth of legal propositions within observable social practice.

A rather separate tradition of legal realism seeks to locate the 'truth' of legal propositions not in the adjudication of disputes but rather in the social function of the law, i.e. the usage that is made, in practice of the rules of law, which may be radically different from the abstract principles within legal language (Renner 1929). Again, the truth of a legal proposition can therefore only be grasped by looking into the social practices concern. This second form of legal realism views the truth of law's content as located within the users' rather than the adjudicators' empirical use of the law. A more complex, and harder to categorise, inheritance of the legal realist movement is the critical legal theory movement, which sought to deconstruct in a more aggressive manner the assumptions and categories of the law, but not simply by trying to relocate these within adjudication or usage (Unger 1983, Kennedy and Klare 1984). Critical legal theory instead builds on the work of post-structuralist and deconstructionist theory in particular to seek to break down categories and assumptions, in particular those which obfuscate or legitimate power structures. For the critical legal scholar, the truth of legal propositions is therefore found in deeper ontological structures which are hidden within ostensibly different legal structures. These are accessed through a complex form of deconstructionist epistemology; however the lineage from the legal realist perspective should be clear, at least for the purposes of the goals of this Chapter. Finally, there exist radically sceptical accounts of the truth of legal propositions, which reject out of hand the notion that there is any form of legal truth as such, at least in an ontological sense. Accounts of economic materialism such as that of Marx see law as simply an ideology upon the genuine economic base of social reality: the truth of legal governed relationships is therefore to be grasped entirely outside the law and in the brute social relationships of the world (Marx and Engels 1970, Pashukanis 1978, Cohen 2000). The difference between the various 'empirical' accounts of legal truth can be understood, broadly, as different views regarding, on the one hand, the nature and importance of rule following practices and, on the other hand, the extent to which the law's ostensible content directly impacts upon such practices.

There exists a broad set of alternative accounts of the truth of legal propositions which takes a radically different view. Rather than seeing the truth of legal propositions as being located, ultimately, within social practice, such theories of law see the law's content as autonomous from social practice to a large extent. Instead such accounts of law see the truth of legal propositions as based on one form of reason or another. Ultimately, while such theories *sometimes* also see such legal phenomena as resting on a shared social practice, they transcend a mere empirical account of law due to their understanding of legal reasoning as capable of being presented in an ideal and often holistic form. There are numerous accounts of the truth of legal propositions of this type, many of which are extremely sophisticated. However, they can be grouped together loosely into a broad typology.

On the one hand, there are those theories of legal truth which see the content of law as somehow immanent, stemming from the internal logic of the legal system. Such accounts are often grouped together under the label 'legal formalism' (Horwitz 1975, Weinrib 1987). The answer to any question regarding the truth of a legal proposition can be gleaned, on this view, from an examination of the inherent structures, institutions and concepts of the legal system. This is particularly applied to private law, that is, the law regulating questions of civil obligations between individuals, such as contracts, which are often subject to logic-type analysis of the structure of legal thought (Weinrib 2012). What is striking about this account of legal truth is that it sees legal truth as entirely resting on matters internal to law. As we shall see in the subsequent section, this is not as misguided as many of its critics often claim, as there is a certain autonomy to legal reasoning which cannot be neglected in the proper understanding of the revealing and indeed generating of legal truth. However, critics of such a view abound, pointing out that the resolution of questions of legal content often stems not from logic but rather from some other aspect of legal reasoning, which leads to the discovery of the truth of legal propositions (Patterson 1999).

However, the most well-known, but extremely varied, family of ideas in this respect are accounts which are loosely known as *natural law* theories (Finnis 1982, George 1994), although this term might be refuted by certain proponents of such ideas. This tradition insists that an understanding of true legal propositions depends on an understanding of the moral purpose, principle or aspirations of the law, or indeed of law in general. For certain natural law theorists, this is a based on an Aristotelean notion of central cases within epistemology (Finnis 1982, chap. 1), while for others it is based on a more prosaic attempt to understand the purpose of law in regulating behaviour (Fuller 1969). Such accounts of law hold that laws which do not reflect morally good content, are, at best, laws in a less central manner. They are, therefore, less true than morally good laws, or laws which meet requirements for morally good laws. Such views of law see legal truth as resting on certain ideals: those of ethics and justice. It is here where one sees the breakdown in the parallel between the dichotomy between the idealist and empiricist visions of truth in law explained here, and the coherence and correspondence theories which characterise the philosophical literature on truth. Accounts of legal truth which rest on moral coherence in fact refer, explicitly or implicitly, to a meta-ethics and an ontology of morals which exists somehow in the real world, to which truth in law corresponds.

On the other hand, certain other accounts of the role of morality within legal content, and hence the truth of legal propositions, seek to explain the inevitably moral component of valid legal propositions through a more coherence-based approach of legal truth. Theorists such as Ronald Dworkin (1986) account for the truth of legal propositions through the importance of the moral interpretation of previous legal decisions and grounds of law, leading to a vision of law in which legal values and principles are diffused across the legal system as a whole. In this manner, Dworkin creates an interpretivist account of law based on the role of moral values within legal thought, but one which echoes the overarching thesis of legal formalism, that is, that legal truth ultimately stems from innate answers already contained within that legal system. The ostensibly similar interpretivist account of Stanley Fish (1980, 1981–1982) sees interpretation as equally central to the question of the truth of legal propositions, but emphasises that the coherence of legal truth stems not directly from moral values, but rather the structures of the legal community's shared practices. Fish's account in this manner fits less neatly into the empiricist/idealist divide which has been constructed here. There exist other accounts of legal truth which are based on other ideals and the law's coherence with them, such as the law and economics movement, which, in its strongest form, sees the truth of legal propositions as resting on their coherence with economic forms of analysis (Posner 1987). It would be equally possible to construct similar accounts of the truth of legal propositions in relation to other ideologically driven accounts of law and its content.

This sweeping survey of legal scholarship and the philosophy of law has revealed that the central questions of legal theory regarding the nature of law can be understood as disagreements about the nature of legal truth. Truth is a fraught thing in that it is difficult to characterise, and this stems from disagreement about the nature of disagreement in law and what such disagreement is about. As we have seen, the theoretical characterisation of legal truth differs slightly from the more general characterisation of truth within philosophy. This can partly be attributed to the purported 'normative' or obligation-generating nature of law, but also to the inherently socially located nature of the legal system, and its complex interaction with the world which it seeks to regulate. Accounts of truth of legal propositions place different weights and accentuations on different elements of these aspects.

However, the closed nature of legal thought, in that it is both a self-contained form of truth, existing for legal purposes alone in many respects and in the sense that each legal system will have its own sets of conditions or approaches for producing and finding the law, means that accounts of post-truth at first glance seem either somewhat forced or superficial in nature. Legal truth differs from truth in a more general sense because it is self-contained, at least to some degree. What is 'true' in one legal system might not be true in another, and might not be true at all when the proposition is removed from the legal context. Legal truth is already removed from other accounts of truth and at times indifferent to this betrayal of other standards of the truth of propositions.

9.5 The transcendence of the legal system and legal post-truth

Twentieth Century legal philosophy has been the site of dramatic disagreements regarding the nature of law, and, as a consequence, the nature of legal truth. This has been animated not only by a desire to fully understand the law's social and moral role, but also due to an attempt to use the law to resolve both complex structural social issues and the most horrendous depths of human individual and collective depravity, such as Nazi atrocities, genocide and war crimes (Fuller 1958, Hart 1958, Messner 1959). However, legal theory has generally focused on law from a different perspective, seeing law as primarily related to its *systemic appurtenance*. For all their differences, legal realists, legal positivists and legal interpretivists see law and legal truth as being contingent on the legal system within which the claim is being made. Those theories of legal truth which do not do this, such as those which see law as based on correspondence with moral or economic theory, can indeed be criticised for failing to take into account this systemic quality of law. In essence, in their starkest form, theories of law which see legal truth as being parasitic on other forms of knowledge, truth or ontology, are insufficiently *legal* in their account. Accounts which see legal truth as doubly bounded by both systemic belonging and a certain account of the epistemology seem to give a more realistic account of legal truth to those familiar with legal processes or the law's social function.

However, it is here where our consideration of legal truth merges meaningfully with a consideration of post-truth. Post-truth is a meaningful term when it fits within a breakdown of traditional epistemic or cognitive frameworks for understanding truth. An examination of the identification of valid propositions in such circumstances might yield either the emergence of a new account of truth, or reveal deeper structures of the nature of truth which are more universal in nature. Legal practice and scholarship has come in recent years to be concerned with an increasingly conspicuous phenomenon which has come to characterise legal processes and practice: legal pluralism (Griffiths 1986, Teubner 1997, Michaels 2009, Itzcovich 2012). Legal pluralism and its close relation, constitutional pluralism (Krisch 2010, Maduro 2012), are observable trends in which more than one legal system occupies the same legal space and purport to give answers to the same legal questions (Walker 2005, Avbelj and Komárek 2008). This might include national law, European Union law, international law, transnational trade law, religious law and sports law also giving different answers to the same question, with no clear rules regarding the hierarchy of such claims. This differs markedly from normative pluralism, a sociological phenomenon in which the law competes with other sources of rules and norms to regulate or structure behaviour, and from the mere co-existence of legal systems, such as two separate national legal systems, whose relationship is regulated by rules concerning the conflict of laws and other frameworks in the case of a potential clash (Twining 2009, Ehrlich and Ziegert 2017). Legal pluralism has emerged in its modern guise due to the proliferation of specialist, international, supranational and transnational legal systems and sources which claims pre-eminence and peremptory status in their role in determining the truth of legal propositions within any given context. The emergence of legal systems such as that of the European Union, said by its own Court to be an autonomous legal order,[2] possessing primacy over national law, even their constitutions,

2 Case 6/64 Flaminio Costa v ENEL [1964] ECR 585.

has underlined the significance of such developments (Avbelj and Komárek 2008, Itzcovich 2012). This becomes a 'live' issue in particular when another legal order refuses to accept the claim of supremacy or primacy in any clash between the demands of the legal system. This has happened on occasion, for instance, within higher courts of European Union Member States, which have refused to accept the general proposition that EU law ranks higher than the fundamental constitutional principles and rights of the domestic legal order.[3] It is in such circumstances that one may speak meaningfully of a legal post-truth within the *post-modern* legal order (Douglas-Scott 2013), characterised by claims of ultimate legal truth and status, but whose validity depends ultimately, it would seem at least, on *perspectival* questions. In conditions of legal pluralism, questions of legal truth seem subject to an inevitable deep epistemic pluralism (Walker 2002), in which one's very way of knowing is relativised. At this point, even if there is a manner of being broadly confident about characterising the truth of legal propositions within legal systems, such accounts become apparently useless when trying to resolve questions of selecting between different answers given by competing legal systems, or indeed seeking to reach a compromise and composite 'third' answer which makes room for both approaches.

This is law's post-truth moment. What can it tell us about either truth in a post-truth world, or legal truth in general? The resolution of conflicts of competing legal truths can, in reality, only be resolved if there is a comprehensible language or mode of thought to mediate between legal putatively separate legal orders. Prominent theorists of this area of law differ as to the mode of resolution of such conflicts. Some accounts embrace the apparently extra-legal nature of this scenario, and claim that such legal answers can only be reached in a non-legal way, as such conflicts are, in effect, political (Krisch 2010). If there is a resolution to such issues they lie outside the usual legal frame of reference and truth conditions or framework. This differs markedly from the traditional adjudication-focused legal realist approach, considered earlier, in that such accounts generally take seriously the idea that in any given legal system one can enumerate with reasonable accuracy the application of general but indeterminate rules. Where the answer depends on radically opposed epistemologies or legal ontologies, such an account also falls short. On this view, the legal post-modern moment is the end of legal truth and a move into a form of post-truth, or perhaps post-legal truth, where law is subsumed by political or other means of resolving legal questions. Alternative visions reject this bleak vision of the interaction of legal 'ways of knowing' and their inability to communicate with each other to provide some account of legal truth. Theorists such as Mattias Kumm (2005, Wiener et al. 2012) argue that legal pluralism creates a forum in which shared values across legal systems can emerge and a dialogue can be created which allows for the discovery of a legal pluralist truth. The possibility of this depends on their being a meta-epistemic frame to allow for the discoverability of such truths, and the overcoming of a stark form of legal perspectivism.

3 BVerfG 73, 339, 22 October 1986 ('Solange II').

Such an account of legal truth is only plausible if the empirical accounts of legal truth based on observable, social practices *and* the idealist accounts of legal truth based on coherence-type theories of systemic legal truth are incorrect somehow, or at least both fail to capture the essence of legal truth. If post-modern legal frameworks of law and legal pluralism can yield circumstances in which a legally valid outcome emerges, the nature of legal truth must be subtly different to the dominant accounts which currently exist, as truth within law must be capable of being uncovered in a manner which is recognisable, at least to some degree, beyond the epistemic and ontological frames of putatively hermetically sealed legal systems. It is the contention of this author that this is, at least in part, the case. This is due to the fact that legal truth is in fact *generated* through certain forms of reason or argument, that is, certain *modes* of reasoning (Bobbitt 1989, Patterson 1999, Altieri 2016). Such a modal account of law flips the correspondence and coherence accounts of law on their head and sees legal truth as produced by certain forms of *qualifying* arguments. Legal answers are not true by virtue of their fitting within a certain framework or corresponding to a set of observable facts. Without the modes of argument which accompany them and indeed justify them, putative legal truths are simply that: putative. Modes of argument within law are not simply ways of *accessing* legal truth which exists somehow beyond those arguments. Instead those arguments *result* in the truth of the proposition. The modes of argument or justification which might justify a certain proposition of law, such as that Article 11 of the ECHR contains a right to strike, might of course depend on the particular legal culture in some ways. However, many of these modes are largely recognisable in one form or another between legal cultures: historical forms of reason based on the grounds of law and their application and interpretation; prudential forms of reason based on the impact of a particular interpretation of the legal grounds; moral considerations of various types; and so on. Once it can be grasped that legal truth is produced by a form of reason, the prospect of legal truth 'existing' when legal systems come into conflict can make a far greater degree of sense. The modes of legal reasoning can still apply to questions beyond the accepted answers within each legal system and can mediate between their answers. Of course, there then exists the second order question of meta-modal levels of reasoning, that is, how one mediates between these different forms of reasoning where they generate different answers. This is a problem which exists both within and between legal systems. The major problem with much legal theory, as can be seen in the previous section, is that it prioritises *one* of these multifarious modes of reasoning and states that legal truth ultimately hangs predominantly or exclusively on that. Ultimately, there is no modal resolution to meta-modal conflict: one can only hope that the confrontation between different modes of thought reveals either synergies between them or discrepancies in the application of one or some. Legal post-truth is ultimately a form of legal truth stripped down to its starkest nature: the result of complex multi-modal forms of reasoning. It is only where we deny the nature of legal truth in the first place that this becomes problematic. Within the legal context, truth is not dependent on a pre-existing realism or ontology: epistemology and ontology are interlinked: legal argument produces legal fact. The possession of legal truth is always the possession of the legal modes which generate that truth.

What does this tell us about the law's ability to shed light on the post-truth phenomenon, and indeed era, more generally? Law's ontological epistemology, or *modal constructivism*, as sketched in this Chapter, helps us to understand how legal truth in both its classical and post-modern contexts depends on a deeper form of engagement with its raw methods, and, potentially, a greater openness in their use to see what kind of result this endeavour might reveal. Within the emergence of the discourse of *post-truth*, and the phenomena that this refers to, the worst perspectivist aspects of post-modernism, initially intended as a form of critique or deconstructivism, have become embedded within the practices themselves. This phenomenon, of displacing appropriate modes of thought with critical or deconstructive perspectives, is also seen regularly within law, such as when economic analysis of law gets mistaken for a higher form of legal reason and substituted for a legal mode of thought. At this point, the classical legal modes of reason must take on the deconstructive role, unpicking the perspectival post-truth in critical fashion. This is equally possible in a more general world of post-truth: what is the norm and what is the radical deconstruction depends on the structures of power and control of the dominant discourse, as the post-modern tradition tells us.

References

Altieri, C., 2016. Some Limits of Postmodernism in Legal Studies: On Dennis Patterson's Law and Truth. *SMU Law Review*, 50 (5), 1663.

Austin, J., 1995. *The province of jurisprudence determined.* Cambridge University Press.

Avbelj, M. and Komárek, J., 2008. Four Visions of Constitutional Pluralism. *European Constitutional Law Review*, 4 (03), 524–527.

Bentham, J.B., 1970. *Of laws in general.* Athlone Press.

Bobbitt, P., 1989. Is Law Politics? *Stanford Law Review*, 41 (5), 1233–1312.

Burgess, A.G. and Burgess, J.P., 2011. *Truth.* Princeton University Press.

Choudhry, S., 1998–1999. Globalization in Search of Justification: Toward a Theory of Comparative Constitutional Interpretation. *Indiana Law Journal*, 74, 819–892.

Cohen, G.A., 2000. *Karl Marx's theory of history: a defence.* Clarendon Press.

Dammer, H.R. and Albanese, J.S., 2013. *Comparative criminal justice systems.* Cengage Learning.

David, M.A., 1994. *Correspondence and disquotation: an essay on the nature of truth.* Oxford University Press.

Dickson, J., 2001. *Evaluation and legal theory.* Bloomsbury Publishing.

Douglas-Scott, S., 2013. *Law after modernity.* Hart Publishing.

Dworkin, R., 1986. *Law's empire.* Fontana.

Ehrlich, E. and Ziegert, K.A., 2017. *Fundamental principles of the sociology of law.* Routledge.

Ewing, K.D., 2013. Myth and Reality of the Right to Strike as a Fundamental Labour Right. *International Journal of Comparative Labour Law and Industrial Relations*, 29, 145.

Finnis, J., 1982. *Natural law and natural rights.* Clarendon Press.

Fish, S., 1981–1982. Interpretation and the Pluralist Vision. *Texas Law Review*, 60, 495.

Fish, S.E., 1980. *Is there a text in this class? The authority of interpretive communities.* Harvard University Press.

Fudge, J., 2004. Labour Is Not a Commodity: The Supreme Court of Canada and the Freedom of Association. *Saskatchewan Law Review*, 67, 425.

Fuller, L., 1969. *The morality of law*. Yale University Press.

Fuller, L.L., 1958. Positivism and Fidelity to Law: A Reply to Professor Hart. *Harvard Law Review*, 71 (4), 630–672.

George, R.P., 1994. *Natural law theory: contemporary essays.* Clarendon Press.

Griffiths, J., 1986. What is Legal Pluralism? *The Journal of Legal Pluralism and Unofficial Law*, 18 (24), 1–55.

Hart, H.L.A., 1958. Positivism and the Separation of Law and Morals. *Harvard Law Review*, 71 (4), 593–629.

Hart, H.L.A., 2012. *The concept of law*. Oxford University Press.

Ho, H.L., 2008. *A philosophy of evidence law: justice in the search for truth.* Oxford University Press.

Holmes, O.W., 1897. The Path of the Law. *Harvard Law Review*, 10, 457.

Horwitz, M.J., 1975. The Rise of Legal Formalism. *The American Journal of Legal History*, 19 (4), 251–264.

Itzcovich, G., 2012. Legal Order, Legal Pluralism, Fundamental Principles. Europe and Its Law in Three Concepts. *European Law Journal*, 18 (3), 358–384.

Joachim, H.H., 1906. *The nature of truth: an essay.* Clarendon Press.

Kelsen, H., 1960. *Reine Rechtslehre: Mit einem Anhang: Das Problem der Gerechtigkeit.* Vienna: Verlag Franz Deuticke.

Kennedy, D. and Klare, K.E., 1984. A Bibliography of Critical Legal Studies. *The Yale Law Journal*, 94 (2), 461–490.

Kirkham, R.L., 1995. *Theories of truth: a critical introduction.* MIT Press.

Kramer, M., 2004. On the Moral Status of the Rule of Law. *The Cambridge Law Journal*, 63 (1), 65–97.

Krisch, N., 2010. *Beyond constitutionalism: the pluralist structure of postnational law.* Oxford University Press.

Kumm, M., 2005. The Jurisprudence of Constitutional Conflict: Constitutional Supremacy in Europe Before and After the Constitutional Treaty. *European Law Journal*, 11, 262–307.

Künne, W., 2003. *Conceptions of truth.* Oxford University Press.

Langille, B., 2009. The Freedom of Association Mess: How We Got into It and How We Can Get out of It. *McGill Law Journal*, 54, 177.

Laudan, L., 2006. *Truth, error, and criminal law: an essay in legal epistemology.* Cambridge University Press.

Leiter, B., 1995. Legal Indeterminacy. *Legal Theory*, 1 (04), 481–492.

Leiter, B., 2007. *Naturalizing jurisprudence: essays on American legal realism and naturalism in legal philosophy.* Oxford University Press.

Luhmann, N., 2004. *Law as a social system.* Oxford University Press.

Maduro, M., 2012. Three claims of constitutional pluralism. *In*: M. Avbelj and J. Komárek, eds. *Constitutional pluralism in the European Union and beyond.* Hart.

Marx, K. and Engels, F., 1970. *The German ideology.* International Publishers Co.

Mason, L., 2014. The intractably unknowable nature of law: Kadi, Kafka and the law's competing claims to authority. *In*: M. Avbelj, F. Fontanelli, and G. Martinico, eds. *Kadi on trial: a multifaceted analysis of the Kadi judgment.* Routledge.

Messner, J., 1959. The Postwar Natural Law Revival and its Outcome. *The American Journal of Jurisprudence*, 4 (1), 101–105.

Michaels, R., 2009. Global Legal Pluralism. *Annual Review of Law and Social Science*, 5, 243–262.

Pashukanis, E., 1978. *Law and Marxism: a general theory*. Ink Links.

Patterson, D., 1999. *Law and truth*. Oxford University Press.

Posner, R.A., 1987. The Law and Economics Movement. *The American Economic Review*, 77 (2), 1–13.

Raz, J., 1975. *Practical reason and norms*. Hutchinson.

Raz, J., 2008. Can there be a theory of law? *In*: M.P. Golding and W.A. Edmundson, eds. *The Blackwell guide to the philosophy of law and legal theory*. John Wiley & Sons.

Raz, J.R., 1980. *The concept of a legal system: an introduction to the theory of legal system*. 2nd ed. Clarendon Press.

Renner, K., 1929. *Die Rechtsinstitute des Privatrechts und ihre soziale Funktion*. Stuttgart: G. Fischer.

Russell, B., 1906. On the Nature of Truth. *Proceedings of the Aristotelian Society*, 7, 28–49.

Sinzheimer, H., 1976a. Das Problem des Menschen im Recht (1933). *In: Arbeitsrecht und Rechtssoziologie : gesamelte Aufsätze und Reden*. Europäische Verlagsanstalt, 53–69.

Sinzheimer, H., 1976b. Die Soziologische Methode in der Privatrechtwissenschaft (1909). *In:Arbeitsrecht und Rechtssoziologie : gesamelte Aufsätze und Reden*. Europäische Verlagsanstalt, 3–24.

Strawson, P.F., 1949. Truth. *Analysis*, 9 (6), 83–97.

Stumer, A., 2010. *The presumption of innocence: evidential and human rights perspectives*. Bloomsbury Publishing.

Sunstein, C.R., 2015. There Is Nothing That Interpretation Just Is. *Constitutional Commentary*, 30, 193–212.

Tarski, A. and Corcoran, J., 1983. *Logic, semantics, metamathematics: papers from 1923 to 1938*. Hackett Publishing.

Teubner, G., 1997. Global Bukowina. *In*: G. Teubner, ed. *Global law without a state*. Ashgate, 1–22.

Twining, W., 2009. Normative and Legal Pluralism: A Global Perspective. *Duke Journal of Comparative and International Law*, 20, 473.

Unger, R.M., 1983. The Critical Legal Studies Movement. *Harvard Law Review*, 96 (3), 561–675.

Vision, G., 2009. *Veritas: the correspondence theory and its critics*. MIT Press.

Walker, N., 2002. The Idea of Constitutional Pluralism. *Modern Law Review*, 65 (3), 317–359.

Walker, N., 2005. Europe's Constitutional Momentum and the Search for Polity Legitimacy. *International Journal of Constitutional Law*, 3, 211.

Walker, R.C.S.W., 1989. *The coherence theory of truth: realism, anti-realism, idealism*. Routledge.

Weinrib, E.J., 1987. Legal Formalism: On the Immanent Rationality of Law. *Yale Law Journal*, 97, 949.

Weinrib, E.J., 2012. *The idea of private law*. Oxford University Press.

Wiener, A., Lang, A.F., Tully, J., Maduro, M.P., and Kumm, M., 2012. Global Constitutionalism: Human Rights, Democracy and the Rule of Law. *Global Constitutionalism*, 1 (01), 1–15.

10 A political and deliberative virtue?

The epistemic trust in trustworthy epistemic authorities

Davide Pala

10.1 Unpacking post-truth. The mistrust in trustworthy epistemic authorities

In 2016 the Oxford English Dictionary defined post-truth as an adjective "relating to or denoting circumstances in which objective facts are less influential in shaping public opinion than appeals to emotion and personal belief".[1] This definition of post-truth is good if we look at its denotative power. It allows us to capture all of those cases that seem instances of post-truth: the election of Trump in the U.S. and Brexit in the U.K., for example, but also the anti-vaccinations movements, the denialism of climate change, and so on.

Notwithstanding, the definition above is problematic. First, by focusing on *personal beliefs*, it ends up either too *opaque* or *misleading*, thus either oversimplifying or misunderstanding post-truth itself. At a first approximation, post-truth seems indeed a highly *multidimensional* phenomenon referring to a vast array of diverse beliefs, which can be subsumed under the label "personal beliefs" only at the price of either oversimplification or misunderstanding. Let me clarify this point. Several speeches given by Trump are arguably better captured by the concept of *bullshit* (Frankfurt 2005) than that of personal beliefs. This is because the feature that stands out in these speeches is more Trump's indifference to truth—which is precisely the hallmark of bullshit—than his personal convictions (which in fact we do not really know). Consequently, in this example the reference to personal beliefs is *misleading*.

As far as *opacity*, instead, the decision to invade Iraq made by the U.S. and allies in 2003 provides an interesting example. This decision, which was grounded on the—we now know, false—belief that Iraq possessed weapons of mass destruction, probably represents an instance of *political self-deception*, in which the personal beliefs of several individuals were part of much more complex cognitive and non-cognitive mechanisms.[2] In this same spirit, then, it would not be too speculative to hypothesize that post-truth comprises also *stubborn beliefs*, forms of *wishful*

1 https://en.oxforddictionaries.com/definition/post-truth
2 See Galeotti 2015.

thinking [3], and *ideological* beliefs. Briefly, the idea of post-truth needs to be unpacked, and to this end the concept of personal beliefs is not very helpful.

Second, in the definition under analysis something important is missing, which prevents us from grasping a feature that is both distinctive and basic of *some* expressions of post-truth. This something is arrived at by noticing that, even if emotions and personal beliefs did not distort our access to objective facts, in several cases an *immediate* and *direct* access to them would be by definition out of reach for most of us. For example, I might be not deeply influenced by my emotions and personal beliefs, and yet, if I am not a medical doctor, I will not have direct access to the objective fact that "vaccines are safe and do not cause autism". Furthermore, I will not have first-hand evidence supporting the belief that "vaccines are safe and do not cause autism", nor will I have the capability to understand the claims relative to the evidence that justifies this belief. Finally, it is likely that I will never acquire the expertise necessary to develop this capacity (Hardwig 1985: 337–339).

The point to stress, then, is that Oxford English Dictionary's definition of post-truth, because of its *outcome-oriented* focus on the neglect of objective facts, lacks an important reference to the recognition that, in all domains in which we are not experts, our access to objective facts is never direct or non-mediated. Rather, it only occurs through *epistemic authorities*, that is, *experts*, and their claims concerning objective facts.[4] In particular, in all of those domains in which we are laypersons, we have access to objective facts only by *trusting* epistemic authorities and their claims about the objective facts. That we *trust* and not merely *rely on* them can be shown in the following way (section 10.2): if my medical doctoral turns out to be an impostor, I will not simply feel disappointed; I will rather feel betrayed, in that I had entrusted her with the task to look after one valuable good, i.e. my health; on the other hand, we will just feel disappointed if Kant breaks his regular habit of having a walk around 5p.m., on which we counted (Baier 1986: 235).

These remarks become more relevant if it is highlighted that we, as human beings with limited epistemic capabilities, and citizens inhabiting complex and specialized societies (Fricker 2006: 225–229), live, in all domains in which we are not experts, in a condition of *epistemic dependence* (Hardwig 1985; section 10.2), which makes us vulnerable to experts. And yet, if the epistemic authorities are *trustworthy*, and their claims are justified on the basis of the standards of scientific inquiry, there are both epistemic and moral reasons to show trust, or better, *epistemic trust* in them and their claims, or so I will argue.

What is then the link between epistemic trust and post-truth? The link is that some expressions of post-truth, such as the anti-vaccination movements and the denialism of climate change, share a distinctive and basic feature, which is precisely the manifestation, within democratic public debates leading to the elaboration of

3 See Lynch 2013.

4 I adopt an intuitive understanding of objective facts, according to which objective facts are phenomena that, differently form thoughts and/or feelings, exist in "external" reality.

public policies, of *mistrust* in *trustworthy epistemic authorities* as for beliefs that are *fully justified* and *almost undisputed* in the scientific community—i.e. beliefs that are justified according to the *non-controversial* standards of scientific inquiry, and on which an *overwhelming* majority of scientists (usually around 97–98%) agree. Look, in this respect, at the Italian anti-vaccinations movements. Although the claim "vaccines are safe and do not cause autism" is fully justified and undisputed within the scientific community, *No-Vax* movements reject it, and show mistrust in immunologists. According to some, immunologists know that vaccines may cause autism, but they do not communicate this information because there are well-paid by pharmaceutical corporations. For others, instead, immunologists are blind to the effects of vaccines to the extent that they are more sensitive to scientific authorities than evidence. Something similar happens in the case of climate change too[5]: climatologists are mistrusted either because they make us believe that there is a scientific consensus where in fact there is none; or they are politically biased—or so we are told by climate change denialists.

Despite their similarities, between these two cases there is a significant difference. While anti-vaccination movements have only partly succeeded in influencing public debates in matter of vaccination policies, the same does not hold for climate change, where denialism is widespread. Data confirm this. On the one hand, climatologists overwhelmingly—i.e. 97–98% of them—agree on the threefold fact: (i) that climate change is occurring; (ii) that this fact is alarming; and that (iii) humans are casually responsible for it. On the other hand, though, if we look, for instance, at American citizens, we notice that (i) 16% of Americans deny that climate change is occurring; (ii) 48% of them question its seriousness; and (iii) 50% think that human activity has no role in causing it (Oreskes 2007: 70–71; Anderson 2011: 149–153; Almassi 2012: 32–33). These discrepancies can be observed in many other countries as well.[6] It is therefore not mere negligence that in the last 30 years we have not taken measures counteracting climate change or its effects.

In this work I propose to understand the manifestations of post-truth mentioned earlier in a way that highlights the role of both epistemic trust and epistemic authorities in our access to objective facts. Manifestations of this kind of post-truth should be then understood as consisting in the attitude of those citizens that, in democratic public debates, mistrust trustworthy epistemic authorities, in regard to beliefs that are fully justified and almost undisputed within the scientific community. This latter fact deserves attention: the beliefs at stake here, which may be covered by the concept of post-truth, are only those on which there is an *overwhelming scientific consensus*—e.g. beliefs such as "vaccines do not cause autism" and "climate change is occurring". Other more disputed beliefs, on which there is *genuine*, as opposed to *illusory*, disagreement among experts, will not be

5 I am assuming that immunologists and climatologists are a good example of trustworthy epistemic authorities. See section 10.5.

6 See www.ipsosglobaltrends.com/climate-change-as-a-result-of-human-activity/

considered, nor treated as a possible manifestation of post-truth, precisely because the disagreement on stage is genuine rather than illusory[7] (section 10.4).

Before proceeding, two caveats are needed. First, one could argue that my account of post-truth is partial to the extent that, besides mistrust, also a more neutral *lack of trust* can be observed in the examples earlier. I agree with this, but I want to stress that mistrust rather than lack of trust is the prevalent attitude, and that in the normative account of post-truth that I will provide this distinction is not particularly relevant. Indeed, both the lack of trust and the mistrust are to be considered *prima facie* bad according to my normative account, in that they show the absence of what I shall call the *political* and *deliberative virtue* of the *epistemic trust* in *trustworthy epistemic authorities* (section 10.3, section 10.5).

Second, it might be objected that my account is still too *outcome*-oriented, because I focus on mistrust rather than its *causes*. I answer this by noticing that it is risky to develop a normative account starting from an analysis of such causes. The resulting account would be dependent on the explicative analysis that has been adopted. Yet, several explanations of the causes of the mistrust in experts can be advanced, and all of them have some plausibility. Some might claim that behind mistrust there are self-deceptive beliefs, and others might point to other forms of motivated irrationality. Also, by focusing on experts rather than laypersons, it can be argued that the mistrust in experts is partly to be traced to experts themselves, as they sometimes fail to effectively communicate their trustworthiness. Moreover, as for scientific experts, one could maintain that the mistrust in them is due to the fact that nowadays science is perceived as threatening, imperialistic, and politically biased (Kitcher 2011: 15–20). Finally, it might be stated that the salient causes of the mistrust in scientific experts are irresponsible mass-media, the segregation of social networks by partisan affiliation, so-called cultural cognition, i.e. the tendency of people to assess risks on the basis of cultural values (Anderson 2011), and/or propaganda made by political parties and corporations (McKinnon 2016). Briefly, there are several possible explanations of the mistrusting attitude shown by citizens toward experts, and all of them capture something *prima facie* true. Hence, instead of trying to show that one explanation has greater explicative power than the others, and then developing a normative framework on such a *probabilistic* and *partial* consideration, I find it theoretically safer to focus first and foremost on mistrust alone, as the most basic fact, and the easiest to ascertain. This does not imply that the causes of mistrust in experts are overlooked. They rather come on stage in a different phase, i.e. the non-ideal phase, when the evaluation of the mistrusting attitude is applied to real citizens (section 10.5).

With this in mind, one could now ask: how should we assess this specific *post-truth attitude*? Which is the most appropriate normative framework? Answering this question is the aim of this chapter. To accomplish this, I will proceed as follows.

7 On *genuine* disagreement among experts and the criteria to employ to choose the epistemic authority to trust: Goldman 2001; Coady 2006.

First, I will provide a definition of three key concepts of my chapter, i.e. epistemic dependence, trustworthy epistemic authority, and epistemic trust (section 10.2). Second, I will advance my main argument, and argue that the mistrust in trustworthy epistemic authorities that is shown by citizens in democratic public debates concerning the elaboration of public policies, as for beliefs that are fully justified and almost undisputed within the scientific community, is *prima facie* bad for democratic societies. The reason is that citizens that show this attitude do not possess what I shall call the political and deliberative virtue of the epistemic trust in trustworthy epistemic authorities (ETITEA), which is of paramount importance for democratic societies. This is so for both *epistemic* and *moral* reasons, as I will show (section 10.3). Third, I will answer some objections that can be raised against my thesis (section 10.4). Finally, I will employ my normative account to provide an evaluation of the post-truth attitude of those citizens that mistrust climatologists regarding fully justified and almost undisputed beliefs such as "climate change is occurring", and argue that such attitude is *prima facie* bad (section 10.5).

10.2 Epistemic dependence and epistemic trust

Our ordinary experiences and interactions show us that we are not *fully autonomous* knowers—provided that one assumes an *evidence-based* account of justified beliefs and knowledge. As for most of the justified beliefs and knowledge that we usually employ, we rather depend on the testimony of others. Moreover, we cannot fully overcome this condition of *dependency*, in which a *division* of the *epistemic labor* is implied (Fricker 2006: 225–227). For example, we normally believe that "smoking cigarettes causes cancer", even if we do not have direct access to the evidence that supports this statement; cannot truly understand and assess the evidence-based reasons that justify it; and will never be able either to have direct access to the evidence that supports this statement, or appreciate the evidence-based reasons justifying it (Hardwig 1985: 337–339). The same, clearly, holds for an incredibly vast amount of beliefs on which we normally count—for example, beliefs such as "planes can fly because, at a certain speed, air pressure is lower above their wings", and "the poor performances of my laptop are due to an old battery". What, then? Should we conclude that we ordinarily believe many things without any justification, i.e. without either evidence or evidence-based reasons supporting them?

As John Hardwig has shown, the answer is negative. According to Hardwig, the beliefs mentioned, and many others, can be rightfully retained by laypersons and understood as justified, in that their justification lies in the appeal to a certain appropriate epistemic authority. That is to say, laypersons can justifiably believe or know that *p*, even if they lack evidence or evidence-based reasons that *p*, to the extent that they know that E, i.e. a *competent* and *sincere* epistemic authority, evidentially believes or knows that *p*. There are, to put it differently, also *non-evidential*, i.e. *testimonial*, but justified reasons for believing or knowing that *p* (Hardwig 1985). A *reductio ad absurdum* can support this claim. If there were no justified testimonial reasons for believing or knowing that *p*, but just evidential ones, then we could justifiably believe or know only those things for which we have first-hand evidence. Yet these things would be very few. Also, historical knowledge would be nonsensical (Fricker 2006: 227), and, actually, the entire scientific enterprise would not properly qualify as knowledge, given that to develop new scientific knowledge epistemic authorities themselves have to rely on the testimonial evidence provided by other epistemic authorities (Hardwig 1991). As these conclusions are implausible, testimonial evidence has to be recognized as capable of providing us with good reasons for believing or knowing that *p*—provided that the epistemic authority on which we rely has some specific features that I will present in a moment.

The justificatory power of testimonial evidence results even more significant if we consider that testimonial evidence is *pervasive*. All of us rely on it most of the time, i.e. in every domain in which we are not experts and, therefore, have no access to the evidence or the evidence-based reasons that support a certain belief that *p*. Not even epistemic authorities in D1 can escape from it, to the extent that in all of those domains that are not D1 they are not experts. This implies that all of us, experts included, live in a condition of *epistemic dependence*, in which we depend on the testimony of others. In other terms, all of us can justifiably believe many things only because these beliefs are justified by the appeal to a certain epistemic authority. As a consequence, a *division* of *epistemic labor*, between lay-persons counting on testimony on the one hand, and epistemic authorities endowed with evidential justificatory power on the other, is part and parcel of both our ordinary lives and knowledge itself. While it is true that this division of epistemic labor makes us vulnerable to epistemic authorities, in that, although sincere and competent, these authorities are not immune to *bona fide* mistakes, at the same time it creates the conditions of possibility for justifiably believing and knowing most things for all of us.

Notice that the condition of epistemic dependence mentioned earlier, to which from now on I will refer as the *fact* of *epistemic dependence*, is not only shared, more or less equally, by everyone, but it is also *inescapable*. Two facts show this. First, as human beings, we are creatures with limited epistemic capabilities. While we can believe all sorts of things, our intellect is too small and life is too short for evidentially justifying all of them on our own (Hardwig 1985: 335). We therefore cannot but depend on the testimony of others. Second, as citizens, we live in complex and sophisticated societies composed of several social sub-systems (e.g. the juridical domain; the economic one; etc.). To be able to understand and appropriately act in each of them, a high degree of expertise is required. Yet, given our limited epistemic capabilities, it is impossible for us to obtain this level of expertise in all of them. Again, then, we cannot but depend on the testimony of others.

At this point, one significant element should be added to the picture. When we come to believe that "smoking cigarettes causes cancer", we are not merely *relying* on the epistemic authority of medical doctors. We are rather showing *epistemic trust* in them. Indeed, when we simply rely on others, we count on their predictable behaviors, i.e. habits or regular patterns due to fear or other reasons, and act on this basis (Baier 1986: 234–235; Jones 1996: 14–15). But this is not what happens when we come to believe that "smoking cigarettes causes cancer" because medical doctors claim so. We do not believe this statement because we count on the fact that medical doctors usually look after their patients' health as a regular habit imposed by their profession or the fear of consequences they would face should they harm their patients—not only, at least. We rather come to believe this statement for stronger reasons, which can be subsumed under the label epistemic trust. The question is then the following: what is epistemic trust? The best way to answer this question is to, first of all, define what *trustworthiness* is. From this definition, the concept of epistemic trust can then be derived straightforwardly (Jones 2012: 61–62; Almassi 2012: 43). Let me then first ask: what is trustworthiness? In particular, what is a trustworthy epistemic authority?

In the literature there is agreement on the fact that an epistemic authority E in domain D can be said to be trustworthy in relation to a certain agent A, if two conditions apply. First, E has a certain level of *competence* in D with regard to p, and, second, it has some *positive motive* toward agent A. Although not precise, this definition is telling. It highlights that to be trustworthy an epistemic authority has to possess two basic features, *epistemic* the first one, and *affective* the second one. Also, the definition mentioned proposes to understand trustworthiness as having a three-place structure (Jones 2012: 62). In other words, to qualify as trustworthy an epistemic authority A has to be (1) competent in domain D as for p, and it has to show (2) some positive motive toward (3) agent A. These elements need some comments.

The first element (1), i.e. competence, is self-justifying. An epistemic authority lacking any kind of competence would not be trustworthy in any meaningful sense of the term, nor would it *sensu stricto* qualify as an epistemic authority. Similarly, the further specifications of the first element—restricting competence to a certain domain, in regard to certain beliefs—are obvious. As stated before, one cannot but acquire competence only in some specific domains. Moreover, in these specific domains the acquired competence will not cover all of the sub-domain areas, but just a few of them.

The second and third elements, instead, referring to (2) some positive motive showed by authority E toward (3) agent A, signal that trustworthiness implies a certain level of awareness from the epistemic authority E that she is counted on by agent A (a) and a disposition to act accordingly (b), without ill will (c). To show this, think about the following three scenarios. In the first scenario (c), medical doctor M knows that we count on her, and yet, she intentionally lies to us about our health, i.e. she shows ill will; in the second scenario (b), M is still aware that we count on her, but, every time we suffer from a disease, she decides not to communicate this information to us, since in her practical deliberation she gives more weight to our husband's desire not to let us be informed about our health than to our explicit willingness to be informed on it—this time M finds that the fact that we count on her is rarely a compelling reason to act accordingly; finally, in the third scenario (a), M is simply not aware that we count on her in regard to our health, so she looks after our health-related interests without including—at least in part—in them our expectations from her (Jones 1996: 9–10). In these scenarios it would be rather hard to call M trustworthy. Trustworthiness, then, comprises both a certain positive disposition of the epistemic authority (2), and an agent whose expectations are taken into account by the epistemic authority itself (3).

Although these considerations are shared in the literature, among scholars there is still disagreement on what specifically means that the authority in question has some positive motive toward us. Moreover, often scholars adopt an intuitive understanding of competence, thereby not unpacking this concept. For example, Annette Baier maintains that having a positive motive is to show a *minimal good will*, intuitively grasped. The expertise component is instead left unspecified, but it is clear that she has in mind a broad idea of competence, and understands it in either technical or moral terms—in this latter sense, also a friend can be competent or not (Baier 1986: 234–236; Cf. Jones 1996: 7). More detailed work is then provided by Ben Almassi and Klaus Kappel, respectively. The first one claims that by positive motive we should mean a *conscientious* attitude in epistemic authority's presentation of testimony that *p*. He then argues that to be trustworthy an epistemic authority has to be competent in a certain domain D, but, besides letting the reader guess that he shares a technical—as opposed to moral—idea of competence, influenced by Alvin Goldman's idea of *expertise* (Goldman 2001), he does not add further qualifications (Almassi 2012: 34 and 43–44). On the other hand, the second one states that a trustworthy epistemic authority is both *sincere* and *competent* in domain D, i.e. the authority can decide questions in D with a high reliability, and likely has many true beliefs as for questions raised in D (Kappel 2014: 2016).

Despite their differences, these proposals share two problems. The first problem deals with how we should specify what counts as a positive motive. To this end, the suggestions made earlier are not very helpful. In detail, the idea of minimal good will (Baier) is misplaced. Indeed, "on a particularly vexatious morning I find myself snarling misanthropically at the whole world, yet I can still come through for some of those who are counting on me, even if not with a smile" (Jones 2012: 67). On the other hand, either conscientiousness (Almassi) or sincerity (Kappel) do not tell us the whole story on the positive motive behind trustworthiness. Indeed, what about honesty, integrity, and the like? Are they not, sometimes, part of what being trustworthy means (Jones 2012: 67–68)? If this is the case, then the best way to define the idea of positive motive is to reason from a more abstract perspective, able to capture the common feature shared by positives motives such as sincerity, honesty, integrity, and so on. In this direction, it comes out that the common feature that is looked for is, as Karen Jones has shown, *responsiveness*. Indeed, when an authority E has some positive motive toward us, this means that, regardless of the specific motive at stake, be it conscientiousness, sincerity, or many others, in any case E will find the fact that we count on her to be a *compelling reason* for acting as counted on—where compelling reasons stand for reasons hardly outweighed by other evaluations (Jones 2012: 71). As far as positive motive is concerned, therefore, being trustworthy is being responsive to the fact that the other is counting on you—no matter the specific motive behind.

The second problem of the proposals mentioned deals with the idea of competence, that is either too broad (Baier) or, even when conceived of in stricter terms (Almassi, Kappel), not well specified. To solve both questions, I propose, first, to adopt the strict rather than broad understanding of competence, namely the more technical meaning, as opposed to the moral one. This choice is justified in that I focus not on trustworthiness *per se*, but rather on *epistemic* trustworthy authorities. Given this, I propose, second, to unpack competence having in mind the features that are commonly attributed to *cognitive* or *intellectual* experts (Goldman 2001: 91–93; Anderson 2011: 146–147). Specifically, my idea is that a competent epistemic authority E in domain D should have the following, necessary but likely not sufficient, characteristics: (1) E has received adequate training in D, and possesses adequate skills and methods to work in D; (2) E possesses a substantial amount of justified beliefs in D and is possibly able to produce new beliefs in D; (3) E's competence is corroborated by several fellow experts; (4) E's competence has a *public* dimension.

Although a full justification of these features is beyond the ambitions of this chapter, some comments are needed. The first feature (1) is meant to highlight two aspects. This first aspect is that E cannot qualify as competent in D if it has a specialization in L; the second aspect is that E can be said to be component in D only if it has at least adequate skills and methods to work in D, where *adequate* means "complying with the methodological standards required by D, and more general standards as well—e.g. E abides by the basic principles of logics". The second feature (2) wants to capture the fact that intellectual competence is not a comparative matter: being competent is more than having more justified beliefs than others; it is rather to have a significant amount of justified beliefs, possibly conjoined with the capacity to develop new ones (Goldman 2001: 91–92). Furthermore, the expression "justified beliefs" is to be read as "beliefs justified according to the justificatory standards of D and more general ones". The third feature (3) is then arrived at by noticing that if the epistemic authority of E is acknowledged by none or just a few followers, then E cannot be considered a competent epistemic authority (Coady 2006). Finally, the last characteristic (4) underscores that the standards certifying competence have to be not only technical, but also publicly approved and acknowledged—in this sense, if E is competent, then it will have (good) institutional credentials.

From this analysis, it follows that a trustworthy epistemic authority E in D is an authority that has, first, *competence* in D, in the sense explained earlier; and, second, it is an authority that is *responsive* to the fact that some agents A count on her.

That said, I can now answer my initial question and provide a definition of epistemic trust—granted that (epistemic) trust has a three-place structure corresponding to the three-place structure of trustworthiness (Jones 2012: 61). In this direction, I claim that A has *epistemic trust* in epistemic authority E that holds that p in domain D, to the degree that A regards E as *competent* in her acceptance of p in domain D, and *responsive* to the fact that A counts on E as for p in D. Hence, A takes E's testimony that p in D as providing evidence for p in D. Conversely, A shows *epistemic mistrust* in E that holds that p in domain D, to the degree that A regards E either as *not competent* in her acceptance of p in D, or as *not responsive* to the fact that A counts on E as for p in D. So, A refrains from taking E's testimony that p in D as providing evidence for p in D (Cf. Almassi 2012: 43).

Two points of this definition deserve attention. The first point is that in my account epistemic trust is understood as a twofold attitude, i.e. both as a *doxastic attitude* and an *affective attitude*: the doxastic attitude is A's judgment about the competence of B, while the affective attitude is A's *optimism* about the responsiveness of B (Jones 1996; 2012). The second aspect to highlight is that the kind of trust here in analysis is *epistemic*, in that it is *evidence contributing*, i.e. we adopt beliefs on the basis of trust (Kappel 2014: 2010).

To summarize, I have argued that we live in a condition of epistemic dependence that is inescapable and exposes us to the need of massively relying on the evidential testimony of others. Furthermore, I have claimed that most of our beliefs are justified by the appeal to an appropriate trustworthy epistemic authority, namely an authority that is both competent in a certain domain, and responsive to the fact that we count on it in that specific domain. Finally, I have specified that the adoption of testimonial beliefs is made possible by epistemic trust, that is the doxastic and non-doxastic attitude according to which we regard an epistemic authority in a certain domain D both as competent in D and responsive to the fact that we count on her in D. Even if these considerations do not exhaust such complex issues, they are sufficient for supporting the main argument of my chapter.

10.3 The (non-exhaustive) ideal of democratic public debates

I now want to advance the main thesis of my chapter. This thesis is the following:

> The *epistemic mistrust* in *trustworthy epistemic authorities* showed by citizens in *democratic public debates* concerning the elaboration of *public policies*, as for beliefs that are *fully justified* and *almost undisputed* within the scientific community, is *prima facie bad* for *democratic* societies. This is so from both an *epistemic* and *moral* point of view.[8]

The main reason for claiming this is that citizens showing this mistrusting attitude do not possess the political and deliberative virtue of the epistemic trust in trustworthy epistemic authorities (ETITEA), which is demanded by the *non-exhaustive*[9] ideal of

8 This mistrusting attitude is *prima facie* rather than *simply* bad, because, in the non-ideal phase of my approach, the acknowledgment of the factors hampering citizens to show ETITEA will lead me to mitigate my initial moral evaluation. See section 10.5.

9 The ideal is non-exhaustive because it only covers the relation between laypersons and experts as for fully justified and almost undisputed beliefs within the scientific community.

the *good citizen* publicly debating in democratic contexts. According to this ideal, in light of the fact of epistemic dependence (section 10.2), citizens publicly debating in democratic contexts trust trustworthy epistemic authorities[10] as for fully justified and almost undisputed beliefs—and these beliefs only, as a way to reduce the *prudential* and *moral* risks engendered by *plainly* and *fully unjustified* beliefs, i.e. beliefs that are not in line with the non-controversial methods and conclusions of scientific inquiry.[11] Specifically, by employing the rawlsian idea of *public reason*, I want to show that ETITEA is required by three ideas characterizing my ideal: (a) the idea of *rational* citizens; (b) the idea of *reasonable* citizens; and (c) the idea of *responsible* citizens. Before clarifying my thesis and elaborating these three ideas in turn, let me expose two assumptions which my ideal takes as starting points, and one remark on ETITEA.

The first assumption of my argument is that I take for granted the rawlsian idea of *public reason*. I assume, in other words, that public debates over the constitutional essentials and questions of basic justice of democratic societies have to be conducted in terms that cannot be rejected by anyone, as their outcomes are implemented through *coercive* acts to be justified to everyone. Also, I postulate that Rawls is right in idealizing citizens debating in democratic contexts both as *rational*, i.e. capable of basic means-end reasoning, and *reasonable*, i.e. endowed with a sense of justice (Rawls 2005).

Differently from Rawls, though, I agree with those scholars arguing that the ideal of public reason should be broadened in scope, to cover every question of justice, rather than only the most basic ones. This is because, in very rough terms, it is hard, if not arbitrary, to distinguish between basic and non-basic questions of justice, and, besides, these issues are strictly interconnected (Greenawalt 1994). Moreover, even if this distinction were clear, in both cases it would be a matter of public debates leading to *coercive* acts, which are to be justified to everyone, i.e. publicly and in political terms, in order to be respectful (Quong 2011: ch. 9). Furthermore, I employ the ideal of public reason for aims that diverge from the rawlsian ones. I do not adopt it as a benchmark for ascertaining the *legitimacy* of public decisions. In my account it is rather a standard enabling us to distinguish between *good* and *bad* attitudes of citizens debating in democratic contexts, where "good" means "consistent with the ideal of public reason", while "bad" means "not consistent with it". Finally, in my account of public reason the idea of both rationality and reasonableness are reinterpreted in epistemic terms. In other terms I ask: what does it mean being a rational and reasonable citizen given the fact of epistemic dependence? This puts my account close to those trying to show the socio-epistemic assumptions of political liberalism (e.g. Buchanan 2002).[12]

10 The assumption here is that in my ideal the trustworthiness of epistemic authorities can be easily ascertained by citizens.

11 I talk about *fully justified* rather than *true* beliefs mainly because a truth-focussed framework would be rejected by skeptics about truth. In other words, the choice to focus on justification rather than truth best serves my *political*—in rawlsian sense—aims. There are also epistemic reasons supporting this choice: e.g. Leite 2010.

12 Furthermore, the conclusions I draw partly challenge the claim that Rawls does not provide us with tools for arguing that public reason must be in line with non-controversial scientific methods and fully justified beliefs. Cf. Jønch-Clausen, Kappel 2016.

The second assumption of my ideal is that I share Allan Buchanan's claim that, in democratic societies, reducing as far as possible the prudential and moral risks engendered by plainly and fully unjustified beliefs is a value of paramount importance. As a matter of fact, beliefs that can be justified only through procedures deeply distant from the standard methods of scientific inquiry or even violating more general norms, such as the principles of logics, too often lead us to commit either serious prudential or moral mistakes, which can even erode the democratic character of our societies. Think of the belief that Jews are an unclean and thieving race, or the belief that blacks are intellectually inferior: the first one has played a relevant role in bringing about Shoah, while the second belief has contributed to the creation and preservation of both slavery and apartheid (Buchanan 2004). To these beliefs I also add beliefs such as "vaccines cause autism" and "climate change is not occurring". Not only because these latter beliefs do not meet minimal standards of scientific justification, as the former, but also because they expose us to risks that are comparable to the aforementioned ones: the belief "vaccines cause autism", if widespread, might cause harmful pandemics; more worrying, the belief "climate change is not occurring" represents a threat to the survival of humanity.

Differently from Allen Buchanan, though, the prudential and moral risks I am thinking about are quite specific. In particular, by *prudential risks* I mean mistakes in *means-end reasoning*, i.e. flaws affecting *rationality*. These risks should not be overestimated. Remember that at stake here there are collectives that in democratic public debates, after finding an agreement on some collective goals to pursue, debate over the supposedly best means allowing to attain these goals. If these means are chosen on the basis of plainly and fully unjustified beliefs, they will likely be inappropriate, not to say counterproductive, thereby not allowing to reach the desired aim. Think about a society whose members have acknowledged that children's health is an important aim to fulfill. In this society, nonetheless, the majority believes that "vaccines cause autism", and, therefore, vaccines are prohibited. Needless to say, the desired aim would not be attained.

On the other side, by *moral risks* I mean two risks. The first risks are *disrespectful behaviors* brought about by *epistemic immodesty*. Even if in the literature this term is used to denote citizens' disbelief that even the best reasoners can disagree about the considerations that they are barred from appealing to (Leland, van Wietmarschen 2012), I understand it as citizens' unwillingness to acknowledge their epistemic dependence, and to act accordingly. This often produces disrespectful behaviors—e.g. arrogant behaviors—directed toward both experts and those citizens that, contrary to the former, acknowledge the social division of epistemic labor (section 10.3.2). The second moral risks I am concerned about, instead, consist in the low or very low consideration for the *reasonably foreseeable* harmful consequences of one's own actions. Indeed, if plainly and fully unjustified beliefs provide the informative basis from which public policies are developed, then foreseeable harms will become ordinary business.

As a consequence of these reflections, it is clear that democratic societies should be concerned with the reduction of the prudential and moral risks engendered by plainly and fully unjustified beliefs.

In light of this, I can now clarify why ETITEA is here developed as a *political*—and *deliberative*—rather than *moral* virtue.[13] It is not simply that the principle justifying ETITEA—i.e. the reduction of the risks engendered by plainly and fully unjustified beliefs is something good—is political in the rawlsian sense (Buchanan 2004; section 10.4), it is also that ETITEA is not about the moral character of individuals, nor does it represent a component of a *flourishing life*. Rather, ETITEA is first and foremost an attitude deriving from the acknowledgment of the fact of epistemic dependence in conjunction with the assumption that ideal citizens of democratic societies have two central powers, i.e. the capacity of basic means-end reasoning and to show a sense of justice. Third, ETITEA is a political rather than moral virtue also because it covers only a very small set of beliefs—as opposed to any sort of belief—i.e. the plainly and fully unjustified ones, in that they expose us to significant prudential and moral risks, which democratic societies should reduce. Besides, ETITEA is political because of its *context-specificity*: it comes on stage only in public debates, but it has nothing to say of what happens in clubs, churches, and so on. Finally, citizens not showing ETITEA are not considered bad citizens. It is just their mistrusting attitude that is said to be *prima facie* bad, because of the risks it produces.

That said, it is now time to develop ETITEA in more detail, by deriving it from the threefold idea of *rational citizens* (section 10.3.1), *reasonable citizens* (section 10.3.2), and *responsible citizens* (section 10.3.3). Let me start with the first one, i.e. the idea of *rational* citizens.

10.3.1 Rational citizens

In my ideal of democratic public debates, citizens are taken to be, first of all, *rational*. This is a minimal assumption, as it simply implies that, in public debates, citizens normally want to act successfully, i.e. they want to choose the most effective *means* to pursue certain common *ends*. In other words, citizens are rational to the extent that they are not disposed to elect means that will likely make their actions either unsuccessful in terms of fulfilling the desired goal, or less successful than those actions that employ other known means. In this regard, rational citizens also know that beliefs that are fully justified and almost undisputed within the scientific community—in those cases in which they are available—lead to successful actions more likely than plainly unjustified beliefs. This is an implication of the idea of rationality advanced: if citizens are rational since they want to choose the most effective means to pursue certain goals, then they will also want to ground their means-related choices on reliable, rather than crude and untested, beliefs.

If this is the case, then in my ideal rational citizens face a problem. As a matter of fact, they can easily ascertain that, in all domains in which they are laypersons,

13 While many scholars have tried to argue that epistemic trust might be a moral virtue, none has understood it as a political and deliberative virtue.

they have not and cannot acquire—exclusively on their own—those fully justified beliefs that would contribute to the success of their actions. This is so because rational citizens are aware that there are too many domains of beliefs and knowledge, and that their intellect is too small to *autonomously* develop fully justified beliefs in all of them. What, then, should rational citizens do, given that they want to act successfully, i.e. on the basis of fully justified beliefs, when they are available, but, on the other hand, they possess fully justified beliefs only in those very few domains in which they have expertise?

My solution to this problem is straightforward. First, to count as rational and, therefore, to be able to choose the most appropriate means to fulfill certain aims, citizens should dismiss the idea of *absolute epistemic autonomy* as *irrational* (Hardwig 1985). Indeed, absolute epistemic autonomy, namely the idea that individuals should keep and act on the basis of only those beliefs for which they can autonomously provide evidence, brings about irrational outcomes. After all, if absolute epistemic autonomy were the epistemic condition on which citizens have to rely, then they would hold (fully) justified beliefs only in those few domains in which they have evidential expertise, while in all of the others, given human limited epistemic capabilities, they would hold beliefs that are crude and untested, i.e. (fully) unjustified. Also, being based on these latter beliefs, the choice of the means to attain the preferred goals would most likely be inappropriate, thus producing unsuccessful actions.

Second, rational citizens should acknowledge their epistemic dependence and show trust in trustworthy epistemic authorities—especially with regard to fully justified and almost undisputed beliefs, given that they most likely lead to successful actions. By trusting trustworthy epistemic authorities and their testimonial evidence, indeed, citizens' actions would arguably be more successful than those actions based on beliefs developed in a condition of absolute epistemic autonomy. That is to say, by showing the virtue of ETITEA, notably in regard to beliefs that are fully justified and almost undisputed within the scientific community, when present, citizens would be in the position to elect the most effective means to pursue their goals. This implies that ETITEA significantly contributes to reducing those prudential risks—i.e. mistakes in means-end reasoning—engendered by fully and plainly unjustified beliefs.

Two key points should then be stressed. First, rationality itself requires that citizens show ETITEA as for fully justified and almost undisputed beliefs, as the best way to choose the most effective means to pursue certain goals. Second, by showing ETITEA, citizens reduce those mistakes in means-end reasoning that are engendered by plainly and fully unjustified beliefs—conversely, by mistrusting trustworthy epistemic authorities as for beliefs that are fully justified and almost undisputed, citizens make something *prima facie* bad from both a prudential and epistemic point of view, in that they do not properly take into account the mistakes in means-end reasoning engendered by fully unjustified beliefs, thereby increasing the probability of bringing about unsuccessful actions.

10.3.2 Reasonable citizens

The second feature that citizens in my ideal possess is *reasonableness*. Reasonableness is a rawlsian concept elaborated to express two basic ideas: very roughly, the first idea is that citizens, provided that they are reasonable, respect a *reciprocity constraint*, therefore they restraint themselves from advancing in public debates sectarian arguments, since they would not be endorsed by everyone; the second idea is that reasonable citizens acknowledge the *burdens of judgment*—i.e. the fact that assessing evidence is complex, weighing political and moral values is difficult, our concepts are inherently vague, and our life experiences show great variations—and, therefore, realize that under conditions of freedom people endorse a plurality of different but reasonable world-views (Rawls 2005: 47–58).

In general terms I share this characterization of reasonableness, and I find it an essential component of a framework that takes seriously the fact of *reasonable pluralism*. Nonetheless, it is incomplete. In particular, as for the burdens of judgment, there is a basic epistemic fact—that is relevant for those caring about the respect that citizens owe each other—which, though, Rawls has overlooked. This fact is that, as far as we know, in every human society there is an *inescapable* and *pervasive social division* of the *epistemic labor*. This can be proved in two ways.

First, we can notice that individuals come to endorse different world-views not, let's say, in "isolation", but rather by trusting certain authorities—and not others. Think about Scientist-Carl and Islamic-Matt: undeniably, both of them have formed their world-views not on their own, but rather via some intellectual authorities. This implies that when one disagrees with others on certain issues, this disagreement is not simply about antagonist personal beliefs, but it is rather an antagonism between a set of diverse but coherent beliefs that belong to different and well-structured structures of thought, all of them *prima facie* deserving respect.

Second, if we take as *basic* the fact that assessing evidence is complex, weighing political and moral values is difficult, our concepts are inherently vague, etc., we should similarly take as *basic* the fact that we live in an *unamendable* condition of epistemic dependence in all domains in which we are not experts. This is something that we experience in our daily life: we depend on the authority of lawyers when we face juridical problems; we rely on physicians when we suffer from a disease; and so on. *A fortiori* this holds true as for those beliefs that are fully justified and almost undisputed in the scientific community: with regard to their validity, we massively rely on the epistemic authorities of scientists. Moreover, the recognition of this *common* condition of epistemic dependence deals with our concern for the respect that citizens owe each other, as I will show in a moment.

In light of this, my proposal is to revise the rawlsian idea of the burdens of judgment in such a way as to include in it the fact of epistemic dependence, i.e. the fact that we have to constantly rely on the evidential testimony of others, in all domains in which we are laypersons. After all, we are creatures with limited epistemic capabilities, whose limits cannot easily be overcome, and, besides, we live in complex societies in which expertise is needed, but at the same time accessible for one single individual in only very few domains (section 10.2).

If my proposal is plausible, then in my idea of democratic public debates reasonable citizens will understand that epistemic dependence is a condition that each of them *more or less equally shares*. In other words, reasonable citizens will conceive of their society as a *network* of *multiple epistemic dependencies*, where everyone relies on others in a roughly similar measure. For example, as for fully justified and almost undisputed beliefs, reasonable citizens will acknowledge that all of us depend on the epistemic authority of climatologists when climate change is at stake; that all of us depend on the epistemic authority of medical doctors when it comes to vaccines; etc.

As in the case of Rawls, some *epistemic* and *moral* consequences follow from the acknowledgment of the burdens of judgment. As for the *epistemic* consequences, by recognizing the fact of epistemic dependence as a condition that all citizens more or less equally share, reasonable citizens should be led to show ETITEA in regard to fully justified beliefs as a way not to result *epistemically immodest* toward themselves and each other—where, to recall it, epistemic immodesty is the attitude of those citizens that deny their constitutive epistemic dependency (section 10.2). To explain this, a fictive scenario might help. In my ideal, reasonable citizens should reason in the following manner: "I depend on many others as for many—fully justified—beliefs, so I need to trust trustworthy epistemic authorities"; and:

> I am not epistemically fully autonomous in more or less the same way as my co-citizens, experts included, thus I should trust trustworthy epistemic authorities, as they do, notably in regard to beliefs that are fully justified and almost undisputed in the scientific community.

As we can see, therefore, an attitude of *epistemic modesty* should follow from the acknowledgment of citizens' common and interlinked epistemic dependence.

The reduction of citizens' epistemic immodesty has an important *moral* consequence as well. Epistemic immodesty, indeed, often translates into *disrespectful behaviors*, which negatively affect both the public respect that citizens owe each other and the moral quality of public debates. If citizens think of themselves as fully autonomous epistemic agents, then, first, they will likely disrespect experts, in that their competence will be disregarded. This could be publicly shown through arrogant statements directed at experts—e.g. "I am as competent in D as you", charges of political bias or even physical threats. Second, those citizens trusting trustworthy epistemic authorities will be considered either not endowed with some minimal epistemic capacities, or biased in favor of epistemic authorities because of self-interest. Needless to say, the moral quality of public debates resulting from a majority of citizens exhibiting epistemic immodesty would be very low. In reverse, by showing ETITEA, reasonable citizens reduce their epistemic immodesty, and this, in turn, involves minimizing the moral risk of being disrespectful toward co-citizens, be they layperson or experts. In other words, if citizens acknowledge that all of them—experts included—rely on the epistemic authority of experts, then immodest and arrogant behaviors will diminish. This is a remarkable result for democratic societies—imagine a society where experts and citizens trusting them were constantly ridiculed or threatened; this society would certainly be in peril from a moral perspective. Additionally, these remarks acquire further weight if one remembers that the focus of my ideal are beliefs that are fully justified and almost undisputed in the scientific community, i.e. beliefs such as "climate change is occurring". As for them, epistemic immodesty of citizens seems wholly misplaced, because of the high level of scientific agreement on such beliefs, and, *a fortiori*, in that disrespectful behaviors deriving from it appear particularly bad.

The key point, then, is that the recognition of the fact of the common epistemic dependence requires that citizens show ETITEA, notably as for beliefs that are fully justified and almost undisputed in the scientific community, as a way to reduce their epistemic immodesty. This, in turn, minimizes the moral risk of exhibiting disrespectful behaviors toward co-citizens, which is something *bad* that democratic societies should seek to avoid.

10.3.3 Responsible citizens

The last feature that citizens in my ideal have is *responsibility*. By this term, I mean that citizens count as responsible to the extent that they do not want their public policies to *unduly* harm others, where "unduly" stands for "without any justification" (Cf. Torcello 2011). To put it slightly differently, responsible citizens have what Rawls calls a sense of justice in that they want to avoid causing *reasonably foreseeable* harms. In more formal terms, then, the idea of responsibility employed here is *outcome* oriented, and for this reason it might be called *outcome-responsibility* (Cf. Miller 2007: 87–90).

Besides this, in my ideal, responsible citizens are aware of two facts. The first fact is that public policies based on fully and plainly unjustified beliefs likely harm others. This follows from the acknowledgment that actions based on an informative basis which is blind to the available evidence or even contradicts it cannot but engender harmful consequences—think of the consequences that people might suffer from if they act on the basis of the fully unjustified belief "vaccines are not safe". The second fact that citizens recognize is that they cannot autonomously shape—fully—justified beliefs in all of those domains in which they are not experts. This is so because they take seriously the fact of epistemic dependence as a condition that everyone shares.

As a consequence of this awareness, responsible citizens should be led to show ETITEA in all of those domains in which they are laypersons—especially when fully justified and almost undisputed beliefs are at stake, given their low probability to cause harms. In this way, first, they let public policies be based on (possibly fully) justified beliefs, and therefore deeply reduce their probability to cause harms—which is their way to act in a responsible manner. Second, the moral risk of not properly taking into account the harmful consequences of one's own actions is significantly reduced. In reverse, citizens commit something *prima facie* bad by mistrusting trustworthy epistemic authorities as for fully justified and almost undisputed beliefs, in that the harmful consequences of one's own actions are not properly considered.

The key point to stress is therefore that the virtue of the ETITEA as for beliefs that are fully justified and almost undisputed in the scientific community is required by the idea of responsible citizens, as a way to reduce the moral risk of not properly considering the harmful consequences of one's own actions.

To sum up, in my ideal of democratic public debates the virtue of the ETITEA with regard to fully justified and almost undisputed beliefs is required by rationality, reasonableness, and responsibility as a way to reduce the prudential and moral risks engendered by plainly and fully unjustified beliefs. Consequently, the mistrust in trustworthy epistemic authorities as for beliefs that are fully justified and almost undisputed within the scientific community is *prima facie* bad.

10.4 Possible objections

Before employing the normative framework just outlined to assess the case of climate change (section 10.5), I want to briefly answer some objections that can be raised against my ideal.

The first objection claims that my ideal does not fit into rawlsian *political liberalism*. This is so (a) either because the core value underpinning it, i.e. the goodness of reducing the prudential and moral risks engendered by plainly and fully unjustified beliefs, refers to a *comprehensive* rather than *political* view, according to which the value of managing such risks should trump other moral considerations—while many doctrines reject this normative primacy (Talisse 2008); or (b) because it is *illiberal* to recommend that citizens should defer to epistemic authorities because of their epistemic dependency. My reply to this is twofold.

As for the first question (a), I want to stress that the core value of reducing the prudential and moral risks engendered by plainly and fully unjustified beliefs is political rather than comprehensive to the extent that, first, it is acknowledged by all those who accept the fact of epistemic dependence, which, as far as I know, is endorsed by both the scientific community and several religions, either reasonable or unreasonable. Second, this core value is retrospectively arrived at by simply employing the threefold idea of rational, reasonable, and responsible *citizens*, which are the *political* building blocks of political liberalism. No further philosophical or religious conviction is employed to this end. Finally, I have not claimed that the value of reducing the prudential and moral risks engendered by plainly and fully unjustified beliefs has absolute normative primacy. It is of course a core value, but other moral values, which I have not discussed might sometimes prevail over it, given certain conditions—think of a democratic society in which trustworthy epistemic authorities are always deferred and never criticized: despite citizens' epistemic dependency, in this society citizens should be clearly encouraged to advance both epistemic and moral objections to experts' claims.

The second question (b) grasps something significant. There is a seeming tension between the *epistemic* reasoning of my argument, on the one hand, and the *political* one, on the other: the former might lead us to demand that citizens defer to experts with regard to any sort of belief, not just the fully justified and undisputed ones, given the fact of epistemic dependence; the latter, instead, requires to preserve citizens' autonomy. This apparent tension, though, is solved, in favor of the political side, if one recognizes that my ideal simply prescribes that democratic societies arrange an epistemic environment where ETITEA can flourish; no-one is forced into showing it. Moreover, in my ideal it is certainly a good thing if citizens rely on experts as for all of those beliefs on which they are not competent. Yet, it does not prescribe so, nor does it reduce the room for disagreement in regard to more disputed beliefs—see more on this later. It just judges *prima facie* bad the mistrust in trustworthy epistemic authorities with regard to beliefs that are fully justified and almost undisputed within the scientific community—and these set of beliefs only, given the *serious* prudential and moral risks that they exhibit. Briefly, my ideal remains within the borders of political liberalism.

The second objection follows the previous one and states that in my ideal citizens are denied their *autonomy*, both as *epistemic* agents and *moral* ones. In my ideal, the objection goes, citizens should simply defer to experts. Yet this focus on citizens' deferential behavior does not match liberal concern for citizens' autonomy. I answer this by noticing that, as for citizens' *epistemic* autonomy, in my ideal it is actually enhanced, for two reasons. First, by stressing citizens' epistemic dependency, citizens are led to embrace a more plausible idea of epistemic autonomy, according to which agents can be epistemically autonomous provided that they trust some trustworthy epistemic authorities, and not in spite of them. To be truly epistemically autonomous is, in other words, to recognize one's reliance on the evidential testimony of others, not to deny it. In my ideal, then, epistemic autonomy is simply reshaped in more plausible terms. Second, in my ideal citizens keep the epistemic capacity to advance objections, even powerful ones, to experts' claims—granted that they have acquired some competence in the domain at stake. The point is that these objections have to be evaluated by experts, as for their validity (Hardwig 1985: 342). But this is not to diminish citizens' epistemic autonomy; it is rather to value experts' competence—experts that are, after all, citizens as laypersons.

On the other hand, from a *moral* perspective, in my ideal, all of the citizens, experts included, are considered on a par, and when it comes to moral and/or political disagreements—concerning, for example, the specific ways to implement a certain policy—they are understood as *epistemic peers*, that is, very roughly, with an equal epistemic power to formulate moral and/or political proposals and objections (Cf. Peter 2013).

The third objection claims that my ideal is partly misguided because, first, even when we take into account fully justified and almost undisputed beliefs, there is always disagreement among epistemic authorities, rather than full consensus; second, it is not true that citizens that mistrust experts choose to exclusively rely on their epistemic autonomy: it is rather that they trust other supposed epistemic authorities.

I reply that, first, it is undeniable that even in regard to fully justified and almost undisputed beliefs there is not full *unanimity* among experts. For example, around 97–98% rather than 100% of climatologists take as fully justified the claim "global warming is occurring".[14] Yet the disagreement at stake here is *illusory* rather than *genuine*—in other words, it is not a matter of disagreement (section 10.1). Indeed, the remaining 2–3% of climatologists not believing that climate change is occurring do not count as trustworthy epistemic authorities in my account, either because they are politically biased or are not truly competent (Oreskes 2007; Oreskes, Conway 2010). Also, this likely holds for many other domains—think about the alleged disagreement on claims such as "cancer is not caused by psychological phenomena". Besides, provided that full unanimity cannot be found on any beliefs, it is a mistake to treat beliefs on which there is an overwhelming scientific consensus as closer to truly disputed beliefs than to beliefs on which in idealized conditions there would be full unanimity. If we conceive of all beliefs as points on a scale where at one extreme there are truly disputed beliefs and, at the other, beliefs on which ideally there is unanimity, it is clear that fully justified and almost undisputed beliefs are closer to the latter extreme.

Second, as for the claim according to which citizens opt to trust other presumed epistemic authorities rather than to exclusively rely on their epistemic autonomy, I answer that social media show that this reading is partly mistaken. In social media, those individuals that mistrust trustworthy epistemic authorities too often show what I have called epistemic immodesty, i.e. they do not recognize their epistemic dependence, and treat experts disrespectfully by means of arrogant claims such as "I am competent in D as you" or "you lie because of self-interest" (section 10.3.2). Only after this initial phase they start looking for alleged epistemic authorities—which in most of the cases are either not trustworthy, or not epistemic authorities at all—able to support their beliefs, as they are continuously and publicly challenged by trustworthy epistemic authorities. The starting point is full epistemic autonomy; the search for supposed epistemic authorities confirming one's own beliefs follows.

The fourth objection can be summarized through the following question: "What if it comes out that trustworthy epistemic authorities are wrong on certain seemingly fully justified and almost undisputed beliefs? In light of this risk, is it still desirable to suggest that citizens should trust them?" The answer is: "yes, it is". This is so because, on the one hand, trustworthy epistemic authorities in D are far less exposed to the risk of making mistakes as for beliefs in D than laypersons. On the other, trust is by definition a *risky* attitude (Baier 1986: 235–240), even when the trustee is a trustworthy epistemic authority. Indeed, both knowledge and the standards of justification are *fallibilist* (Leite 2010), and, besides, *bona fide* mistakes may occur.

Finally, the last objection states:

> in ideal conditions it is not hard to understand which epistemic authorities are trustworthy among the available ones, but this is not true in the real world, where many circumstances hamper an easy identification of them. Similarly, in non-ideal scenarios it is difficult for citizens to ascertain whether on certain beliefs there is an overwhelming consensus or not.

14 Oreskes 2007; Anderson 2011.

I reply by stressing that, while both claims detect real difficulties (section 10.5), it is likewise true that, as Elisabeth Anderson has argued, citizens, even those with a low level of education, can identify trustworthy epistemic authorities and verify whether on certain beliefs there is an overwhelming consensus by simply surfing Wikipedia (Anderson 2011).

10.5 Conclusions. The case of climate change

I have argued that the mistrust in trustworthy epistemic authorities, as for beliefs that are fully justified and almost undisputed within the scientific community, that is showed by citizens within democratic public debates leading to the elaboration of public policies is a peculiar manifestation of post-truth (section 10.1). I have then advanced my main argument. In particular, after providing a definition of three core concepts of my chapter, i.e. epistemic dependence, trustworthy epistemic authorities, and epistemic trust (section 10.2), I have claimed that this post-truth attitude is *prima facie* bad for democratic societies—from a prudential point of view, an epistemic perspective, and a moral one. I have defended this thesis by stating that citizens showing it do not possess the political and deliberative virtue of the ETITEA, which is demanded by the non-exhaustive ideal of the good citizen publicly debating in democratic contexts. I have developed this ideal and shown that, in light of the fact of epistemic dependence, citizens publicly debating in democratic contexts should trust trustworthy epistemic authorities as for fully justified and almost undisputed beliefs, as a way to reduce the prudential and moral risks engendered by plainly and fully unjustified beliefs—and these beliefs only. In detail, by employing the rawlsian idea of public reason, I have argued that ETITEA is required by three ideas characterizing my ideal: (a) the idea of rational citizens; (b) the idea of reasonable citizens; and (c) the idea of responsible citizens (section 10.3). Finally, I have answered some objections (section 10.4).

To draw some conclusions it can now be useful to briefly reason on a real-word case, i.e. the case of climate change. As for it, I have already noticed that, if one looks, for example, at American citizens, the situation to address is the following. On the one hand, 97–98% of climatologists agree on the threefold fact (i) that climate change is occurring; (ii) that this fact is alarming; and that (iii) humans are casually responsible for it. On the other hand, (i) 16% of Americans deny that climate change is occurring; (ii) 48% of them question its seriousness; and (iii) 50% think that human activity has no role in causing it. In other words, in regard to the beliefs i–iii, 16%, 48%, and 50% of Americans, respectively, show either a lack of trust or explicit mistrust in climatologists as for three fully justified and almost undisputed beliefs (section 10.1). How should we judge this attitude?

If my ideal is sound, and, besides, we take for granted that climate experts in climate change are trustworthy epistemic authorities, their trustworthiness is publicly acknowledged and more or less easily verifiable by citizens, and, finally, the beliefs i–iii provide a good example of fully justified and almost undisputed beliefs, then it follows that Americans' public mistrust in climate experts as for climate change is *prima facie* bad for their democratic society.

Specifically, first, this mistrusting attitude shows a failure in *rationality*, to the extent that it contributes to choosing the alleged best means to address the environment on an informative basis that is crude and untested, thereby reducing the probability of fulfilling the desired aim. The prudential risk of not electing the appropriate means to attain the preferred goal, i.e. the preservation of environment, is therefore not properly acknowledged. Second, the public mistrust in climatologists showed by Americans is *unreasonable* because, by not taking into due account the fact of citizens' common epistemic dependence, an attitude of epistemic immodesty follows. This, in turn, increases the moral risk of having disrespectful behaviors directed at both experts and those laypersons that trust climatologists. Third, this mistrusting attitude toward climatologists and their claims is *irresponsible*, since citizens that show it run the moral risk of not carefully considering the likely harmful effects of the public policies they are contributing to shaping.

This is not the whole story, though. One should also investigate, on a non-ideal level, if there are relevant obstacles, for which citizens are not wholly responsible, that, nonetheless, prevent them from showing the virtue of the ETITEA—in climatologists, in the case here at stake. The acknowledgement of these obstacles might prompt us to mitigate our moral judgment. And this is precisely the path that we should undertake as for climate change. As a matter of fact, it has been convincingly argued that propaganda made by multinational corporations, with strong interests in not tackling the problem of climate change (McKinnon 2016), and, on the other side, irresponsible mass-media, presenting climatologists' beliefs on climate change and non-experts' contrary ones as if they were on a par (Anderson 2011), have played an important role in preventing citizens from showing epistemic trust in climatologists. In light of this, the moral evaluation of the mistrust in climatologists as for climate change developed here should be understood as provisional. Further work, in which more detailed non-ideal considerations on those factors impeding citizens from showing ETITEA are taken into account and weighted, is needed.

To sum up, I have developed a normative framework enabling us to understand why the mistrust in trustworthy epistemic authorities that is showed by citizens in democratic public debates concerning the elaboration of public policies, as for beliefs that are fully justified and almost undisputed within the scientific community, is *prima facie* bad for democratic societies. I have argued that this mistrust is *prima facie* bad as it exposes citizens to the *prudential* risk of choosing inappropriate means to pursue their own collective aims, and the *moral* risk of both disrespecting each other, and not taking properly into account the harmful consequences of their public policies. Complementarily, I have shown there are both *epistemic* and *moral* reasons for showing trust in trustworthy epistemic authorities as for beliefs that are fully justified and almost undisputed in the scientific community. Finally, I have suggested that as propaganda made by corporations through complicit politicians on the one hand, and irresponsible mass-media, on the other, have contributed to preventing citizens from showing ETITEA, politicians and mass-media have the twofold duty to stop behaving irresponsibly, and to create an epistemic environment where the ETITEA as for fully justified and almost undisputed beliefs can flourish.

References

Almassi, B. (2012). Climate Change, Epistemic Trust, and Expert Trustworthiness. *Ethics and the Environment, 17(2)*, pp. 29–49.

Anderson, E. (2011). Democracy, Public Policy and Lay Assessment of Scientific Testimony. *Episteme, 8(2)*, pp. 144–164.

Baier, A. (1986). Trust and Antitrust. *Ethics, 96*, pp. 231–260.

Buchanan, A. (2002). Social Moral Epistemology. *Social Philosophy and Policy, 19(2)*, pp. 126–115.

Buchanan, A. (2004). Political Liberalism and Social Epistemology. *Philosophy & Public Affairs, 32(2)*, pp. 95–130.

Coady, D. (2006). When Experts Disagree. *Episteme, 3(1–2)*, pp. 68–79.

Frankfurt, H. (2005). *On Bullshit*. Princeton: Princeton University Press.

Fricker, E. (2006). Testimony and epistemic autonomy. In: J. Lackey, E. Sosa (eds.), *The Epistemology of Testimony*. Oxford: Oxford University Press, pp. 225–250.

Galeotti, A. E. (2015). Liars or Self-Deceived? Reflections on Political Deception. *Political Studies, 63*, pp. 887–902.

Goldman, A. (2001). Experts: Which Ones Should You Trust? *Philosophy and Phenomenological Research, 63(1)*, pp. 85–110.

Greenawalt, K. (1994). On Public Reason. *Chicago-Kent Law Review, 69(3)*, 668–689.

Hardwig, J. (1985). Epistemic Dependence. *The Journal of Philosophy, 82(7)*, pp. 335–349.

Hardwig, J. (1991). The Role of Trust in Knowledge. *The Journal of Philosophy, 88(12)*, pp. 693–708.

Jones, K. (1996). Trust as an Affective Attitude. *Ethics, 107(1)*, pp. 4–25.

Jones, K. (2012). Trustworthiness. *Ethics, 123(1)*, pp. 61–85.

Jønch-clausen, K., Kappel, K. (2016). Scientific Facts and Methods in Public Reason. *Res Publica, 22(2)*, pp. 117–133.

Kappel, K. (2014). Believing on Trust. *Synthese, 191*, pp. 2009–2028.

Kitcher, P. (2011). *Science in a Democratic Society*. New York: Prometheus Books.

Leite, A. (2010). Fallibilism. In: J. Dancy, E. Sosa, and M. Steup (eds.), *A Companion to Epistemology*. Oxford: Blackwell, pp. 369–370.

Leland, R. J., van Wietmarschen, H. (2012). Reasonableness, Intellectual Modesty, and Reciprocity in Political Justification. *Ethics, 122(4)*, pp. 721–747.

Lynch, K. (2013) Self-Deception and Stubborn Belief. *Erkenntnis, 78(6)*, pp. 1337–1345.

Mckinnon, C. (2016). Should We Tolerate Climate Change Denial? *Midwest Studies In Philosophy, XL*, pp. 205–2016.

Miller, D. (2007) *National Responsibility and Global Justice*. Oxford: Oxford University Press.

Oreskes, N. (2007). The scientific consensus on climate change: how do we know we're not wrong? In: J. F. C. DiMento, P. Doughman (eds.), *Climate Change: What It Means for Us, Our Children, and Our Grandchildren*. Cambridge, MA: MIT Press, pp. 65–99.

Oreskes, N., Conway, E. (2010). Defeating the Merchants of Doubt. *Nature, 465*, pp. 686–687.

Peter, F. (2013). The Procedural Epistemic Value of Deliberation. *Synthese, 190*, pp. 1253–1266.

Quong, J. (2011). *Liberalism without Perfection.* Oxford: Oxford University Press.

Rawls, J. (2005). *Political Liberalism.* New York: Columbia University Press.

Talisse, R. (2008). Toward a Social Epistemic Comprehensive Liberalism, *Episteme, 5*(*1*), pp. 106–128.

Torcello, L. (2011). The Ethics of Inquiry, Scientific Belief, and Public Discourse. *Public Affairs Quarterly, 25*(*3*), pp. 197–215.

11 Truth, facts, alternates and persons

Or, whatever has happened to post-modernism?

Tracy B. Strong

For, dear me, why abandon belief
Merely because it ceases to be true.
Cling to it long enough, and not a doubt
It will turn true again, for so it goes.
Most of the change we think we see in life
Is due to truths being in and out of favor.
Robert Frost, "The Black Cottage"

Hamm: Did you ever think one thing?
Clov: Never.
Samuel Beckett, *Endgame*

As we all know, the news is filled these days with discussion of "post-truth," "alternate facts," "lies," "misleading statements," and much more. "News" itself is called into question as "fake." Many worry that a significant portion of the US population, and in particular much of its present administration, reject the validity of science and any objective determination of what are "facts." It is worth noting here that while of a new intensity, these immediate political concerns are not in fact new – they certainly date back to the George W. Bush administration and likely in a perhaps attenuated form to prior administrations.

Some might call this a consequence of (at least part of) post-modernism – and some have. And there appears to be a certain amount of credible evidence that during the 1970s, the CIA actively promoted interest in post-modernism (J. Derrida, R. Barthes, M. Foucault, G. Deleuze, and so forth) in order to undercut the authority of more Marxist oriented thinkers (L. Althusser, J-P. Sartre, M. Merleau-Ponty, S. de Beauvoir).[1] In the late 1960s and early 1970s, several of my friends in graduate school wrote dissertations on Marx – good ones – only to find that three years later no one seemed interested. Indeed, some decades ago, I wrote a basically sympathetic review of Hubert Dreyfus and Paul Rabinow's book

1 See Gabriel Rockhill, "The CIA Reads French Theory: On the Intellectual Labor of Dismantling the Cultural Left," *The Philosophical Salon. Los Angeles Review of Books*, 28 February 2017.

on Foucault, only to ask at the end why the name of Karl Marx was not mentioned.

In the face of all this, and having spent much of my professional career in an attempt to understand and make the thought of Friedrich Nietzsche and others available, what am I to do? Nietzsche, after all, appears explicit: "Against that positivism which stops before phenomena, saying 'there are only facts,' I should say: no, it is precisely facts that do not exist, only interpretations..."[2] Elsewhere he asserts that "*there are no things in themselves, that the very notion of a 'thing' is itself a construction.*"[3] Not only are there no facts, but Nietzsche will push the point further. In an entry entitled "The Researcher," he writes: "There are many kinds of eyes. Even the sphinx has eyes – and consequently there are many kinds of 'truths' and consequently there is no truth."[4] Nietzsche's point, however, is not to provide support for the Trump administration press secretaries.

Nietzsche's point is not that truths are many – a kind of becoming pragmatic pluralism – but that anything that can be designated as true necessarily contains multiplicities and contradictions. "All truth is simple – is that not a double (*zweifach*) lie?"[5] This aphorism from *Twilight of the Idols* is a short version of the more extended *Nachlass* entry: "All truth is simple: that is a double lie (*zweifach*). Everything that is simply is plain imaginary, it is not 'true.' However what is real, what is true, is neither single (*Eins*) nor indeed ultimately reducible to singularity."[6] What is at stake is rather the concept of what a "fact" is.

Philosophically, the matter *is* more complex – one forgets the impact that the publication of the *Critique of Pure Reason* had on the world. Kant had shown that in fact we never perceive the world as it is *an sich* but only that which our senses make available to us. His achievement in the *First Critique* was to have shown the following. First, all experience is experience of and only of appearances; second, that whatever it is that appearances are of is something that cannot be the object of experience; third, that we can know only how it is that we have experiences; and fourth, that it is in reflecting on how it is that we have experience and knowledge of experience that we can ground reason. This was immediately recognized as the source of a radical new conception of philosophy, one that admitted the full force of skepticism but did not remain mired in it. It was also recognized as having released what in 1792 Jacob Oberreit called a "gigantic horror" on the world. The replacement, as it were, of God with the noumenal (that about which nothing is knowable) changed the human position in the world. As Nietzsche remarks in *Schopenhauer as Educator*:

2 F. Nietzsche, *The Will to Power* (Random House. New York, 1967), 481.
3 F. Nietzsche, *Kritische Studien Ausgabe* (de Gruyter. Berlin, 1998), 12.141 (henceforth KSA, volume number and page number).
4 KSA 11.598.
5 KSA 6.59: *Twilight of the Idols.*
6 KSA 13.478–9. I am assisted in the passage by B. Babich, *Nietzsche's Philosophy of Science* (Albany, NY, SUNY Press, 1992), 112–113.

> This danger of the despair of truth attends every thinker who sets out from the Kantian philosophy providing he is a vigorous and whole man in suffering and desire and not a mere clattering thought – and calculating – machine... As seen, however, as Kant might start to exercise a popular influence we shall be aware of it in the form of a gnawing and disintegrating relativism and skepticism.... We cannot decide whether what we call truth is really truth or rather it only appears to us to be such.[7]

One might compare this to contemporary bloodless interpretations of the First Critique.

Nietzsche does seem to me to describe, already in 1874, pretty much the situation that concerns us today, now not only in the rarefied air of epistemology but in everyday political life. How did it come about?

By the middle 1960s, two separate but related intellectual forces were taking root in American social sciences and humanities. Both were a response to the positivism that had dominated the professions in the period immediately following the Second World War. The appeal of that positivism was wide-spread – in social science, in philosophy, in the New Literary Criticism – and was itself in great part a reaction to what appeared to have been an extremely dangerous subjectivism and irrationalism in the 1930s. It is worth noting here that most of the Anglophone political theory written since the Second World War has been done so on the more or less explicit basis of making sure that "it never happened again." I have written an entire book trying to get away from this prejudice. In any case, both of these reactions – to be discussed – had the effect of breaking the intellectual hold – or were at least taken to have broken the hold – of the positivist understandings of the social world and of how one should go about trying to understand that world.

I shall deal shortly more directly with the question of positivism and its survival. Nietzsche did not think it dead.

What were the philosophical or conceptual developments of the period? Into this positivist vision of the world came a critique that was branded with the shorthand name of "Kuhn." Thomas Kuhn's book, *The Structure of Scientific Revolutions*, argued that claims about the world carried with them participation in a broader understanding – to some degree social, historical and epistemological in nature – without which those claims would not be possible. Kuhn called these broader understandings "paradigms." Kuhn, in other words, appeared to question the distinction between two forms of speech or knowledge, between the expressed and the un- or inexpressible.

Soon, everyone was citing Kuhn.[8] Crudely, what most people took him to have done – whether or not they approved of it – was to have brought "values" or

7 KSA 1.355 (SE 3). See also B. Babich "Ex aliquod nihil: Nietzsche on Science, Anarchy and Democratic Nihilism," *American Catholic Philosophical Quarterly*, 84.2 (Spring 2010): 231–256, to which I owe the quote from J. Oberreit, a Swiss doctor and philosopher, partly responsible for the recovery of the Nibelungen sagas.

8 And the matter was broader: the term "Social Construction" as in Peter Berger and Thomas Luckmann's 1966 book, *The Social Construction of Reality*, stood in for or rather with Kuhn in the social sciences. Citations were at 50–60 a year in the early

cultural commitments back in scientific discourse. It is important to realize that in this reading of Kuhn, however, "values" were still understood precisely in the terms that positivism had cast them in. They were, in other words, the not-objective, the non-cognitive and so forth. Kuhn was thus accused by many of irrationalism. That facts, as one learned to say, were "theory [or value] laden," and "embedded" in "webs of meaning" did not, however, in fact join culture, value or meaning any more tightly to the world, nor make knowledge of these things any more shareable. The emphasis was rather in the other direction – a scrim of "values" before all those places where we might look for facts supposedly loosened the grip of world on facts.

This terrain was fertile enough to foster a second development. Pretty soon, those who read Kuhn in this manner – whether favorably or not – were or had been reading Wittgenstein and allowing themselves free passage between paradigms, pictures, forms of life and language-games. Central here was the claim taken from Wittgenstein that language, or certain linguistic conventions, so shape our understanding of the world that we do not see around their corners. Wittgenstein's apothegm that "a picture held us captive" came to stand for a peculiar kind of blindness forced on one through language itself.[9] For many who were favorable to this so-called "linguistic turn,"[10] however, Wittgenstein's proposition about imprisonment became rather a slogan of supposed liberation. For if what seemed to constrain our thought was *merely* a picture, then it would certainly seem one could get out of it, or at least change pictures – or so it appeared. The irony here is that Wittgenstein's passage actually expresses rather a *disappointment* with knowledge. Wittgenstein continues: "And we could not get outside it, for it lay in our language and language seemed to repeat it to us inexorably." The irony is compounded in that *two* disappointments are captured here simultaneously: the initial one, a disappointment with the failure of knowledge to satisfy its own inveterate demands (in the *Investigations* this appears as the demand or hope for a crystalline pure ideal of language), and the succeeding one, a disappointment with this initial disappointment – a finding of the latter to be in effect empty, a disappointment with success. It is this second disappointment that drives Wittgenstein to his famous turning around of the axis of his investigation (PI 108) – the equivalent for him of an earlier *periagoge* in an even more famous cave. I shall have more to say about such turnings later.

In the social sciences, however, it was not long before some were proclaiming that "what you see depends on where you sit."[11] Kuhn's paradigms – already

1970s, jumped to 120 in 1974, and then ranged between 140 and 160 a year until the early 1990s. See Andrew Abbott, *Chaos of Disciplines* (Chicago. University of Chicago Press, 2001), Chapter 3 and esp. pp 89ff. Were one to add such books as Burkhart Holzner's *Reality Construction in Society*, the count would go much higher.

9 Ludwig Wittgenstein, *Philosophical Investigations* (Oxford. Basil Blackwell, 1958), paragraph 115. (Henceforth PI in the text.)

10 The term was originally Gustav Bergman's. See the discussion in the "Introduction," in Richard Rorty, ed. *The Linguistic Turn* (Chicago. University of Chicago Press [1967]).

11 I believe that Graham Allison gave this expression currency, generalizing a maxim of Douglas Price. See Graham Allison, *Essence of Decision* (Boston. Little Brown, 1971).

carried from scientific practice into socio-politico analysis – were now radicalized by being located in the plurality of "language games" that were suddenly found to mark the differences among everything from academic disciplines to political projects. Ironically, since Wittgenstein's earlier work, the *Tractatus Logico-Philosophicus*, had been a central document in the rise of positivism (whether properly understood or not), his later work, the *Philosophical Investigations*, acquired its prestige in part as a recantation of an earlier "positivism."[12]

I shall not be concerned here directly with the status and importance of Kuhn's work for the social sciences. However, leaving aside the question of whether or not those who read Kuhn got him right – and the answer to that would have to be for the most part "no" – it is important to realize that Kuhn's work drew heavily on those developments in philosophy just noted, developments associated with the designation "ordinary language philosophy," a practice of philosophy variously associated with the work of J.L. Austin and Ludwig Wittgenstein. Its most prominent contemporary American practitioner is Stanley Cavell, who has extended Austin and Wittgenstein beyond any point that might have otherwise seemed obvious. Kuhn was himself a colleague of Cavell's at Berkeley and is clearly influenced by him. Kuhn was also influenced – as he later admitted and this is relevant to the debates of the status of science – by Ludwig Fleck, *The Genesis and Development of a Scientific Fact*, in which Fleck introduced the notion of a *Denkstil* and a *Denkkollectiv* – the clear parents of "paradigm." As one commentator has written, Fleck argued:

> that a pure and direct observation cannot exist: in the act of perceiving objects the observer, i.e. the epistemological subject, is always influenced by the epoch and the environment to which he belongs, that is by what Fleck calls the thought style.[13]

Many of us greeted these developments with enthusiasm and furthered them in print. How do they tie it to the developments which we now resist, or rather make fun of, in the political realm?

Linda Zerilli, to take just one case, finds herself distressed that in the present political context "truth is quickly becoming a casualty."[14] What about truth? Can one place a claim to "truth" in a larger context? Or, are such claims against which one cannot argue: facts are not values and the world merely needs to be understood accurately and appropriately. Let me take up the point by Nietzsche that truth is always many. Yet it is not clear that the context should not shape our

12 The work of Cora Diamond and James Conant has called this into definitive question.

13 Sofia Siwecka, "Genesis and Development of the 'Medical Fact'. Thought Style and Scientific Evidence in the Epistemology of Ludwik Fleck," *Dialogues in Philosophy, Mental and Neuro Sciences*, 4.2 (2011): 37–39. For a fuller discussion see Babette Babich, "Calling Science Pseudoscience: Fleck's Archaeologies of Fact and Latour's 'Biography of an Investigation' in AIDS Denialism, and Homeopathy," *International Studies in the Philosophy of Science*, 29.1 (2015): 1–39

14 In her contribution to the symposium in *Theory and Event* (JSTOR on line) 9.4

judgment. Take the following case having to do with distress over scientific truths or facts.

In 1925, Tennessee passed the Butler Act forbidding the teaching of evolution in the state and providing for a fine of between $100 and $500 for each offence. Williams Jennings Bryan, several times presidential candidate, Secretary of State under the first Wilson administration, had been an important force behind the bill. He was one of the most politically progressive white politicians in the country: among his other accomplishments were strong support for the direct election of Senators (1913), for the progressive federal income tax (1913), female suffrage (1920) and Prohibition (1920).

The state of Tennessee also required the teaching of a text book by George W. Hunter called *Civil Biology* (1914), which clearly, if briefly, set out what it understood as a kind of theory of evolution. On page 196, the text concluded its discussion of race by indicating that there have evolved five races of humans, to wit, the Ethiopian, Malay, American Indian, Mongolian and "the highest type of all, the Caucasian". This last was the only race to whom the predicate "civilized" was applied and the text continued by suggesting some possibilities for the improvement of the race.

A group of citizens in Dayton, Tennessee got together and persuaded a local teacher, John Scopes, to claim that he had, in using this text book, taught evolution and was hence in contravention of the law. A trial ensued, with Bryan a central figure in the prosecution and Clarence Darrow, fresh from having obtained a sentence of life in prison rather than a death penalty for the confessed and brutal 19-year-old murderers Nathan Leopold and Richard Loeb, both from very rich families. In his summation for that case, Darrow had invoked the following:

> Nature is strong and she is pitiless. She works in mysterious ways, and we are her victims. We have not much to do with it ourselves. Nature takes this job in hand, and we only play our parts. In the words of old Omar Khayyam, we are only 'Impotent pieces in the game He plays Upon this checkerboard of nights and days, Hither and thither moves, and checks, and slays, And one by one back in the closet lays.' What had this boy had to do with it? He was not his own father; he was not his own mother....All of this was handed to him. He did not surround himself with governesses and wealth. He did not make himself. And yet he is to be compelled to pay.[15]

The children (19 years old), he successfully argued, were products of the mercilessness of nature, hence not (fully) responsible.

Bryan was an evangelical Christian who believed in the truth of the Bible. He also knew a good deal about Darwin, more in fact than the defense. And he certainly knew more about the Bible than did Darrow. The point here is that Bryan's opposition to the teaching of evolution had to do *both* with his Christian fundamentalism *and* with the fact that the theory of evolution appeared to justify the

15 Online at www.larryfike.net/darrow/

claim that some beings (or races) were superior to others and could be used, as he pointedly reminded Darrow, to mitigate responsibility for a confessed vicious murder. He also knew that during the First World War German militarism had legitimated itself by appeals to Darwin.

Bryan had prepared a speech by which to respond to Darrow but never got to give it for the judge ruled the direct examination of him by Darrow to be irrelevant. Here is part of what he would have said:

> Science is a magnificent force, but it is not a teacher of morals. It can perfect machinery, but it adds no moral restraints to protect society from the misuse of the machine. It can also build gigantic intellectual ships, but it constructs no moral rudders for the control of storm tossed human vessel. It not only fails to supply the spiritual element needed but some of its unproven hypotheses rob the ship of its compass and thus endangers its cargo. In war, science has proven itself an evil genius; it has made war more terrible than it ever was before. Man used to be content to slaughter his fellowmen on a single plane—the earth's surface. Science has taught him to go down into the water and shoot up from below and to go up into the clouds and shoot down from above, thus making the battlefield three times a bloody as it was before; but science does not teach brotherly love. Science has made war so hellish that civilization was about to commit suicide; and now we are told that newly discovered instruments of destruction will make the cruelties of the late war seem trivial in comparison with the cruelties of wars that may come in the future. If civilization is to be saved from the wreckage threatened by intelligence not consecrated by love, it must be saved by the moral code of the meek and lowly Nazarene. His teachings, and His teachings, alone, can solve the problems that vex heart and perplex the world....[16]

Except probably for the last two sentences, I imagine that most of us here would generally agree with the rest of this statement. My point here is that there is no such thing as a claim by science or even a "scientific truth" divorced of contexts – and the plural is important. One context of science adduced here by Bryan is that science destroys. Can one speak of science without regard to the worlds in which it exists and which it fosters – a negative answer is the lesson that we might learn from Heidegger's analysis of technology?

What about this? In response, someone might make a distinction between what one might call "evolutionism" and evolutionary theory. The former would be associated with Thomas Huxley, Herbert Spencer and others who sought to use what they understood of Darwinism to claim the superiority of the more advanced species. The second would be the refusal to attribute "superiority" to those species that survived. It is, however, the case that still today the idea of progress is associated with evolution and with science. Like it or not, however, as Judith Schulevitz wrote in *The New York Times Books Review* on January 22, 2006, many

16 Online at www5.csudh.edu/oliver/smt310-handouts/wjb-last/wjb-last.htm

people (on both sides of this fence) remained "convinced that evolution has large scale social and theological (or anti-theological) implications." (See the interview with Daniel Dennett in the *NY Times Magazine* the same day and the review of his most recent book in *New York Review of Books* by Thomas Nagel.)

Yet for most of us, "science" plays a central role – we are as disturbed, it appears, by the proposal to teach "intelligent design" in American secondary schools as we are by Bush's administration's justification of the war in Iraq or Trump's gutting of the EPA and Global Warming policies – or, more accurately, we think them part of the same syndrome. Prior to 1925, evangelical Christians such as Bryan were among the socially and politically most progressive forces in the United States. Today, for most of us, evangelical Christians are very often allied with the forces that have brought us the Iraq War, the gutting of EPA, the skewing of the tax code in favor of the very wealthy, and so forth. My point, however, is that the teaching of evolution or of anything always takes place in a context and that politically this matters as to what we conceive of as science. All is maculate.

Thus a second question: Can the scientific teaching of evolution be considered independently of (a) the political contexts in which it sits, and (b) the fact that it is taught as if a scientific theory were simply true? Actually, to begin to understand the theory of evolution properly one needs a good knowledge of cellular and even molecular genetics – and this shows us that there are still a lot of unexplained spaces in the theory. This question, however, means that one must rely on what counts as authority in this particular case. The question here is if any authority is final. Hobbes' objection to Boyle was in fact political rather than scientific; it was an objection to the kind of authority the Royal Society and the experimental community claimed (see Steven Shapin and Simon Schaffer, *Leviathan and the Air-Pump*, 1985). Steven Shapin has shown in *A Social History of Truth* (1995) that positive results were always validated by named gentlemen, whereas negative ones were referred to unnamed underlings.

What might be done? Suppose someone were to argue something like this: in our world correct political judgment has been made increasingly difficult or impossible due, as Jeremy Elkins has claimed, to the "leveling of strong institutions and institutional norms under the weight of raw political will".[17] The institution often thought to be much at fault has been the weakness of the contemporary American press. Against this some hold out the "ideal of an independent press" as the "singly most important potentially countervailing non-governmental institution in a democracy" (11). An independent press is one committed to "the *truth*" (his italics) and to contributing to an "informed political dialogue." It should be "independent of partisan considerations" (13) although it "cannot avoid" being a political actor. It is to be "independent," "to continually examine its assumptions," and this is importantly necessary "for a democracy that aims to be deliberative and discerning in its judgments" (15–16).

Who could be distressed by this? Well, consider what claims are implicit: (1) democracy is a deliberative process; (2) deliberation depends on having a commitment to the truth; (3) "truth" is independent of partisan considerations; (4)

17 Jeremy Elkins in *Theory and Event*, op cit. cited by page in text.

the press is or should be beholden to no one but its own professional standards, which include "informing the public on matters of public importance." We are not far from *The New York Times*' professed motto "All the news that is fit to print."

In such a vision, truth is conceptually separate from "facts" for simply "publishing *whatever* facts one has most easily at hand" will not do. This seems to me quite right. But Elkins and others usually continue the argument in a manner I find wrong. It is said that the press needs to report those facts that "conduce towards reasoned public understanding, deliberation, and judgment." And here I have a number of problems or questions.

In the first place, what is "the press"? One of the consequences of transformations in the technologies of communication is that there are multiple presses and sources. Anyone caring to seek out the kinds of facts that a person might think relevant to furthering discourse could have done so. The problem is the proliferation of media sources such that *everything* is reported in one place or another. In the United States, for most liberals this is *The New York Times*, it would seem, or National Public Radio: one should read the economist Paul Krugman (which I do avidly). On my cable network, however, I count at least 20 different news sources, including Chinese TV, Al Jazeera, Fox News, BBC, etc. It is not that the news that a liberal might want is not available but that there is, as it were, too much of it. The very proliferation of sources is fragmenting – at one point (until say the late 1960s), everyone listened to more or less the same popular music because there were relatively few stations. Today the FM band (and now a fortiori with broadcast systems like Sirius Satellite, Spotify) has something for every taste and can in no way contribute to the forming of common tastes. What used to bring people together into a few complex and not-coherent groups with multiple and only partially overlapping values now divides people. People can go to what they know rather than have what they do not know come to them. The proliferation of media sources is also a proliferation of what is designated as fact. And any claim to fact is, for the sake of fairness, entitled to its 15 minutes of prime time.

Secondly, the particular medium of television is important. At least two thirds of Americans get most of their news from TV and over half get all their news that way. Particularly here, the medium exists in an economic system that demands profit and profit is gained by increasing the number of listeners. Two solutions to this demand are prevalent: the first is a reliance on voyeurism, epitomized as "if it bleeds, it leads." The second is more insidious: the cutting down of the attention time needed for any issue, such that something new is always appearing. Dan Hallin[18] has shown that the average length of a clip in which the president spoke on national news shows went between the 1960s and the 1980s from close to two minutes a night to around 18 seconds. American half-hour evening news programs did not start until 1963. And it is in that context that everything is shorter. This is not an argument that more time leads to truth, but that less time does not lead to thought.

18 Hallin is a member of the UCSD Department of Communication.

A third issue exacerbates these tendencies. Coast to coast live television was not possible before 1951 and not standard until the 1960s, but now almost all broadcasts from chains with the resources to have extensive staff are national. This means that their broadcasts are now oriented towards no audience in particular, and must try to offend the least number of viewers possible. As a result almost no political news that is politically relevant locally gets broadcast. John Gaventa, then of the Highlander Center, found that two different communities of miners in two different Tennessee valleys both got their news from Nashville and had no knowledge of the similarity of their problems. The consequence of the second and third factors is that very few people have access to issues that affect them directly.

It is thus not enough to call for deliberation. As Lynn Sanders points out: "Deliberation is a request for a certain kind of talk: rational, contained, and oriented towards a shared problem".[19] In the first place, these issues *are* partisan issues – it would be personally wrong – I would harm myself were I – to agree with, or acknowledge the possibly at least partial correctness of, some of those who hold positions different from mine. In the second, the media technology and the structure of the communication industry mitigate against the provision of supposedly necessary information and will continue to do so. Thirdly, "deliberation" is in any case not precisely what is needed. What is need is the formation of groups of people sharing overlapping sets of problems, the solution to any one of which is not compatible with the solution to some other, such that they realize they are not alone – partisanship formed from the need to accept contradictions. In 1967, while I was canvassing about the Vietnam War, I found that in household after household, on the same street, I would be told, "Well, I am against the war, but no one else here is." Michael Schudson, in his *Discovering the News* (1978), argues that the highly partisan Penny Press of the end of the eighteenth century was essential to the development of a politically democratic (and market oriented) society. I have some sympathy with Speaker of the House of Representatives Joseph Cannon's pronouncement that in the days before the idea that the press should be independent:

> men representing papers in sympathy with the party in power were alert to present the record their party was making so that the people would know its accomplishments, and those representing the opposition party were eager to expose any failures on the part of the Administration.

When this gave way to "independent" journalism as an ideal (and hence to the development of a professional class), Cannon continued, "The cut of a Congressman's whiskers or his clothes is a better subject for a human interest story than what he says in debate." (This from Cannon's autobiography of 1925, *Uncle Joe Cannon.*) The helplessness of the would-be "independent" media in the face of the present administration's planting of stories (which are then quoted as factual news *by the planter* on *Meet the Press*), the practice of hiring supposed reporters to

19 Lynn Sanders "Against Deliberation," *Political Theory*, June 1997, p. 370.

ask soft-ball questions, the development of media channels dedicated to a particular ideological point of view – why are these sources so popular? (*The O'Reilly Factor* on Fox has been the top "news" show). All of these practices are such that the solution is not going to come from dedication either to producing more deliberation or to "the truth." Schudson again: "When a news story is written so that the readers do not know whether to cheer or boo, this represses emotional identification with political issues, persons and parties."[20]

For me, the problem lies as much in the fact that the role of institutionalized groups formed by partially overlapping consensus*es* (we used to call them political parties) has been greatly attenuated over the last 50 years – you have only to look at the 11 candidates for the recent Presidency election in France, each with their new "Party" – and that this is encouraged by the idea of an "independent" press. A political party lays "claim to the whole individual and the partisan act by requiring a consolidation of reference groups, a decision as to which loyalties the individual values most."[21]

Informed deliberation is not the way most people make decisions, nor should it be. I do not by and large go out to gather all possible information, examine all sides of the issues and debate them: and I have a lot more disposable time and more education than do most people. Instead I make decisions based on what the people I trust and work with decide to do. This is not always true and it was in the past more true than in it is now. If I bowl alone it is not just that I lack social capital: *I lack the opportunity to share political feelings and judgments.*[22]

I find myself, however, in partial disagreement with any reference to "the community" finally having to decide whether to "teach the science of human origins at all" (p.32). Elkins immediate reifies "the community" (as "it") and indicates that if "it" decides to teach evolution, it must do so scientifically (and not in any of the religious or pseudo-scientific frameworks that now proliferate). As I read him, Elkins wants to deal with the issue by raising the question of the "various kinds of truth claims" and indicate that some of them are not the kind "with which a pluralistic-agonistic political ideal is concerned."

Let me take up here these questions. First, I am simply in the dark about what pre-existing entity "the" community refers to. I should have thought that *establishing* communiti*es* (in the plural) was the problem. Second, much more attention has to be given to the rather casual claim that if evolution is taught it must be taught "scientifically." That idea needs to be taken apart (that is what we call deconstruction). What does this entail? In a recent film, *The March of the Penguins*, we are astonished by the fact that Emperor penguins each year undertake in the Antarctic winter to march together 70 miles to the same brooding area; after conception and delivery of the egg, the females march back the 70 miles to get

20 Michael Schudson, "In All Fairness. Definitions of fair journalism have changed over the last two centuries." *Media Studies Journal*, Spring/Summer, 1998, 40.

21 Cited from Wilson Carey McWilliams, *The Idea of Fraternity in America* (Berkeley and Los Angeles. University of California Press, 1973), 71.

22 See Christopher Beem, *The Necessity of Politics. Reclaiming American Public Life* (Chicago. University of Chicago Press, 1999).

food, returning two months or so later to the spot where the foodless males are taking care of the eggs (through the Antarctic winter!). Why do they do this? We (scientifically) ascribe their ability to do this to "instinct." "Instinct," however, is simply a word for the fact that we have no idea how the penguins manage to accomplish this feat, let alone of why they do it. Note that to ascribe their behavior to traits acquired during "evolution" is similarly to cover over the fact of not knowing how or why. "Instinct" and "evolution" are in fact terms we use to avoid saying that we don't know. Since we "know" – science tells us – that animals do not get together and form a plan, give each other reasons, organize themselves coherently, they must make these treks because of "instinct," an empty suitcase of a word. (And here recent work on animals raises all sorts of fundamental questions.) Likewise with intelligent design: we "know" that it is a crock scientifically. What this in fact means, however, is that we have an account that humans could have evolved into what we see without that account requiring that there be a Creator (or a designer). But logically speaking, the fact that we can give an account that does not need a Creator does not mean that there is none, unless we take Ockham's razor to be the foundation of all thought (in which case an analogous argument would apply). I am not saying there is a creator, nor do I believe there is or was one: I am simply pointing to the fact that the claim that there is *not* one is part of the *assumptions* of evolutionary science as we know it. Not needing a factor is insufficient: LaPlace's response to Napoleon will not do.

And this involves some intellectual problems. In the *Timaeus*, Plato proposes an account of the origins of human beings, a model of an ideal city, and a cosmological account of the universe. "Pre-scientific myth," one tends to conclude. Yet have convincingly argued that the *Timaeus* operates on an axiomatically based scientific model, "in the strong contemporary sense."[23] Plato even allows (*Timaeus* 54–55) that anyone who could propose another model that fits the facts better would have a better theory. The authors conclude generally that if a theorem contains more information than is to be found in the set of axioms of the system of which it is a part, that the theorem is therefore formally undecidable. This holds as true for Plato in the *Timaeus* as it does for modern Big Bang and other theories (including that of evolution). And I won't even raise the question of string theory. *This is a necessary quality of all claims to knowledge*: the world will always be more than we can make of it. To hold any theorem about the world therefore requires the acceptance of some assumptions that are not logically compelled. This is one of the reasons that science is not only never fixed but cannot be. The Stanford anthropologist Tanya Luhrman, in *When God Talks Back* [24], has shown that evangelical Christians have a highly developed discourse of verification of claims about God talking to one, and the claims one might be entitled to make.

23 L. Brisson and F. Walter Meyerstein, *Inventing the Universe: Plato's Timaeus, the Big Bang, and the Problem of Scientific Knowledge* (Albany, NY. SUNY Press, 1999), 18.
24 T. Luhrmann, *When God Talks Back* (New York. Vintage Reprint, 2012).

11.1 Third question: Is science (just) about truth? Is there not (also?) a lot more?

Doing science means participating in a pre-existing and changing community of discourse. As Wilfred Sellars argued, in *any* inquiry, one is required to:

> think thoughts of the form 'We (one) shall do (or abstain from doing) actions of the kind A in circumstances of kind C.' To think thoughts of this kind is not to classify nor to explain but to *rehearse an intention.* [25]

Thomas Kuhn argues that science holds as values (*not* as rules), "accuracy, scope, fruitfulness and simplicity." And it is not always obvious which approach is "more" fruitful, "more" accurate and so forth, nor what to do when these values conflict, as they often do.[26] That the earth rotates on itself rather than is rotated around may become a more fruitful understanding but for some time it left up in the air the question of why objects fall in a straight line. (See on related issues Ludwig Fleck, *The Genesis and Development of a Scientific Fact* (1979).) We are approaching Nietzsche's complexity here. Even someone as supposedly committed to the fact-value distinction as Max Weber knew that all thought must operate on necessarily unquestioned presuppositions. He writes: "Kant's epistemology … proceeded from the assumption that 'scientific truth exists and it is *valid*' and then went on to in quire what intellectual assumptions are required for this to be (meaningfully) possible."[27] Note what he calls "an assumption."

We should be under an obligation to reconstruct axiomatically any theory we have of the world. That those axioms *exclude* certain other ones is true: but they do not *disprove* them. This is why Nietzsche referred to science as the newest form of the "ascetic ideal." Suppose one asked a fundamentalist Christian what he or she saw if and when he or she looked at modern science. I suspect they would see something like that first part of my earlier citation from Bryan (the part I claimed the audience considered here also agreed to).[28] And here they would also be the inheritors of Nietzsche's claim that after the death of God humankind will see wars the like of which have never been seen before. Science, it would appear, is about conquest (as Bacon saw, scientific knowledge is power). This is part of the axiomatic structure of science. It is also true that science gives us flush toilets, the Airbus A380 and safety razors. Whether or not one can have one without the other is, to me, not an obvious matter.

25 Wilfred Sellars, *Science, Perception and Reality* (London. Routledge and Keagan Paul, 1963), 42.

26 Thomas Kuhn, "Reflections on my Critics," in I Lakatos and Musgrave, *Criticism and the Growth of Knowledge* (Cambridge. Cambridge University Press, 1970), 262.

27 Max Weber, "Science as a Vocation," *The Vocation lectures*, Owen and Strong (eds) (Hackett, 2004), 28–29.

28 On the centrally important question of how to speak with such groups, see Romand Coles, *Beyond Gated Politics: Reflections for the Possibility of Democracy* (Minneapolis, MN. University of Minnesota Press, 2005) and Luhrmann, op. cit.).

Let me take now the claim that much in our world displays a "contempt for the truth" – or simply ignores it. There are four possible forms of contempt here. The first is a kind of Platonic "noble lie" – the fact that someone – often with power – feels that something not being true is less important than the good that it allows. The second is something like what Adorno said in *Minima Moralia* about the Germans, that they never tell a lie that they don't believe to be true. A third is that one just does not care.

Let me expand just a bit: There are three possibilities and they need to be distinguished. First would be that those in power simply do not need to care for truth when it is a matter of power and conflict. This is the stuff of empires. "Of the gods we believe, and of men we know, that by a necessary law of their nature they rule wherever they can," say the Athenians to the Melians, and they go on to indicate that such has always been and always will be the law for those with power.

Second is the attitude that actions should *appear* as founded in and on truth. Here it is politically useful that people at least believe that the government is telling the truth when it gives reasons for its actions. This raises the question of the relation between truth and the appearance of truth. This is a kind of debasing of Platonism or of Edmund Burke's "politics well-wrought veil." It is also dangerous in that after a while, as Nietzsche pointed out, when something is repeated long enough, you yield to it.

Third, there is the question of what the actors themselves believe. It is conceivable (and I indeed think it the case) that Bush/Cheney/Rumsfeld and now Trump, Bannon, Kushner actually believe that they are bringing or trying to bring if not social justice to those who have been pushed aside by the tyranny of Saddam Hussein or now by neo-liberalism, then at least "greatness" to a realm in which it had supposedly been notably lacking under the previous regime. They are not cynical but serious. Here the problem is not so much a contempt for the truth such as the fact that claims to truth are not necessarily checked by the world. I should note here that some years ago a lot of people who complained about the apparently non-moral *Realpolitik* of Henry Kissinger suddenly then found themselves complaining about the apparently moral aims (bringing democracy to Iraq) of the Bush administration. ("There's a higher Father that I appeal to," answered Bush when queried by Bob Woodward about what his father thought of his policies.)[29] Should an American not want for the administration to do what will make his or her country great again – especially if your experience of the last 20 years has not been great? Should one not want to bring democracy to Iraq?

The answer is that, given what I have said, these are the wrong questions, and cannot be posed until other issues are dealt with. ***I think then that the concern with lies whether they be Platonic, or Adornoesque, and thus with "truth" is the wrong approach to our situation.*** I have given some reasons to doubt about the actuality of "truth," certainly as it pertains to the socio-political world, although I would argue it also pertains to the "scientific" one – and gave some reasons for

29 Cited from Bob Woodward, *Plan of Attack* (New York. Simon and Schuster, 2004), 421.

that also. It is not clear that the "truth will set you free" as the old civil rights song had it – a song I sang in a company of those who firmly believed it.

Now the most important truth-claims formulated in speech for politics are *factual* truths – they are synthetic, I think a posteriori, and, most importantly, they can be and are talked *about* – thus they have the quality of never being compelling but of always being contingent: they can always be called into question. Therefore, the case is not that the truth will set you free but that it is only in and by allowing ourselves to be subject to the compulsions of our freedom to speak as we must that we can save what could be called truth. But what does this freedom involve? First, it means acknowledging and accepting the claim that freedom makes on us. At least one of the things that Rousseau meant by "forced to be free" was that freedom had the quality of compulsion.[30] Freedom requires of us that the path we take be our own path – *dein eigenes Weg*, as Kant put it. The central question here is what is meant by "own." We can, of course, always refuse this compulsion and most often we do so, as Theodor Adorno, Erich Fromm and others have shown.

Second, *knowing* the truth is in any case not the problem. It is rather, I borrow a term from Stanley Cavell, "acknowledging it." What does this mean? Picture: You are late. You know you are late. I know you are late. I know you know you are late. You know I know you know you are late – this is the third man problem in philosophy. Such *knowledge is not enough.* You have to *do something specifically appropriate to the particular situation* – in this case likely say something like: "I am sorry I was late, I ..." and fill in an *appropriate* excuse (your child was sick; the car broke down; there was an accident on the highway; but probably *not* "I was having too much fun in bed"). When Trump says something false it is not that he does not *know* that it is false that matters, but that he does not, perhaps cannot, acknowledge it. And to not acknowledge it is to be missing something about himself much more than it is an attempt to deceive.

What is he missing? And this understanding has, for me, the consequence of making our political situation even more perilous than one might have thought. The problem is not that the administration lies; the problem is not that people do not or cannot deliberate. The problem is rather that the administration lacks any sense of responsibility to that human capacity that can make discourse public. And to lack that responsibility is to be a tyrant.

In what does tyranny consist? In the *Persian Letters*, Montesquieu argued that it consists in requiring that others have no existence for oneself except that which one allows them. This seems to me exactly right. What is missing in Trump et al. is an acknowledgement that there are those who, still to some shrinking degree, think that they (the administration) are of the same community as he. (I lack this sense increasingly: I note with *political* distress that

30 See Steven Affeldt, "The Force of Freedom: Rousseau on Forcing to be Free," *Political Theory* (June, 1999) and Tracy Strong, *Jean Jacques Rousseau and the Politics of the Ordinary*, second edition (Lanham, CT. Rowman and Littlefield, 2002), 299–333.

when Trump comes on the TV, I turn to the World Poker Tour.) It is not simply a matter of knowing (all there might be to know) something about citizens, but acknowledging (by the administration) what the administration does and did know. Cavell again:

> Acknowledgment goes beyond knowledge not in the order, or as a feat, of cognition, but I the call upon me to express the knowledge at its core, to recognize what I know, to do something in the light of it, apart from which this knowledge remains without expression, hence perhaps without possession. Acknowledgment of the other calls for recognition of the other's specific relation to oneself, and that this entails the revelation of oneself as having denied or distorted that relationship.[31]

The key word is *specific* – there is no universal quality. To allow the other a voice is to recognize something about one's relation to the other – that there is the relation of being human – and to recognize one's constant temptation to deny that relation. My existence as human depends on theirs and this in turn on the acknowledgment that no one's soul or self or body is his or her own.

11.2 Last question: What have we lost with this administration? What have they lost?

There is a fourth possibility, to which I have some more sympathy but about which I am not completely clear. It occurs at the end of John Ford's great account of the price one pays for civilization, for commonalty, the price of the valence of liberty. I refer of course to *The Man Who Shot Liberty Valance.* Briefly: a frontier town. Two men are outside of or beyond the law: one a good man, John Wayne; the other a vicious brute, Lee Marvin. To the town comes an Eastern lawyer, Jimmy Stewart. Stewart, who is incompetent with a gun nevertheless, gets himself into a gun battle with Marvin. Unbeknown to any except Stewart, Marvin is shot by a hidden Wayne (Wayne and Stewart are both in love with the same woman). Stewart is greeted as a hero, marries the woman, eventually elected governor, then Senator, then ambassador to the UK. At Wayne's death many years later, he and his wife come back to the town for the funeral. Stewart is interviewed by the paper and tells the story of what actually happened the night Liberty Valence was killed. At the end of the account, the editor tears up his notes; a young reporter says "aren't you going to print that?" The editor turns to him and us: "This is the West, young man. When the legend becomes fact, print the legend." Legends do become facts: my country is now facing competing legends, or more accurately one side has a legend and the other may be searching for one. Hence what will be facts is necessarily politics. Or, in the words of Kurt Vonnegut at the end of the

31 Stanley Cavell, *The Claim of Reason* (Oxford. Clarendon Press, 1979), 428.

introduction to his novel *Mother Night*, "You are what you pretend to be; therefore be careful about what you pretend."[32]

I hope that with this the import of my epigraphs has become clear:

> For, dear me, why abandon belief
> Merely because it ceases to be true.
> Cling to it long enough, and not a doubt
> It will turn true again, for so it goes.
> Most of the change we think we see in life
> Is due to truths being in and out of favor.
>
> Robert Frost, "The Black Cottage"

> Hamm: Did you ever think one thing? Clov: Never.
>
> Samuel Beckett, *Endgame*

Frost's poem appears to be relativistic or even conservative but it is in fact a version of the last thesis on Feuerbach: "All previous philosophy has merely interpreted the world. The problem, however, is to change it"[33] – this is not a call to the barricades but a claim that our epistemological and philosophical problems derive from the form of life that we live. Thus also, Wittgenstein in *Remarks on the Foundations of Mathematics*:

> The sickness of a time is cured by an alteration in the mode of life of human beings, and it was possible for the sickness of philosophical problems to get cured only through a changed mode of thought (*Denkweise)* and mode of life, not through a medicine invented by an individual.[34]

Beckett tells us that no thought is an island, apart from a main. And hence *the* truth is a misnomer. To sum up: I have at the start adduced a citation from Nietzsche about positivism and his resistance to it: what this entails, we can, I think, now see better.

What follows from this is challenging. I return to my promissory note about positivism. Central to positivism had been three claims. The first was that there was a clear-cut conceptual separation between facts and values and that, in consequence, values were subjective, not of the world, and could and should be kept apart from one's analysis of social reality. This was not a denial that values were "important" but it was a denial that values were objects of knowledge.[35] I have denied this.

32 Kurt Vonnegut, *Mother Night* (New York. Delta Reissue, 1998), vi.

33 Karl Marx, *Theses on Feuerbach, XI. Marx-Engels Selected Works* (Moscow. Progress Publishers, 1969), 15.

34 Wittgenstein, *Remarks on the Foundations of Mathematics*, (57 – translation modified).

35 See James Conant, "Must We Show What We Cannot Say" in Paul Guyer and Hilary Putnam, eds. *The Senses of Stanley Cavell* (Bucknell, PA. Bucknell University Press, 1998), esp 252–253.

The second claim was parent to the first. It was a claim that propositions about the world could and should be made to speak for themselves – thus that propositions about the world should have a validity independent of he or she who advanced them. One could and should clearly separate the speaker from the spoken, for if one did one's work right not just empirical claims about the world but concepts themselves would stand independently of the speaker. In its simplest form, the claim was that a statement like "mass equals force times acceleration" was true independently of who said it and of when, where and of what it was said. I have denied this also.

The third claim derived from the first two. It held that certain forms of discourse (claims to knowledge) were responsible and responsive to the real world in ways that other forms (one might think of them as emotive, or expressive) were not.[36] In the first form honesty towards the world required something of the thinker; in the second anything (apparently) went. IT followed form this that should a statement about the world not be "true," over time the world would provide the means of rejecting it. I have denied this separation.

What does it commit me to? **These rejections commit me to the position that the validity of a statement – its truth value – depends first of all on who is making it to whom**. The first judgment should be about the soul, only then about what is claimed as fact. This is gnomic: perhaps too much. It is, however, much like what Wittgenstein noted down in 1931:

> It seems to me that the story of Peter Schlemihl should read like this: He makes his soul over to the devil for money. Then he repents it and the Devil demands his shadow for ransom. But Peter Schlemihl still has a choice between giving the Devil his soul, or sacrificing, along with his soul, life in community with other humans.[37]

Like Huck Finn, we must choose life and community and accept that this may entail going to hell. Why does the devil demand the shadow? In *King Lear* (Act I, sc 4), Lear

36 See the discussion in Stanley Cavell, *Themes Out of School* (Chicago. University of Chicago Press, 1984), 36.

37 Ludwig Wittgenstein, *Culture and Value* (Chicago. University of Chicago Press, 1980), 14. LW changes the story. In the story, Schlemihl sells his shadow to the Devil for a bottomless wallet (the gold sack of Fortunatus), only to find that a man without a shadow is shunned by human societies. The woman he loves rejects him, and he himself becomes involved in guilt. Yet when the devil wants to return his shadow to him in exchange for his soul, Schlemihl, as the friend of God, rejects the proposal and throws away the bottomless wallet besides. He seeks refuge in nature and travels about the world in scientific exploration, with the aid of seven-league boots. When overtaken with sickness, he is reconciled with his fellow men who take care of him, and in regard for his sickness do not look for his shadow. Finally, however, he returns to his studies of nature and finds his deepest satisfaction in communion with nature and his own better self.

asks "who is it who can tell me what I am?" The Fool answers: "Lear's shadow." Rather than take "shadow" to be what Lear is, we might also read this passage as telling us that it is our shadow that can tell us who we are. For only bodies have shadows. What might we lose if we lose our shadow, what may we have already lost? Our shadow, our soul, our body, our self? No wonder we flail at the insubstantial.

12 The post-truth in painting

Enrico Terrone

Experience-based theories of depiction (e.g. Wollheim 1980, Hopkins 1998), just as recognitional theories (e.g. Schier 1986, Lopes 1996), rest upon two pillars. The first one is seeing-in broadly understood, that is, the visual experience of what is depicted that a picture elicits from a suitable viewer. The second one is the standard of correctness, that is, the norm that seeing-in should abide by in order to count as an appropriate experience of what is depicted. While seeing-in is elicited by the picture's appearance, the standard of correctness is established by the picture's history.

Surely, much more theoretical effort has been devoted so far to figure out seeing-in rather than the standard of correctness. The latter has been discussed almost exclusively with respect to the distinction between intentions and causal mechanisms involved in the production of a picture. In this respect, there is a significant consensus among scholars on the fact that the maker's intentions normally fix the standard of correctness in the case of handmade pictures while causal mechanisms normally do so in the case of photographs (cf. Newall 2011). However, some scholars have pointed out the relevance of intentions to the standard of correctness of photographs (cf. Hopkins 1998) while others have emphasized the relevance of causal mechanisms to the standard of correctness of handmade pictures (cf. Lopes 1996).

In this chapter I argue that there is a distinction that is more essential to the standard of correctness than that between standards fixed by intentions and standards fixed by causal mechanisms. The former distinction, indeed, does not concern what fixes the standard but what the standard itself does. In this respect, there are three different ways in which the standard of correctness can be conceived, namely, with respect to kinds, individuals, and standpoints. I will call them kind-standard, individual-standard, and standpoint-standard. In sections 12.1–12.2, I will analyze the role that each of them plays in our relationship to pictures. I will argue that the kind-standard and the individual-standard can be relevant also to ordinary perception, whereas the standpoint-standard is specific to the pictorial experience. In section 12.3, I will illustrate my account of the standard of correctness by examining a famous controversy on Van Gogh's painting "Shoes" (1886). Then, in sections 12.4–12.6, I will propose an ontology of depiction according to which a picture is constituted by both its visual appearance and its standard of correctness. Finally, in section 12.7, I will explore the consequences of this ontological account for what concerns the relationship between pictures and post-truth.

12.1 The kind-standard and the individual-standard

The notion of a standard of correctness has been introduced by Richard Wollheim in his essay "Seeing-as, seeing-in, and pictorial representation", included in the second edition of his book *Art and its Objects* (Wollheim 1980). Wollheim states that the visual experience elicited by a picture, namely seeing-in, is necessary but not sufficient for an appropriate appreciation of that picture. Even though seeing-in puts significant constraints on what we can recognize in a picture, it only provides us with a visual appearance that might correspond to several things. For instance, in face of Goya's "El niño azul", seeing-in allows us to exclude that the object depicted is an eagle or an apple, but it does not allow us to establish whether this is a child or a doll. And even if we successfully guess that what is depicted is a child and not a doll, we still need to establish who that child is.

Wollheim characterizes the standard of correctness as the norm that establishes what is depicted by a picture among the things that one can see in it: "What the standard does is to select the correct perception of a representation out of possible perceptions of it" (Wollheim 1980, 137). This characterization by Wollheim involves a commitment to some conceptual penetration of perception, so that a grasping of the standard can change the *perception* of what is depicted. I think it would be better to avoid this commitment. That is why, in what follows, I will opt for a more neutral formulation: what the standard of correctness does is to select the correct *understanding* of a representation out of possible *understandings* of it. While seeing-in just provides us with some possible understandings of a picture, the standard of correctness allows us to select the correct one out of them.

In order to exemplify the standard of correctness, Wollheim (1980, 138) considers two cases:

> The standard, it will be observed, applies both to representations of particular things and to the representations of things of a particular kind as the following examples bring out. In a certain sixteenth-century engraving, ascribed to a follower of Marcantonio, some art-historians have seen a dog curled up asleep at the feet of a female saint. Closer attention to the subject, and to the print itself, will show the spectator that the animal is a lamb. In Holbein's famous portrait in three-quarters view (coll. Thyssen) I normally see Henry VIII. However, I may have been going to too many old movies recently, and I look at the portrait and, instead of seeing Henry VIII, I now find myself seeing Charles Laughton. In each of these two cases there is a standard which says that one of the perceptions is correct and the other incorrect, this standard goes back to the intentions of the unknown engraver or of Holbein, and, in so far as I set myself to look at the representation as a representation, I must try to get my perception to conform to this standard.

From Wollheim's perspective, the standard can establish both the kind and the individuality of what one sees in a picture. In the case of the sixteenth-century engraving, the standard establishes that what one sees in the picture *belongs to* the kind "lamb", not to the kind "dog". In the case of Holbein's portrait, the standard establishes that the individual one sees in the picture *is* Henry VIII, not Charles Laughton. According to the terminology introduced earlier, the former is a kind-standard whereas the latter is an individual-standard.

At this point, one might wonder whether any picture has both an individual-standard and a kind-standard for all the things depicted. This seems excessive. For many pictures, the kind-standard seems to be sufficient. It would be awkward to state that an appropriate experience of Renoir's "Bal du moulin de la Galette" requires that one knows the identity of all the persons depicted. In this case, recognizing them as belonging to the kind human being seems to be enough. What matters in this case, as suggested by the title, is rather the correct identification of the location in which the scene depicted occurs. An appropriate understanding of this painting requires that one treats that dance as occurring in Paris in the 1870s. Treating that dance as occurring, say, in Naples in the 1830s would be compatible with the seeing-in experience elicited by "Bal du moulin de la Galette" but not with its standard of correctness. This shows that the standard of correctness can concern not only kinds and individuals, but also places and times. In the following section, I will argue that the standard concerning places and times is specific to the pictorial experience whereas the requirements on kinds and individuals can also apply to ordinary perception.

12.2 The standpoint-standard

If I show you something saying "look at that", your response can be assessed according to something like a standard of correctness. Going back to Wollheim's examples, if I show you a lamb but you wrongly treat it as a dog, your response is inappropriate with respect to a sort of kind-standard. Likewise, if I show you Roger Federer over there but you mistake him for your friend Alan Smith, your response is inappropriate with respect to a sort of individual-standard. In this sense, one can extend both the kind-standard and the individual-standard from the domain of pictorial experience to that of ordinary perception. Yet, with respect to place and time, there is a crucial difference between ordinary perception and pictorial experience. In the case of ordinary perception, the place of the scene seen is here, in front of us, and the time when it occurs is now, when our very perception is occurring. By contrast, the pictorial experience, as such, does not tell anything about the place in which and the time at which the scene depicted occurs.

In fact, ordinary perception warrants that the perspective from which we perceive a certain scene is the standpoint that is currently occupied by our body. Thus, ordinary perception automatically informs us about the place in which and the time at which the scene perceived occurs, namely, here (i.e. where our body is) and now (i.e. when our experience occurs). By contrast, in pictorial perception the perspective from which we perceive a certain scene does not correspond to the standpoint that is currently occupied by our body. Thus, pictorial perception, as such, does not tell us anything about the place in which and the time at which the scene depicted occurs. In principle, we can locate the scene depicted at different places and times. We need the standard of correctness in order to associate the perspective from which we see the scene depicted to a certain standpoint having its own spatiotemporal location. This is what I call the standpoint-standard, which allows us to select the correct spatiotemporal location of the scene depicted out of possible spatiotemporal locations of it.

There is a category of pictures for which the standpoint-standard is clearly crucial. These are the pictures supplied by surveillance cameras and CCTV systems. An appropriate perception of what is depicted by a surveillance camera requires that one knows where the camera is placed, as well as whether it is recording now or, if not, when it recorded the scene depicted.

In the pictorial perception provided by a surveillance camera, the kind-standard and the individual-standard are as dispensable as they are in ordinary perception, in which we can see something moving over there without knowing what it is. But the standpoint-standard is indispensable. If one watches a surveillance camera without abiding by its standpoint-standard, one surely is not having an appropriate understanding of the scene depicted.

The standpoint-standard can play an important role not only in surveillance cameras and CCTV systems, but also in other categories of pictures. For instance, digital cameras now typically include metadata specifying when and where (viz. date, time, longitude, latitude) a certain photograph was taken. In old analog photographs, a similar role was often played by the title. Consider Cartier-Bresson's photograph "Juvisy, France. 1938". The standard of correctness of this photograph does not require that we know who is the man sitting on the left, or which kind of wine he is pouring in his glass, or which kind of food he has left in his dish. Rather, what matters for an appropriate appreciation of this photograph is the information provided by the title, which tells us that the standpoint from which we see the scene depicted is at a certain location in Juvisy at a certain moment in 1938. In fact, the standard of correctness of this photograph requires that we see the scene depicted as what one could see from such a standpoint.

The same is true for many paintings. I have mentioned earlier Renoir's "Bal du moulin de la Galette" but one can easily find other examples. Consider for instance Constable's "Beaching a Boat, Brighton". The title provides us with an indication of the kind of event that we should see in the picture (viz. the beaching of a boat) but it also specifies a place (viz. Brighton), which one can supplement with a time if one considers the year in which the painting was made (viz. 1824). Thus, an appropriate appreciation of "Beaching a Boat, Brighton" requires that one associates the perspective from which one sees the scene depicted with a standpoint located in Brighton in the 1820s.

So far I have characterized the standpoint-standard in terms of place and time, but there is a third parameter that is worth considering, namely world. In paintings such as "Bal du moulin de la Galette" or "Beaching a Boat, Brighton", let alone photographs such as "Juvisy, France. 1938", the standpoint is implicitly located in the actual world. Yet, there are pictures in which the standpoint is located in a possible world which is different from the actual world. For instance, both Gericault's "Le Radeau de la Méduse" and Bosch's "The Ship of Fools" depict people on a boat, but the standpoint-standard of the former prescribes to locate the scene in the actual world whereas the standpoint-standard of the latter prescribes to locate the scene in a possible world. Just as it is crucial to a proper experience of "Le Radeau de la Méduse" that one perceives the scene depicted as having its place in the actual world, it is crucial to a proper experience of "The Ship of Fools" that one perceive the scene depicted as having its place in a world created by Bosch's outstanding fantasy.

In the case of moving pictures such as films, the standpoint-standard is what allows one to distinguish documentaries, which involve standpoints in the actual world, from fiction movies, which involve standpoints in fictional worlds. In principle, the pictorial experience does not tell one whether what is depicted occurs in the actual world or in a fictional world. One needs the standpoint-standard in order to draw this distinction. This is especially evident in the case of mockumentaries such as Peter Greenaway's *The Falls* (1980) or Peter Jackson's *Forgotten Silver* (1995), i.e. fiction movies that disguise themselves as documentaries in order to deceive a spectator who ignores their true standpoint-standard.

Figure 12.1 Van Gogh's "Shoes" (1886)

12.3 Van Gogh's shoes

As an illustration of disagreement concerning the standard of correctness, let us focus on Van Gogh's painting "Shoes" (1886). In his understanding of this painting, philosopher Martin Heidegger applies a kind-standard to it, treating the thing depicted as belonging to the kind "pair of peasant shoes". He writes:

> In van Gogh's painting we cannot even tell where these shoes stand. There is nothing surrounding this pair of peasant shoes in or to which they might belong, only an undefined space. [...] A pair of peasant shoes and nothing more. And yet. From the dark opening of the worn insides of the shoes the toilsome tread of the worker stands forth. In the stiffly solid heaviness of the shoes there is the accumulated tenacity of her slow trudge through the far-spreading and ever-uniform furrows of the field, swept by a raw wind.
> (Heidegger 1964, 662–63)

Art historian Meyer Schapiro criticizes Heidegger's understanding of the painting and proposes an alternative kind-standard, namely, "pair of city-dweller shoes". Schapiro relies on documents that show that Van Gogh was living in town when he painted those shoes, thereby concluding that those should be city-dweller shoes, not peasant shoes. He writes:

> In reply to my question, Professor Heidegger has kindly written me that the picture to which he referred is one that he saw in a show at Amsterdam in March 1930. This is clearly de la Faille's no. 255; there was also exhibited at the same time a painting with three pairs of shoes [...] But from neither of these pictures, nor from any of the others, could one properly say that a painting of shoes by van Gogh expresses the being or essence of a peasant woman's shoes and her relation to nature and work. They are the shoes of the artist, by that time a man of the town and city.
> (Schapiro 1968, 204)

Interestingly, Schapiro does not limit himself to propose an alternative kind-standard, namely "city-dweller shoes" instead of "peasant shoes". He also introduces a sort of individual-standard, arguing that the shoes depicted belong to a particular individual, namely Van Gogh himself. According to Shapiro, in order to enjoy an appropriate appreciation of the painting we should treat the shoes depicted as the shoes of the painter as a city-dweller.

In his book *The Truth in Painting*, philosopher Jacques Derrida criticizes Schapiro's criticism of Heidegger, arguing that the fact that Van Gogh was living in town when he made that painting does not entail that he depicted the shoes of a city-dweller, let alone his own shoes. Even if Van Gogh was living in town, he might have remembered or imagined some peasant shoes and painted them consequently.

Furthermore, Derrida puts into question the basic kind-standard that both Shapiro and Heidegger presuppose, that is, the fact that the two shoes painted by

Van Gogh constitute a pair. He writes: "For where do they both – I mean Schapiro on one side, Heidegger on the other – get their certainty that it's a question here of a pair of shoes?" (Derrida 1987, 261). In fact, if one carefully scrutinizes the shapes of the shoes painted by Van Gogh, one can notice that they are quite similar; in particular, they seem to be both left shoes. If this was right, the kind-standard would state that what is depicted are two things both belonging to the kind "left shoes", not one thing belonging to the kind "pair of shoes".

Derrida's conclusion is that, lacking definitive pieces of evidence, we should limit ourselves to apply the very general kind-standard "shoes" to this painting, giving up any attempt to apply more specific kind-standards such as "pair of peasant shoes" or "pair of city-dweller shoes", let alone an individual-standard such as "the shoes belonging to Van Gogh". Therefore, he states: "Quite simply these shoes do not belong, they are neither present nor absent, there are shoes, period" (Derrida 1987, 274).

I argue that Derrida's conclusion is too hasty. Even if we assume that he is right in his criticism of Schapiro, we are not forced to reduce the standard of correctness of this painting to the generic kind-standard "shoes". On closer inspection, the standpoint-standard keeps playing a role. An appropriate experience of the painting requires that we see these shoes not simply as shoes, but as shoes located somewhere in Western Europe in the 1880s. These are not just "shoes, period". Rather, these are shoes that exist in a certain historical context on which the painting supplies a peculiar standpoint. The fact that we cannot establish whether these shoes constitute a pair, or whether they are peasant shoes or city-dweller shoes, or whether they belong to Van Gogh, does not prevent us from seeing them as shoes belonging to the historical context in which they were painted. Indeed, even in ordinary perception one might perceive two shoes *from a certain standpoint* without being able to establish whether they constitute a pair or not, whether they are peasant shoes or city-dweller shoes, and to whom they really belong.

12.4 Pictures as public artifacts

Even if one tries to minimize the role of the standard of correctness, as Derrida does, one cannot give it up completely. In fact, Derrida's conclusion on Van Gogh's painting: "there are shoes, period" still presupposes a kind-standard according to which what one sees in this painting belongs to the kind "shoes" and not, say, to the kind "toy shoes". This suggests that the standard of correctness is not just a possible enrichment of a picture, but rather a constitutive element of it. From this perspective, a picture is more than its visual appearance. A picture is a pair constituted by both a visual appearance and a standard of correctness.

Such an ontology of depiction allows us to explain why two pictures can share the same visual appearance and yet be different pictures. They can do so in virtue of having different standards of correctness. Consider for instance two pictures, P_A and P_B, which portray two twins, A and B, in the same posture on the same background. P_A and P_B are numerically distinct in spite of their having an identical appearance because the standard of correctness of P_A states that the individual depicted is A whereas the standard of correctness of P_B states that the individual depicted is B.

Ultimately, we can conceive a picture as an artifact whose function consists in eliciting a specific experience from a suitable viewer. This specific experience is determined not only by the picture's visual appearance, which elicits a certain seeing-in state, but also by the standard of correctness, which selects the correct understanding out of the possible understandings that are compatible with that seeing-in state. In the example, P_A and P_B can elicit the same seeing-in state but their different standards of correctness allow the viewer to select different correct understandings (viz. a recognition of A and a recognition of B). Therefore, P_A and P_B are distinct particular artifacts in virtue of having different standards of correctness.

Pictures, so understood, belong to the category that Amie Thomasson (2014, 47) calls "public artifacts": "While all artifacts are indeed mind dependent, public artifacts do not depend merely on the *individual* intentions of their makers; they also depend on public norms". My point is that the public norm that governs the functioning of a certain picture as a public artifact is its standard of correctness. The latter can derive, and often actually derives, from the intentions of the maker of a certain picture, but does not boil down to them. The standard of correctness is a norm, not an intention.

Depending on its standard of correctness, a picture can function in at least three different ways. First, a picture that only has a kind-standard just provides us with information about the features of a certain kind. The illustrations that one can find in ornithology books are of this sort. Second, a picture that has both a kind-standard and an individual-standard – but lacks a standpoint-standard – provides us with information about the features of a certain individual regardless of the particular situations in which that individual might find herself. The photographs included in documents such as passports or identity cards are of this sort. Third, a picture having not only a kind-standard and an individual-standard but also a standpoint-standard provides us with information about what is going on in a particular place at a particular time. The pictures provided by surveillance cameras and CCTV systems are of this sort.

Even though some pictures may lack an individual-standard, the kind-standard seems to remain an indispensable constituent of the vast majority of pictures. Indeed, one finds it hard to conceive of a picture to which no kind-standard applies. Maybe some works by painters such as Miro, Tanguy, Klee or Kandinski are of this sort. We just see things with certain shapes and colors but we do not know what kinds they belong to. Yet, in such cases, one might wonder if these pictures really depict something, i.e. these really are *pictures* and not just mere images (i.e. mere generators of seeing-in experiences). Thus, one is faced with two alternatives.

On the one hand, if one denies that these are *pictures*, these cannot count as counterexamples to the claim that *pictures* essentially require a standard of correctness. On the other hand, if one treats these as *pictures*, one is at least committed to the claim that these provide us with a perspective on a world different from ours, a world inhabited by individuals whose kinds we completely ignore. In this case, such pictures have at least a standpoint-standard, which prescribes us to treat what we see as occurring in a world that is different from our actual world.

12.5 Where is the standard of correctness?

It is tempting to identify a picture with its visual appearance since the latter is all we see when we look at a picture. Yet, we should resist this temptation since the fact that something cannot be seen does not mean that it does not exist. If we conceive of pictures as artifacts whose functions consist in eliciting an appropriate experience from a suitable viewer, we should acknowledge that a picture is constituted not only by a visible component, namely its visual appearance, but also by a hidden component, namely its standard of correctness. Unlike the picture's appearance, which has its place in front of the viewer, the standard of correctness lacks a precise location in space (even though it has a beginning in time). The ontological nature of the standard of correctness is not that of a visible thing. Rather, the standard of correctness is a sort of norm that remains implicit in practice even though it can be made explicit by means of texts such as titles, labels, catalogs, encyclopedia entries, works of art history, etc.

The standard of correctness is a norm that a cultural community implicitly accepts – often through deference to some experts – and applies to a certain picture. In principle, this norm is determined by the intentions of the maker of the picture or by the causal mechanism that produced it, depending on whether the picture is handmade or not. Yet, the standard of correctness that is actually in force for a picture – in a certain historical period, within a certain cultural community – depends on the pieces of information possessed and by the attitudes adopted by the members of that community. If detailed information about the intentions of the maker or the circumstances of the relevant causal process is no longer available, the standard of correctness is redefined by the members of the relevant community on the basis of the pieces of evidence that are at their disposal.

What happens in such cases is the realistic version of a thought experiment suggested by Michael Newall:

> While intention does provide the standard of correctness for manugraphic pictures, this is not a matter of logical necessity. We can, for instance, imagine a situation in which manugraphic pictures operate according to a different standard of correctness. Imagine a community in which painters put their images to a popular vote in order to determine their meaning. Voters would be required to consider the various items that they find that each picture surface can occasion a visual experience or recognition of, and then choose one of these and write its name on a ballot. The picture's subject matter is then the item with the most votes.
>
> (Newall 2011, 4)

Newall treats this hypothesis as a merely theoretical conjecture, arguing that "To do away with a standard of correctness based on intention would be to make pictures much less useful to us. Understandably, this function is something that no culture that makes use of images appears to have sacrificed" (Newall 2011, 4). Yet, he seems to overlook that there are pictures for which reliable information on the makers' intentions (or on the circumstances of the relevant causal processes) is no longer available, and yet we still want to provide these pictures with standards of correctness on the basis of the few pieces of evidence that we possess. In such cases, we resort to some procedures of the sort imagined by Newall. Certainly, we do not write our preferences on a ballot thereby establishing the standard of correctness by selecting the kind or the individual or the standpoint with the most votes. However, we rely on an implicit negotiation that proceeds along similar lines and pursuits the same purpose. Alberto Voltolini makes a similar point when he writes:

> Upon closer examination, we find that it is not the case that the aboutness of an opaque picture in question is always settled by authorial intentions. Let us consider the famous moai figures, found on Easter Island. We take them to be statues representing the gods of the Polynesian community living on the island before its discovery by the Europeans. Yet who knows? Maybe the artists who sculpted the moai had altogether different intentions. [...] Hence, already in the case of opaque pictures, their intentional aboutness is a matter of negotiation between their producers and their consumers.
>
> (Voltolini 2015, 72)

As the outcome of a negotiation, the standard of correctness rests upon the attitudes of the member of the relevant cultural community, as well as on the documents (catalogs, encyclopedia entries, works of art history, etc.) that have recorded them. If such attitudes and documents change, the standard of correctness changes in turn. This is not surprising, if we acknowledge that the standard of correctness is a public norm, and public norms can change over time, just as juridical laws do.

Ultimately, pictures, as public artifacts can change in both their components. On the one hand, the appearance of a picture can change as a consequence of changes of its material supports. On the other hand, the standard of correctness can change as a consequence of changes in the information possessed and in the attitudes adopted by the members of the relevant community. In principle, the standard of correctness of a picture is easier to preserve than its visual appearance, since the former can be easily recorded in written documents whereas the latter may be embodied in delicate material objects such as painted canvas. However, the fact that the standard of correctness is an invisible component of a picture that usually remains implicit in practice can lead people to take it for granted thereby overlooking the possibility of losing it as time goes by. If this is right, a proper preservation of a picture should involve taking care not only of its visual appearance but also of its standard of correctness. In this sense, the art restorer and the art historian participate to the same enterprise, namely, preserving a picture. While the restorer takes care of the visual appearance of a picture, the historian takes care of its standard of correctness.

12.6 What good is the standard of correctness?

What holds true for preservation also applies to appreciation. As Nelson Goodman (1968, 111–112) puts it:

> The aesthetic properties of a picture include not only those found by looking at it but also those that determine how it is to be looked at. This rather obvious fact would hardly have needed underlining but for the prevalence of the time-honored Tingle-Immersion theory, which tells us that the proper behaviour on encountering a work of art is to strip ourselves of all vestments of knowledge and experience (since they might blunt the immediacy of our enjoyment), then submerge ourselves completely and gauge the aesthetic potency of the work by the intensity and duration of the resulting tingle. The theory is absurd on the face of it and useless for dealing with any important problems of aesthetics; but it has become part of the fabric of our common nonsense.

If one considers the behavior and listens to the comments of the visitors of a gallery, one can notice that – half a century after the time when Goodman wrote these lines – the "Tingle-Immersion theory" still has a significant quantity of followers. In particular, it is quite common, when one visits an art gallery, to encounter visitors who are limiting themselves to looking at paintings, without caring at all about the standard of correctness. If what I have argued in this chapter is right, such visitors fail in having an appropriate appreciation of the paintings they see. They use such artifacts in the wrong way, that is, as mere generators of seeing-in states. The ignorance of the standard of correctness prevents them from selecting the correct understanding of a picture out of possible understandings of it. They misuse a picture by ignoring the norm that governs its use, just like an incompetent driver would misuse a car. The latter, of course, is much more dangerous than the former, but what is going on in both cases is a misuse of a public artifact. The truth in painting, which was warranted by the standard of correctness, gives way to the post-truth in painting.

The visitors of a gallery who misuse a picture are not necessarily responsible for their ignorance. Sometime pictures are exhibited without some accompanying labels so that a visitor who ignores the standard of correctness lacks an easy way to get it. Sometimes the labels are there but the information they convey is too vague or too anecdotal to lead one to grasp the standard of correctness. Something similar holds true for gallery guides, who may succeed or fail in highlighting the standard of correctness of a picture depending on the pieces of information with which they provide their followers.

More generally, the appropriate appreciation of a picture is a matter of education. It is up to art courses in schools to promote the awareness that a picture is constitute not only by its visual appearance but also by its standard of correctness, and that a proper appreciation of a picture requires them both. In this sense, there are two basic ways in which education can contribute to promote appropriate practices of picture appreciation. First, an art teacher can directly teach her students the standards of correctness of several masterpieces of art history. Second, an art teacher can teach her students a method allowing them to acquire the relevant pieces of information in order to figure out the standard of correctness of a certain picture that they encounter for the first time. In carrying out these educative tasks, art teachers rely on the outcomes of disciplines such as art history and art theory.

This leads us to stress the key role that art scholars play in the enforcement of the standard of correctness. In fact, art historians and art theorists are among the epistemic authorities to whom we defer the researches and negotiations aimed at establishing the standards of correctness of the pictures we live with. In particular, we rely on art scholars in order to enjoy appropriate appreciations of paintings, that is, in order to use them as "public artifacts", in conformity with the functions they should fulfill and with the norms that govern their use. If one considers, for instance, a milestone of art history and art theory such as the work of Erwin Panofsky – e.g. his essays *Early Netherlandish Painting, Its Origins and Character* (Panofsky 1953), *Meaning in the Visual Arts* (Panofsky 1955), *Renaissance and Renascences in Western Art* (Panofsky 1972) – one can acknowledge how these disciplines can improve our understanding and appreciation of pictures by highlighting their standards of correctness. What Panofsky calls "iconography" is, indeed, a systematic method for individuating the standard of correctness of specific classes of paintings.

10.7 Pictorial post-truth

The standard of correctness is crucial not only for a proper aesthetics appreciation of paintings but also for a proper understanding of pictures in general. When the connection between the visual appearance of a picture and its standard of correctness is broken, the former becomes a potential bearer of what I call "pictorial post-truth". This is a situation in which the picture's appearance, split from the corresponding standard of correctness, is no longer understood but rather misunderstood.

Remember that what the standard does is, first of all, to compensate the epistemic limitations of pictorial perception with respect to ordinary perception. In the latter we experience things in their context, whereas in the former we experience a scene detached from its context. Thus, the standard allows us to somehow reconstruct the missing context. When the standard is lacking, a misleading purported context can replace the true one. Here is where post-truth enters into the picture.

In fact, digital technology significantly increases the repeatability of pictures. As flagrantly shown by the web, in the global era pictures allow us to see almost any place from any other place. Yet, with respect to pictures, repeatability is a double-edged sword. It spreads a picture by exponentially increasing the number of its instances but also risks to weaken the intelligibility of a picture because the more the instances the more the difficulty to keep all of them in contact with the picture's standard of correctness. At a certain point, the picture becomes a mere visual appearance to which wrong interpretations can be attached. Let us consider two paradigmatic cases.

The first one is a photograph of film director Steven Spielberg on the set of his film *Jurassic Park* (https://eu.usatoday.com/story/news/nation-now/2014/07/12/steven-spielberg-triceratops-facebook-jurassic-park/12574887/). The standard of correctness of this picture reveals what we see as a relax moment in the staging of a fiction film. Yet, disentangled from its standard of correctness, this picture might become the portrait of a hunter with his prey, thereby eliciting indignation from supporters of animal rights, or at least troublemakers purporting to do so, namely trolls. The second example is a photograph of the Pink Floyd concert in Venice in 1989 (www.ilmessaggero.it/primopiano/cronaca/libia_concerto_pink_floyd_bufala-3836132.html). This picture, severed from its standard of correctness, has recently been diffused on social networks, in a spirit of racist propaganda, as a purported picture of migrants leaving Libya for Italy.

This is the way in which pictorial post-truth works. Firstly, the picture's appearance is detached from the picture's standard of correctness. Then, the standard of correctness is replaced by some misinformation. Finally, the picture is interpreted according to such misinformation thereby becoming a carrier of post-truth. In some cases pictorial post-truth can be fun, but in others it can contribute to deteriorate civility. Therefore, taking care of the standard of correctness of pictures is not only a matter of aesthetic appreciation; it has a significant impact also on the social and political dimensions of our lives.

References

Derrida, J. 1987, *The Truth in Painting*, Chicago: University of Chicago Press (*La Vérité en peinture*, Paris: Flammarion, 1978).

Goodman, N. 1968, *Languages of Art: An Approach to a Theory of Symbols*, Indianapolis: Bobbs-Merrill.

Heidegger, M. 1964, "The Origin of the Work of Art", in A. Hofstadter and R. Kuhns (eds.), *Philosophies of Art and Beauty*, New York: Random House, pp. 649–701. ("Der Ursprung des Kunstwerkes", in *Holzwege*, Frankfurt: Klostermann, 1972)

Hopkins, R. 1998, *Picture, Image and Experience: A Philosophical Inquiry*, Cambridge and New York: Cambridge University Press.

Lopes, D. 1996, *Understanding Pictures*, Oxford: Clarendon; New York: Oxford University Press.

Newall, M. 2011, *Pictures and the Standard of Correctness*, in "Esthetica". (www.estheticatijdschrift.nl/magazine/(2011)/depiction/pictures-and-standard-correctness).

Panofsky, E. 1953, *Early Netherlandish Painting, Its Origins and Character*, Cambridge, MA: Harvard University Press.

Panofsky, E. 1955, *Meaning in the Visual Arts*, Garden City, N.Y.: Doubleday.

Panofsky, E. 1972, *Renaissance and Renascences in Western Art*, Boulder: Westview Press.

Schapiro, M. 1968, "The Still Life as a Personal Object – A Note on Heidegger and van Gogh", in *The Reach of Mind: Essays in Memory of Kurt Goldstein*, New York: Springer, pp. 203–209.

Schier, F. 1986, *Deeper into Pictures*, Cambridge: Cambridge University Press.

Thomasson, A. 2014, "Public Artifacts, Intentions, and Norms", in M. Franssen, P. Kroes, T. A. C. Reydon, P. E. Vermaas (eds.), *Artefact Kinds: Ontology and the Human-Made World*, Dordrecht: Springer, pp. 45–62.

Voltolini, A. 2015, *A Syncretistic Theory of Depiction*, London: Palgrave Macmillan.

Wollheim, R. 1980, *Art and its Objects: An Introduction to Aesthetics, 2nd edn. Revised*, New York: Harper and Row.

Index

For Product Safety Concerns and Information please contact our EU representative GPSR@taylorandfrancis.com
Taylor & Francis Verlag GmbH, Kaufingerstraße 24, 80331 München, Germany

www.ingramcontent.com/pod-product-compliance
Ingram Content Group UK Ltd.
Pitfield, Milton Keynes, MK11 3LW, UK
UKHW011015180926
475701UK00004B/759

* 9 7 8 0 3 6 7 7 2 9 0 2 8 *